TAGORE IN PRINT

ABOUT THE AUTHOR

Partha Pratim Ray M.A., M.Lib. I.Sc., M.Phil., in Library and Information Science is a working librarian and guest faculty in the Institute of Education, Visva-Bharati. Dr. Ray has contributed more than twenty-seven research papers in journals of national and international repute. Presently, he is engaged in bringing out a volume of his published papers. Besides Tagore's literature his area of specialization includes role of information communication in society and bibliometric study.

TAGORE IN PRINT

A Comparative Study Before and After Expiry of Copyright

PARTHA PRATIM RAY

CONCEPT PUBLISHING COMPANY PVT. LTD.
NEW DELHI-110059

ISBN-13 : 978-81-8069-870-5

First Published 2012

Published and Printed by

Concept
Since 1974

Concept Publishing Company Pvt. Ltd.
A/15-16, Commercial Block, Mohan Garden
New Delhi-110059 (India)
T: 25351460, 25351794, *F*: 091-11-25357109
E: publishing@conceptpub.com, W: www.conceptpub.com
Editorial Office: H-13, Bali Nagar, New Delhi-110 015, India.

Cataloging in Publication Data--*Courtesy:* D.K. Agencies (P) Ltd. <docinfo@dkagencies.com>

Ray, Partha Pratim.
Tagore in print : a comparative study before and after expiry of copyright / Partha Pratim Ray.
p. cm.
Includes bibliographical references (p.) and index.
ISBN 9788180698705

1. Tagore, Rabindranath, 1861-1941—Criticism and interpretation. 2. Tagore, Rabindranath, 1861-1941—Bibliography. 3. Bengali literature—Publishing. 4. Indic literature (English)—Publishing. 5. Copyright—India. I. Title.

DDC 891.4409 23

Dedicated
to
My father
Late Sadananda Ray
for
Always Having
Belief and Trust
on me.

Preface

Rabindranath Tagore a renaissance figure, breathtaking in vigour, volume and variety, put forward Indian literature to the world. Essentially known as poet, but he was a dramatist, writer of short stories, novelist, a social, political, religious, aesthetic thinker, educational innovator, pioneer of rural reconstruction programme in India, a believer of *One World* concept "*Yatra Visvam Bhavatyekanidam*" (where the world makes its home in a single nest). Rabindranath, the composer of two National anthems, has sketched the picture of people with personal touch in his numerous writings. His untranslatable songs known as *Rabindra Sangit* have become a symbol of cultural ethos of both West Bengal and Bangladesh. Rabindranath took painting late in life and yet achieved distinction as a painter. Rabindranath was more than a literary icon, a cultural ambassador, a real myriad-minded universal man.

Rabindranath not only expressed his vision on society, religion, aesthetics, education, rural development, nationalism, internationalism in his writings but tried to give concrete shape with the establishment of his experimental school at *Santiniketan* and rural development programme at *Sriniketan*, which in course of time became an academic and cultural centre of national importance known as *Visva-Bharati*. The same was declared as a central university in 1951. Rabindranath, during his life time, gave treasure of his manuscript and copyright (in the year 1907) to *Visva-Bharati*. The publishing department of *Visva-Bharati* known as Visva-Bharati Granthan Vibhaga (termed as VBGV) was responsible for publishing Tagore's literature (Tagoreana) with the motto of publishing complete writings of Tagore ('*Samagra Rabindranath*'), at affordable cost ('*Sulabh Rabindranath*') accurately ('*Bisuddha Rabindranath*'). But after expiry of copyright in 2001, it has become free for private publishers to publish Tagoreana.

The present study is not directed towards assessing, interpreting or criticizing the treasure of Tagoreana, but to assess how far the uniqueness or quality of Tagoreana is being maintained by private publishers after the expiry of copyright. Intellectual output of Rabindranath has a universal acceptability and implications too. So, it is the responsibility of intellectual community to maintain a vigil on the quality of publication of the thought content of this *viswamanab* (Universal man). The present work is a humble effort towards this direction.

In this study effort has been made to use Bengali names and words sparingly, to give relief to the reader not familiar with Bengali language. Many names and places mentioned in this work have no widely agreed spelling such as Santiniketan/Shantinikatan. In such case/s commonly used or reasonably consistent spelling is used in this study. The name of the city Calcutta is now changed to Kolkata. But in this study both the names Calcutta and Kolkata used as all the compared titles of Tagoreana (last edition during Tagore's life time) published by Visva-Bharati Granthan Vibhaga bears the name Calcutta as place of publication and Tagoreana published by private publishers bears the place of publication as Kolkata. In case of Bengali works of Tagoreana, there is an effort to use a spelling that reproduces the sound not the orthography of Bengali.

Partha Pratim Ray

Acknowledgements

I owe a deep sense of gratitude to several persons—my teachers, friends, colleagues, and institutions for accomplishment of the work. It is difficult to express my gratitude to all the persons by name. Yet, firstly I express my deepest gratitude to Dr. Bidhan Chandra Biswas, Department of Library and Information Science, University of Kalyani and Professor (Retd.) B.K. Sen, Department of Library and Information Science, University of Malaya , Malaysia for their untiring guidance and supervision in spite of their busy academic engagement.

My heartiest gratitude goes to Prof. Juran Krishna Sarkhel, Head, Department of Library and Information Science, University of Kalyani, for his valuable suggestions, encouragement and all kinds of help.

The researcher also acknowledges his gratitude to the members of the Board of Studies, Department of Library and Information Science, University of Kalyani for their valuable suggestions.

The author also acknowledges the pleasant memories of spending many evenings and being enriched while having discussions with Prof. Ganapathy Subbiah, Department of Ancient Indian History, Culture and Archaeology, Visva-Bharati. The author is also thankful to Dr. Atanu Sasmal, Reader, Sainthia Abhedananda Mahavidyalaya, Dr. Kahnu Charan Sahoo, and Dr. Sanat Kumar Rath, Department of Education, Visva-Bharati whose encouragement and help in finding various references have been an asset to this researcher. The author is much indebted to his brother-in-law Susanta Kumar Chakraborty, colleagues Ananda Mukherjee and Atanu Kumar Sinha for the constant zeal they have shown which inspired the author to complete this work in time.

It is a pleasure to acknowledge gratitude to the staff members of the Central Library, Institute of Education Library, Kala-Bhavana Library, and Sangit-Bhavana Library of Visva-Bharati for their co-operation in extensive use of the libraries.

It is the author's privilege to express gratitude to the Curator and the staff-members of the Archives, Library as well as Audio-Visual section, Rabindra-Bhavana, Visva-Bharati, for their kind co-operation and help.

It is also a pleasure to acknowledge gratitude to all the staff members of the Department of Library and Information Science, Librarian and other library professionals of Central Library and the staff members of central administration, University of Kalyani, for their kind co-operation.

Last but not the least, the author is thankful to his mother Sunity Ray, mesomosai Bijay Gopal Dutta, wife Bani, and kids Pitam and Antara for their moral support and sacrifice of leisure without which the timely submission of this thesis would not have been possible.

Partha Pratim Ray

Contents

List of Table

1

Introduction

1.1 Introduction

An ancestor of Rabindranath's family Daksha was one of the five Brahmins who came to the Hindu kingdom of Bengal "to help in reviewing orthodox Hinduism in Buddhist-ridden Bengal." [1] But later on two Brahmin brothers Kamadev and Jayadev, trusted officers of the Muslim Governor Pir Ali Khan of Jessore (now in Bangladesh) were converted to Islam through a cruel joke. A Brahmin turned into Muslim Pir Ali Khan as a result, later came to be known as Pirali Brahmins [2].

Purushottam, the son of Jagannath Kushari, had married into the Pirali Brahmin family. Jagannath was ostracized as he married a non-Brahmin. He and his family were forced to leave to their home town Khulna (now in Bangladesh) and settled in Jessore and later on in the village of Govindapur (now in Calcutta). As the villagers of Govindapur were low caste fisherman, they used to address Panchanan (seventh generation of Purushottam) [3] as '*Thakur Masai*', means 'Lord' in respect of higher social status. He worked as a sort of stevedore for the merchants, who put him as '*Tagore*' in their ledger book. Thus *Thakur* in Bengali becomes '*Tagore*' (Tagoure) in English [4]. The descendants of the family prospered and succeeded in business.

Dwarakanath (1794-1846) grandfather of Rabindranath Tagore, addressed as Prince was born in this family. He was known to be rich, shrewd and learned. He was closely associated and actively involved with Raja Rammohun Roy for the promotion of higher education and social welfare [5]. He ventured into different branch of business including agriculture, mining and trading. He was appointed as collector of 24 Parganas district and later revenue officer of the tax and excise department [6]. Dwarakanath was also associated with the establishment of Hindu College in 1816 (now known as Presidency College) and the establishment of medical college and hospital in 1835 in Calcutta [7].

Debendranath, father of Rabindranath had to take the responsibility of his family, debt-ridden business in young age as his father Dwarakanath passed away in England. But he was able to pay off all the debts and also keep father's promises of charity (for that reason he was called as '*Maharshi*'—the Great Sage) and make the family business financially viable and more prosperous. Debendranath saved enough so that the family was never in want of money for day-to-day requirements [8]. On the other side he was a very spirited man with vast knowledge of religion and philosophy and believed in universal religion.

Rabindranath Tagore (1861-1941), the fourteenth child of Debendranath Tagore (1817-1906) and Sarada Devi (1826-1875), born on 7th May, 1861 in the ancestral mansion of the Tagore family at Jorasanko, in central Calcutta. The family had a great impact on Rabindranath. His father's piety, honesty, love of nature and sense of beauty, made a great impression on Rabindranath for whom the father remained a kind of ideal and model [9]. Ramananda Chatterjee, renouned literary personality of Bengal referred the family as "the most gifted in Bengal in the realms of religion, philosophy, literature, music, painting and the histrionic art"[10]. According to Rabindranath "*most of the members of my family had some gift; some were artists, some poets, some musicians and the whole atmosphere of our home was permeated with a spirit of creation*" and he acknowledges "*one great advantage which I enjoyed in my younger days was the literary and artistic atmosphere which prevailed in our house*" [11].

Maharshi Devendranath Tagore, the father of Rabindranath Tagore, founded Santiniketan Asrama in 1863. Two years earlier Maharshi had passed through this site, which is about 140 km. from Calcutta, on his way to visit the state of Bhubanmohan Singh of Raipur village of Birbhum district of West Bengal. The land was then barren and deserted with the exception of a couple of *chhatim* (*saptaparna*) trees under which he took rest. He felt a strange calm and elation as he sat and meditated facing a bare horizon behind which the sun was setting. Maharshi decided to establish "*Asrama*" at that place. Accordingly, he bought twenty *bighas* of land and built a two-storied rest house in 1864 and named it '*Santiniketan or Abode of Peace*'. In 1888 he made a trust deed providing an annual grant for maintenance of the house and the grounds, and dedicated it to all seekers of truth, who were free to come and stay to meditate on the *Supreme Being*, without discrimination to caste, creed etc. No injury to animal life and no worship of idols were to be practised. On the objective of the development of education the deed indicates—"In pursuance of the need of enhancement of the quality of living in the Asrama the trustees were empowered to establish a Brahmavidyalaya at Santiniketan and a library" [12]. Accordingly, *Santiniketan Asrama* was established on 19th October, 1888 and converted to '*Brahmacharyasram*' by Rabindranath on 22nd December, 1901.

In December 1921 Visva-Bharati was publicly inaugurated as a "National University" with the international outlook, as a centre of learning where the cultures of East and West may meet in a common fellowship. According to Tagore, "*Visva-Bharati represents India where she has her wealth of mind which is for all. Visva-Bharati acknowledges India's obligation to offer others the hospitality of her best culture and India's right to accept from others their best*"[13].

On 14th May, 1951, during the Prime Ministership of Pandit Jawaharlal Nehru, the Parliament of India by Act XXIX of 1951 declared Visva-Bharati as an institution of national importance and declared its functioning as a unitary, teaching and residential university. In introducing the bill and again while winding up the debate, the then Minister of Education, Maulana Abul Kalam Azad assured the house that the object of the bill was "not to give Visva-Bharati the status of an ordinary university, but to preserve and promote the ideals for which the great institution was established"[14]. Since then Visva-Bharati is receiving all kinds of grants from the Central Government.

Rabindranath is known to the world for his extraordinary quality and versatility as a poet. But he also left his indelible mark on other areas as a playwright, novelist, philosopher, composer and singer, innovator in education and rural development, actor, director and painter, cultural ambassador and what not. Rabindranath, more than any other person in history, illustrated what in the Italian renaissance was called the archetype of *l'uomo univesale* (the universal man). His inheritance belongs to mankind, but the presence of his many splendoured geniuses is ubiquitously felt at his experimental school at *Santiniketan* (Abode of Peace) and rural reconstruction programme at *Sriniketan* (Abode of Sri Lakshmi) [15]. As recognition for his contribution to literature Rabindranath was awarded with the Nobel Prize in the year 1913.

Rabindranath gave copyright of all his works to Visva-Bharati. The first volume of *Vichitra Prabandha* (Miscellaneous Essays), published in 1907 with the declaration "*the copyright of these works rest with Bolpur Brahmacharyashram*" [16]. So Visva-Bharati enjoyed the copyright of literary works as well as musical notation of Rabindranath through its publications unit Granthan Vibhaga and Musical Board in Calcutta up to December 2001.

1.2 Statement of the Problem

Tagore in Print: A Comparative Study Before and After Expiry of Copyright

1.3 Definitional Analysis

Tagoreana

Rabindranath has a huge number of writings in different literary forms. *Kavi-Kahini* (Verse) published in 1878 was the first publication of Rabindranath in book form. The poet's year of departure, i.e. 1941 from this earthly abode was also marked with the publication of five books entitled *Arogya* (Verse), *Janmadine* (Verse), *Galpasalpa* (Stories and poems), *Sabhyatar Samkat* (Address), and *Asramer Rup O Vikas* (Essays). Rabindranath has written twenty volumes of poetry, fifteen plays, ninety-five short stories, eleven novels, thirteen volumes of essays, prepared textbooks, penned more than four thousand letters, composed more than two thousand songs, and created more than two thousand paintings. All these writings were not published during Tagore's lifetime. Many creative works of Rabindranath appeared in print as posthumous publication. All these writings and paintings, in other words, all his creative and intellectual output of Rabindranath is termed as Tagoreana.

Copyright

Encyclopaedia Britannica defines copyright as "the exclusive, legally secured right to publish, reproduce and sell the matter and form of literacy, musical, dramatic or artistic work. Copyright is designed to protect an artist, publisher or other owner against any unauthorized copying of his works—as by reproducing the work in any material form, publishing it, performing it in public, filming it, broadcasting it, causing it to be distributed to subscribers or making any adaptation of the work. A copyright supplies a copyright holder with a kind of monopoly over the created material, which assures him of both control over its use and the pecuniary benefits derived from it." Thus it protects the labour, skill and judgement that someone—author, artist or some other creator expands in the creation of an original piece of work.

Copyright is a legal protection for a limited period against unauthorized reproduction of any published/unpublished scientific/artistic work. So, in simple words, copyright means to protect the rights of authors as well as the public. The author has to be given credit as well as the financial rewards for his/her intellectual labour and creation. The public is also given a chance to use as a right the new ideas, creations, theories and literary creations of the great minds, which is a good contribution to the progress of the society and the nation.

1.4 Rights under Copyright

Rights under copyright are of two types:

(i) *The Economic rights*: The rights of reproduction, broadcasting, public performance, adaptation, translation, public relations, public display, distribution, etc. and

(ii) *The Moral rights*: The author's right to object to any distortion, mutation or other modification of his/her work that might be prejudicial to his/her honour or reputation.

Both the rights belong to the creator who can exercise them, i.e. he/she can use the work himself/herself, can give permission to someone else to use the work or prohibit someone else from using the work. The general principle is that copyrighted works cannot be used without the authorization of the owner of rights. The registration of a work under the Act is not compulsory, but once the particulars of a work are entered in the 'Register of Copyright' it constitutes the *prima facie* evidence of ownership in the work [17]. It is desirable to mark, print or display the copyright registration of any work with the symbol "© Copyright" along with copyright registration number, year of registration and the name of the owner of copyright to inform the public about the existence of copyright in the work and warn them from illegal use or copy.

1.5 Types of Copyright

According to Copyright, Designs and Patents Act, UK (1988) the following categories of works are covered under copyright:

- **Literary:** song, lyrics, manuscripts, manuals, computer programmes, web page designs, commercial documents, leaflets, newsletters, articles, etc.;
- **Dramatic:** plays, dance, etc.;
- **Musical:** recordings and score, etc.;
- **Artistic:** photography, painting, sculptures, architecture, technical drawing, diagrams, maps, logos, etc.;
- **Sound recordings:** may be recordings of other copyright works, e.g. musical and literary;
- **Films:** documentary and feature films, broadcasts and cable programmes;
- **Typographical arrangement of published editions:** magazines, periodicals, etc.;
- **Computer programmes:** the Copyright (Computer Programmes) Regulations, 1992 extended the rules covering literary works to include Computer programmes [18].

Rabindranath's creative works cover literary, artistic (paintings and drawings), musical, sound recording. Thus Visva-Bharati enjoyed the copyright of Rabindranath's creation in these areas.

1.6 Period of Copyright

The copyright holder enjoys the copyright for the following span of time:

- For literary dramatic, musical or artistic works (excluding photograph) during the lifetime of the person and till 60 years after his death;

- For joint authorship till 60 years after the death of the author who dies later;
- For anonymous work till 60 years from the year in which the work was first published;
- For photograph/cinematograph, film/audio record, government or public understanding work till 60 years from the year in which it was first published.

It is worth mentioning that a broadcasting authority is the owner of the broadcast production right up to 24 years of the first broadcast of a programme [19].

The term Related Rights is used to cover rights that, while they are not concerned with copying copyrighted materials, are linked to the duration of copyright. These rights include public rental or hire, public lending, so-called moral rights and so-called neighbouring rights. This last term includes rights such as performing and broadcasting rights, recording rights and film distribution rights.

1.7 Owner of Copyright

The owner of copyright can be an individual or an organization. In an organization an employee who creates something as part of the course of his/her normal duties passes ownership of the copyright to his/her employer. UK law uses the word 'author' in its broadest sense, to apply to, say, not only a novelist but also a playwright, composer, photographer, artist and so on. Any work originated by a corporate body that show no personal author are protected as 'anonymous works'. Copyright can change hands by assignment. A novelist or an author of a learned article typically assigns to a publisher the right to reproduce copies of his/her work.

The law gives rights of protection not only to originators but also to those who create particular physical formats for general distribution or sale, such as publishers of printed books, producers of audiovisual media and providers of broadcasting services. Certain rights are also given to performers of plays and other works.

It is important to note that copyright is a negative right [20]. Copyright can only occur provided a work is 'fixed' or recorded in some form. It does not give someone the right to copy items; it gives the owner the right to prevent others copying items. After the period, copyright ends and the materials are said to 'fall into the public domain'; they are then usable without restriction by third parties.

1.8 Copyright Act and its Implications in India

In the year 1914 the first copyright act was enacted in India, which was a copy of the British Act of 1911. It codified and consolidated the earlier acts on different work to make it applicable to British. It also abolished the common law copyright and introduced a term of life of the author plus fifty years.

In independent India, the Copyright Act, 1957 was passed on 4th June, 1957 by both the Houses of Parliament and ratified with the assent of the President. This Act was amended in the years 1983, 1984, 1987, 1992 and both the Houses of Parliament passed the last amendment on 11th and 13th May, 1994. The enactment of Indian Copyright Act of 1957 replaced the Act of 1914. The Act of 1957 came into force on 21st January, 1958 with the intention to cope with the new problems in the law of copyright created by advances in communication, broadcasting, motion pictures, litho photography, microfilming, cinema, sound recordings, etc. It was according to universal copyright convention. But at that time, it was not well in force as most of the population was illiterate. This Act covered books, periodicals, music, cinematographic works and latest reprographic techniques and computerized storage.

The Copyright Act, 1957 amended on different occasions to cope with the changing technological advances protects the right of copyright holder. In 1984, amendments were made to discourage and prevent the widespread piracy prevailing in video film and records. Again amendment was made in 1987 to protect creativity of creative artists. In the amendment of 1992 the tenure of copyright extended as author's life plus sixty years after his death instead of existing fifty years. This was done especially to benefit and to protect the work of the great author Rabindranath Tagore. In June 1994, the amendment was made especially to cover computer and electronic devices, which was called 'Software Copyright Act of 1994'. This is also known as Digital Documents Protection (Copyright) Act in India.

Authors create the thought contents of the documents while the publishers make provisions for publication, distribution and sale of the works. Libraries as a social and cultural institution acquire, process, organize, preserve, disseminate and provide access to the works of intellectual contents in order to satisfy the information need of their users, including those that have lost market viability or became out of print. On the other hand they are intended to support the needs of authors/copyright owners to obtain a fair economic return on their intellectual property [21]. Considering two such circumstances, IFLA, on the one hand supports the effective enforcement of copyright and recognizes that libraries have a crucial role to play in controlling as well as facilitating access to the increasing number of local and remote electronic/digital information resources, and on the other hand, maintains that overprotection of copyright could threaten democratic traditions and impact on social justice principles by unreasonably restricting access to information and knowledge. Considering the overall perspectives of "fair use" or "fair deal" (as mentioned in the Indian Copyright Act) it is recommended that:

- Library and information centres are legally permitted to browse, take notes or print the copyrighted material for self-study, research and educational purpose.
- Licensing agreements for digital products and services should ensure that libraries be allowed to share the products for fair use and should also be allowed to download a part of the information in electronic format.
- Libraries and information centres should be permitted to print electronic copyrighted work even in full measures for preservation purposes.
- Time period for copyright protection for digital work should be minimized at five years. Then, the same should be allowed to be used by public free of cost.
- Libraries and archives are permitted to make maximum copies of unpublished copyrighted works for the purposes of preservation, security or for deposit for research use in another library or archive.
- Libraries can also make maximum three copies of a published work or replace a work in their collection if it is damaged/deteriorated/lost and the format of which has become obsolete.

Libraries and the information professionals can play a valuable role, as the organizer and facilitators of digital property beyond the transformation of information to an electronic state. Library professionals are in the best position to evaluate the value of information in any form to an individual or to an organization, a role undeniably ignored now. Indeed, this role, the "capacity to make use of information effectively", will be crucial in the digital environment. The library and information professionals should have a fair use/fair deal arrangement as in the case of printed works.

1.9 Objectives of the Study

The study aims:

i. To trace the range and sequential order of publication of Tagoreana.
ii. To find out the publication track of Tagoreana before and after the expiry of copyright.
iii. To assess the standard of publication of Tagoreana after the expiry of copyright.
iv. To evaluate the responsibility discharged by Visva-Bharati Publication Unit before and after the expiry of copyright.
v. To find out whether Tagore's writing follows bibliometric theories.

1.10 Research Question

Rabindranath gave copyright of all his works to Visva-Bharati. First time it was declared in *Vichitra Prabandha* (Miscellaneous Essays), with the declaration "*the copyright of these works rest with Bolpur Brahmacharyashram*" [22]. As a result Visva-Bharati enjoyed copyright of Tagoreana according to the then existing law up to December 1991, but Indian Parliament enhanced the copyright period keeping in mind the Tagore's work and Visva-Bharati, for the period from 50 years to 60 years after the expiry of the author. The main argument was to provide Tagore's work easily and cheaply. The extended period was also over. The questions that arise now are:

- How far the uniqueness or quality of his writings are maintained by publishers of all sorts, particularly in the case

of impression, illustrations, composition, font size, compilation, etc.?
- What kind of publication should be treated as standard?
- Is the Tagoreana being published simultaneously by large private publishing houses as well as small and new publishers in Bengali?
- Are the private publishers maintaining any standard with regard to Tagoreana?
- What percentage of Tagoreana is being published by private publishers?
- Are the Visva-Bharati publications more costly?
- What will be the fate of less popular/commercially non-viable writings of Tagoreana?

All these questions have to be addressed in the background of range and sequential order of writings as well as publications of Tagoreana. In this context efforts will be made to examine interrelationship between rank and frequency of words in Tagoreana, to observe whether the poetic language also follows some kind of law through the application of Zipf's law.

The present study is an attempt to address the aforesaid research questions with the help of Tagoreana, biographical, bibliographical sources. Bibliometric technique has been used for statistical and mathematical analysis. It will also assess quantitatively the intellectual content of Tagore's writings in respect of different places, times and family conditions and translation of his works during his life time.

1.11 Need and Significance of the Study

Tagoreana is a wealth of not only of Bengal (India) but also of the world, as Rabindranath was a *viswamanab* (universal man) and his intellectual output has a universal acceptability. Power of Rabindranath as a person, as a name and as a writer is universally accepted [23]. His writing covers all aspects of human life such as society, religion, aesthetics, education, rural welfare, nationalism, internationalism and all branches of literature besides drawings and paintings. Thus Tagoreana not only enriches modern Indian literature but also world literature. So it is the responsibility of intellectual community to maintain quality of intellectual output of the great scholar of India. Before the expiry of copyright the responsibility was vested with Visva-Bharati his own institution. But after the expiry of copyright how far quality control in respect of physical as well as intellectual part of Tagoreana is maintained by private publishers needs to be reviewed. In this connection the role of Visva-Bharati in the publication of Tagoreana and its quality also needs to be evaluated. The study is also significant to have an understanding of relatively less popular or commercially non-viable publications. Here the question arises whether Visva-Bharati has a good role to play in respect of these publications.

1.12 Review of Literature

Review is a retrospective activity implying the collection and examination of evidence and information. A literature review discusses published information in a particular subject area, generally within a certain time period. A literature review can be just a simple summary of the sources, but it usually follows an organizational pattern and combines both summary and synthesis. A summary is a recap of the important information of the source, but a synthesis is a reorganization and reshuffling of that information.

Review of literature acts as a handy guide, gives an overview or acts as a stepping stone to a particular topic. It keeps scholars up-to-date about latest development in their respective subject field. Thus comprehensive knowledge of the literature of the field of interest is essential for research. For the present study both macro- and micro-documents in the form of book and journal articles were consulted for literature review.

Books

Sen, Pulinbehari. *Rabindra granthapanji*. (1973) [24]. The author in brief narrates the history of publication of bibliographies of Tagoreana with reference to Prasanta Chandra Mahalanobis [*Rabindra-Parichaya*, published in Prabashi in 1328, 1329 (B.S.)], Edward Thompson and Prabhatkumar Mukhopadhyay. The book provides a chronological account of publication of Tagoreana from *Kavi-Kahini* (1878) to *Raja O Rani* (1889) with details bibliographical information, correction/change made by Tagore in different editions, number of copies published, even copy of title page of some first publications, criticism in contemporary journals etc.

Mukhopadhyay, Prabhatkumar. *Rabindragrantha parichiti* (1978) [25]. It is an annotated index of Tagoreana from *Kavi-Kahini* (1878) to *Vyangakautuk* (1907). This edition provides special stanza-wise description of publications. Besides bibliographical details information regarding first publication in journals, change of text from first publication to book form is also provided. Many of the first publications especially in journals are rare but details information about it would open new avenues of research. Information regarding some unsigned writings of Rabindranath before the publication of *Kavi-Kahini* such as *Bharatbhumi, Delhi-Durbar* etc. are also provided.

Thompson, Edward. *Rabindranath Tagore: Poet and Dramatist.* (1979) [26]. The author analyses Tagoreana dividing it into five important segments: (i) early life and poetry (1861-1886), (ii) the Shileida and Sadhana period (1887-1897), (iii) unrest and change (1898-1905), (iv) the *Gitanjali* period (1905-1919), and (v) internationalism (1919-1941). According to the author Tagore's published verse and dramas amount to 15,000 lines or their equivalent. His non-dramatic prose, novels, short stories, autobiography, criticism, essays of many kinds, are more than twice as much, and there are a mass of uncollected materials.

Kripalani, Krishna. *Rabindranath Tagore: a biography*. (1980) [27]. The author married Tagore's granddaughter Nandita, lived and worked with Tagore at Santiniketan from 1933. Thus, this biographical work is a detailed study of Tagore's life and works. The work gives a picture of a complete man through his many achievements but partial expressions of a restless vitality and inexhaustible zest in living. The author also showed how Tagore contrived to show India to herself and the importance of his contribution to her (India) reawakening was stable and deep-releasing and feeding hidden fountains of creative activity.

Bandyopadhyay, Somendranath. *Rabindra-chitrakala: Rabindrasahityer patabhumika*. (1982) [28]. This treatise deals with overall perspective of Tagore's paintings and drawings in the background of history of painting, theme and form. It also analyses Tagore's writings on paintings in the perspective of art as well as literature. This is a pioneering work surveying drawings and paintings as an essential component of Tagoreana.

Kundu, Ashokumar. *Rabindra dinapanji* (1986) [29]. This book provides a day-to-day account of Tagore's life with the objective to remember Tagore in our everyday's work. The author enlisted date-wise activity of Rabindranath in first part against a date and in the second part writings on that date along with its literary form, place and date of writing.

Majumder, Swapankumar. *Rabindra granthasuchi*. (1988) [30]. Detailed information about 123 titles of Tagoreana in 21 different sections (A to U) is provided in this book. Information regarding publisher with full address, printer and its address, cover and its designer, year of first publications, number of copies printed, size, printing place, font, folio, binding, pagination, dedication, introduction written by author or other, etc. are given against an entry. Sections A to F provide information about persons behind publication, G to O physical bibliography, P to R information about main text, S to U index feature.

Robinson, Andrew. *The Art of Rabindranath Tagore*. (1989) [31]. Work deals with Rabindranath Tagore's paintings and drawings in the background of Eastern and Western responses as these occupy a place of major importance like his equally formidable output of novels, short stories, plays, essays, letters and songs. It also reproduces 175 plates of Rabindranath's paintings and drawings, and includes discussion thereof in respect of medium used, painting materials, size and signature put by Rabindranath.

Pal, Prasantakumar. *Rabijibani*. (1990) [32]. This biography of Rabindranath Tagore is written with a new approach providing detailed information and interpretation on Tagore's personal life and literary career. There is a perfect blend of Rabindranath's personal life, literary career in national and even international perspective. One special feature of this publication is that each chapter deals with one year of Tagore's life and for that reason it becomes more authentic, informative and well documented, at the same time retains literary flavour.

Datta, Bimal Kumar. *Rabindra sahitye granthagar* (1989) [33]. Tagore's vision on library in the form of its nature, function, provision of service, role of the librarian etc. are discussed in his book. Thus it covers both philosophical and functional aspects of library. Besides it gives an account how Tagore's vision of library was reflected in Tagoreana.

Mukhopadhyay, Prabhatkumar. *Gitabitan: kalanukramik suchi* (1992) [34]. This classic work on music gives an account of the books on *gan* (music) by Rabindranath starting from *Rabichhaya*

(1292 B.S.) to *Gitabitan* (1339 B.S.). Thus it helps to sketch the growth of song as part of growth of Tagoreana. In the text year-wise production of songs, date of composition, place of writing, first publication date, source of notation of songs and also *sur-tal* (musical time and measures) are given.

Mukhopadhyay, Prabhatkumar. *Rabindrajibani o Rabindrasahitya-prabashak.* (1994) [35]. The title Rabindrajibani o Rabindrasahitya-prabashak itself denotes that it is not only a biography but also acts as an entry point to the thought content of the treasure of Tagoreana. The books in four volumes Vol. 1 (1861-1901), Vol. 2 (1901-1918), Vol. 3 (1918-1934) and Vol. 4. (1935-1941) covers the entire personal as well as literary career of Rabindranath with ample documentation of notes, reference and cross references. A substantial amount of information was collected from Rabindranath himself as the first edition of this legendary work was published during Tagore's lifetime in December 1933.

Mallick, B.P., Nara, T. and Bhattacharaya, N. *Gitanjali: linguistic statistical analysis* (1994) [36]. This monograph is based on the work done by the Institute for the Study of Languages and Cultures of Asia and Africa (ILCAA), Tokyo. ILCAA has transferred a number of prose and poetical works of Rabindranath Tagore written in Bengali language to computer tape and has published word counts and concordances for some of these works. The project team of Indian Statistical Institute (ISI), Calcutta has carried on further studies on *Gitanjali* data of ILCAA. This study of pioneering nature includes statistical as well as linguistic analysis and interpretation of *Gitanjali*.

Dutta, Krishna and Robinson, Andrew. *Rabindranath Tagore: the myriad-minded man.* (1995) [37]. This beautifully illustrated biography is the product of long research of a Bengali and an English writer. The East and the West are polarities as old as the hills. Tagore's perception that they would be compelled to meet one day is the essence of this book. It highlights those works of Tagore that have universal appeal and illuminate his global views and 'myriad-mindedness'.

Mukhopadhyay, Arunkumar. *Rabindra-samiksha.* (2005)[38]. The author observes that totality of the great 'myriad-minded genius' Rabindranath Tagore manifested itself gradually in conjunction with his later output. 'In earlier days he was marked as a spiritualist and a believer in the *Upanishads*, little account was taken of his pure poetic imagination and solid humanism.' After his demise in 1941, there arose an interest in Tagore, the humanist and the seer. Since then a comprehensive study and understanding of his literary creation and paintings, social and political thoughts has been presenting him in a much more clear perspective of his humanistic, uninhibited and healthy values. This volume *Rabindra Samiksha* (a critical appreciation of Rabindranath) has attempted to evaluate Tagore as a poet and a seer, as a great humanist of radical outlook and an intellectual giant.

Das, Anathnath. *Visva-Bharati Granthan Vibhaga*. (2008) [39]. It is an edited book of collection of profiles of selective learned bodies of West Bengal including Visva-Bharati Granthan Vibhaga. The article deals with the origin, growth and development of the Granthan Vibhaga since its inception in 1923 by Rabindranath. It covers publications, first board of directors and their heartily involvement, turn over in the initial years, measures taken for quality control, above all Tagore's concern about its smooth functioning discussed.

Journal Articles

Das, Anathnath. *Publication of Rabindranath, copyright and copy left* (2002) [40]. In this paper a brief history of the publications of Tagoreana starting from publication of *Kavi-Kahini* (1878) is narrated. This paper suggests that poor quality of publication of Tagoreana immediately after the expiry of copy right is just one phase of publication. No one should be hopeful or disappointed studying these publications only. The author is hopeful about quality production in future. The author offers his suggestion to Visva-Bharati Granthan Vibhaga to be more active in editing, rearrangement of writings at affordable price to reach the masses keeping in view its glory of the past.

Ghosh, Nityapriyo. *Publication of Tagoreana, with pleasure*. (2002) [41]. The article criticizes some publications of Tagoreana with examples that came out after expiry of copyright with the change in titles matching with the titles of popular movies that were based on Rabindra fiction. The author mentioned violation of copyright by publishers copying *Granthaparichaya* which is not written by Rabindranath and mistakes due to poor proof reading. Also discussed Rabindrasangit sang by some singers violating notation even during copyright period with pleasure.

Basuchowdhury, Alokranjan. *Copyright free Rabindra creation: reaction of periodicals.* (2002) [42]. The paper discusses various articles published in Bengali newspapers like *Aajkal, Pratidin* etc. Criticises their criticism about poor quality cheap production of Tagoreana by private publishers and suggest waiting sometimes for quality production after the initial craze for publication. The articles also criticises Visva-Bharati's activity for not being able to publish complete Tagoreana even after 60 years of enjoying copyright. Mentioned copying *Granthaparichaya* is a clear violation of copyright as it is not written by Rabindranath.

Saha, Jadu. *Problem and prospects of publication of translated works of Rabindranath after expiry of copyright.* (2002) [43]. This paper criticises Visva-Bharati for not being able to circulate Rabindranath world-wide. It discusses scope of translated works of Tagoreana produced for world market along with problem of translation. The author is hopeful about the prospect of good market of Tagoreana in the copyright free environment.

Ray, Partha Pratim. *Vision of Library in Tagoreana: a bibliometric approach.* (2004) [44]. Ever since Debendranath Tagore founded Santiniketan Asrama and Rabindranath Tagore conceived the idea of Visva-Bharati, collection and preservation of books were an integral part of this institution. Tagore's concern in this regard is amply reflected in many of his speeches and writings wherein his concern for both philosophical as well as functional aspects of library science finds a poignant place. The paper aims to recapture Tagore's writing on library with the application of bibliometric technique.

The reviews of books reveal that most of the books deal with bibliographical and biographical information. The bibliographical information helps to understand the growth of Tagoreana. However, the coverage of the publications is not exhaustive, for example Pulinbehari Sen's work covers publication up to *Raja O Rani* (1889), Prabhatkumar Mukhopadhyay's work up to the publication of *Bangakautuk* (1907), and Swapankumar Majumder's study covers only 123 titles of Tagoreana. Thus only from biography of Rabindranath written by Prabhatkumar Mukhopadhyay and Prasantakumar Pal, a complete picture of growth of Tagoreana can be drawn. A comprehensive bibliography is essential for this study because only by comparing post-copyright publications of Tagoreana by private publishers with pre-copyright publications of Tagoreana conclusions could be drawn.

The reviews of journal articles reveal that authors are not satisfied with post-copyright publications of Tagoreana by private publishers. They, however, hope that quality publication will appear in future. They also mentioned cases of violation of copyright by private publishers, e.g. copying *Granthaparichaya* and suggested Visva-Bharati for rearrangement of titles at affordable price and for wide circulation.

For literature review besides the above cited documents different journals devoted to Bengali literature like Baier Desh (Anandabazar Patrika Limited), Jijnasa (Renaissance Publisher), Sanditsa (Sriaurobindo Bhavana, Calcutta) etc. and also journals of Library and Information Science were consulted. But no article related to the present study could be traced out. Articles on different aspects of Tagorean vision like education, rural development, co-operative movement, concept on agrarian reform, ideas on nationalism etc. could be found. Only two articles 'Tagore's vision of knowledge and its communication' [45] and 'Information communication in Tagore's model of rural development' [46] focus some light on the Tagorean perspective of information, knowledge and its communication.

1.13 Research Methodology

Research is the systematic approach towards purposeful investigation. It is an activity undertaken for generating fresh knowledge. *The Encyclopaedia of Social Science* defines research as "the manipulation of things, concepts or symbols for the purpose of generalizing to extend, correct or verify knowledge, whether that knowledge aids in construction of theory or in the practice of an art" [47]. According to Ostle research is "an inquiry into the nature of, the reason for, and the consequences of any particular set of circumstances, whether these circumstances are experimentally controlled or recorded just as they occur. Further, research implies the researcher is interested in more than particular results; he is interested in the repeatability of the results and in their extension to more complicated and general situation" [48]. To achieve good results to generalize it as a solution, scientific methods based on logical consideration are followed in research. As scientific method is the process of "experimentation, observation, logical arguments from accepted postulates and a combination of these three in varying proportions" [49] or it "is the method of all logically trained minds...the unity of all sciences consists alone in its methods, not in its materials; the man who classifies facts of any kind whatever, who sees their mutual relation and describes their sequences"[50]. For the purpose of generating new knowledge or solution of a problem, research comprises defining and redefining problems, formulating hypothesis or suggested solutions, collecting, organizing and evaluating data, making decisions and drawing conclusions and testing it.

A research method is the method or technique the researcher uses in performing research operations. Research methodology is the way to systematically solve the research problem. The systematic methods involve a series of processes such as formulating research problem, extensive literature survey, development of hypothesis, preparing research design, determining sample design and collecting data. For the present study systematic sampling technique had been followed for collecting data from population. A sample is "a part of the population which is studied in order to make inferences about the whole population" [51]. A sample as a representative of population is concerned with *how many* units of *what particular description* and *by what method* has been chosen for research purpose [52]. In the case of present study the unit comprises Tagoreana published before and after expiry of copyright by Visva-Bharati publishing unit and private publishers in Bengali language.

Methodology can be viewed as the essence of scientific investigation. Because of the interdisciplinary nature of library and information science, different research methods (like questionnaire, field survey, interview etc.) may be considered depending upon particular problem under study. As the research question of this study is to know the publications of Tagoreana and its quality in respect of physical bibliography as well as intellectual content of it after expiry of copyright, it requires a comparative study. For comparative study of the items such as publisher, printer, year of publication, page, size, price, ISBN (International Standard Book Number), copyright, illustrations, introduction etc. the entire publication of Tagoreana by Visva-Bharati and private publishers has been considered. But to access the quality of the literary text, comparison was made in respect of change or deletion of punctuation marks, use of additional punctuation marks, mistakes in spelling, omission/addition of words/sentence, clubbing of paragraph/lines, etc. in Tagoreana (published by Visva-Bharati) before and after expiry of copyright; and post-copyright publications by private publishers at the first page and at the interval of every ten pages. Last edition of Tagoreana published during Tagore's lifetime is considered as standard publication. Because Rabindranath himself used to correct his manuscripts of first publication in journals or books. The evidence of such kind of corrections can be observed from the first edition of many titles Tagoreana like *Europe-Pravasir Patra, Sesh Raksha, Sahaj path 1, Gitabitan, Chandalika* etc. preserved in Rabindra Bhavana. Research on such kind of corrections had been conducted based on comparative textual study of different editions of Tagoreana published during Tagore's lifetime. Examples of such studies are *Pathantar Chayan: Rabindranather Upanyas* [53] (selections from different editions: Rabindranath's fiction) *Sonar Tari: Bishoy Pathantar* [54] (Sonar Tari: Subject: Selection from different editions) etc.

To record the result of comparative study, bibliometric technique is followed, as it "has clearly become established as a sub-discipline with the application of history and sociology of knowledge in communication and information science" [55]. As the present study is concerned with quantitative and qualitative publication of Tagoreana and as such "it is a quantitative evaluation of publication patterns of all macro- and micro-communication along with their authorship by mathematical and statistical calculus" [56]. Bibliometric technique has been considered and applied as the essential tool for this purpose.

Bibliometrics can also be described as a "branch of information theory that attempts to analyse quantitatively the properties and behaviour of recorded knowledge" [57] or "the quantitative treatment of the properties of recorded discourse and behaviour pertaining to it" [58]. In this study (such as to study growth of Tagoreana) statistical bibliographic technique is followed as it "... sheds light on the process of written communication and of the nature and course of development of discipline by means of counting and analyzing the various facets of written communication" [59]. Thus, bibliometrics applies mathematics and statistical methods to book and other media of communication. Rolland Stevens considers bibliometrics as a quantitative science and divided it into two categories: (i) descriptive and (ii) evaluative [60]. Descriptive bibliometrics includes the study of the number of publications in a given field or productivity of literature in the field for the purpose of comparing the amount of research in different countries, the amount produced in different periods or the amount produced in different subdivisions of the field. This kind of study is made by a count of these writings in the field. Evaluative bibliometrics is the study of the literature used by research worker in a given field. For this study more emphasis is given on descriptive bibliometrics.

Bibliometric laws are statistical expressions, which seek to describe the working of science by mathematical means. Hulme in the year 1923 used the term 'Statistical Bibliography' to refer the application of quantitative techniques to libraries [61]. Three fundamental laws, namely Lotka's Law (1926), Zipf's Law (1933) and Bradford's Law (1934) laid the solid foundation of bibliometrics.

A.J. Lotka describes the methods of ranking of words frequency in a particular set of documents. The law is symbolically expressed as:

$$Y_x = b/n^{2:ca}, \text{ where, } a > 0, X = 1, 2, 3\ldots\ldots$$

Y_x is the relative frequencies of authors publishing X papers.

The results obtained showed surprising regularity which allowed Lotka to derive the equation, $\mathbf{x^n y = c}$ where **x** stands for the number of contributions, **y** for the number of authors, and **c** is constant [62]. Suppose, on a subject 1800 authors have contributed one paper each. Then it is likely that $\mathbf{2^2 y = 1800}$, i.e. 450 authors will have contributed 2 papers each, and $\mathbf{3^2 y = 1800}$, i.e. around 200 authors will have 3 papers each, and so on.

Bibliometrics offers one of the most puzzling phenomena in quantitative linguistics which is called Zipf's law after the name of George Kingsley Zipf, a professor of Philosophy of Harvard University. Zipf proposes an inverse relationship between the rank of a word in order of decreasing frequency and the frequency of its occurrence in a long natural language text. In other words the product of the rank and the frequency tends to be constant. This relationship is mathematically expressed as:

$$r \times f = c$$

Where r is the rank of a word, f is the frequency of occurrence of the word and c is constant.

Zipf's work on *Selected Studies of the Principle of Relative Frequency in Language* published in 1932 based on James Joyce's novel *Ulysses,* four Latin plays of *Plantus, Iliad* of Homer and the old English of *Beowulf* [63]. Zipf further advanced his study with the publication of the "*Psychobiology of Language*" based on frequency table in decreasing rank prepared by Dr. Miles L. Hanley and associates on *Ulysses* which contains 2,60,430 running words of which 29,899 are unique words. This work shows Zipf's first diagram of reciprocal relationship between log f (frequency) and log r (rank) [64].

Zipf further developed the theory of "*Human Behaviour and Principle of Least Effort*". Here Zipf attributed rank-frequency relationship to the human nature of economizing effort which is reflected in the economy of words to convey the meaning of the text. According to Zipf, "The principle of least effort means... that a person... will strive to solve his problems in such a way as to minimize the total work that he must expend in solving both his immediate problems and his probable future problems" [65]. This law is further expanded by Benoit Mandelbrot [66].

Bradford's law of scattering of articles on a particular topic over different journals. It is expressed as:

$F(X) = a + b \log x$ (where $F(x)$ = cumulative number of references contained in the first x most productive journals, a and b are constants).

Bradford argued that if scientific journals are arranged in order of decreasing productivity of articles on a given subject, they may be divided into a nucleus of periodicals more particularly devoted to the subject and several groups or zones containing the same number of articles as the nucleus, when the number of periodicals in the nucleus and succeeding zones will be as $1: n: n^2...$ [67].

Out of these three fundamental laws Zipf's law has been considered for this study as the law basically indicates the relationship between the rank of a word and the frequency of its appearance in a long literary text.

1.14 Source

To conduct research on "*Tagore in Print...*" it is necessary to study the growth of Tagoreana (all writings of Tagore in the form of poetry, fiction, drama, music, letters as well as paintings). For this bibliographical study primary and secondary sources in the form of original works or first editions were consulted. Moreover a wide range of secondary sources in the form of books and articles in Bengali and English were consulted to corroborate and critically evaluate for the purpose of interpretation.

For biographical material, sources that Tagore himself produced, i.e. *Reminiscences* at the age of fifty and *My Boyhood Days* at the age of eighty in particular and other biographical glimpses that can be found in his numerous writings were consulted. For more biographical information major biography written by three renowned Tagorean scholars, i.e. Prabhatkumar Mukhopadhyay [68], Krishna Kripalani [69] and Prasanta Kumar Pal [70] were consulted. Amongst other relevant sources, writings of Henn [71], Roy [72], Thompson [73], Dutta [74], Ghose [75], and Ghosh [76] are worthy to mention.

For comparative study of Tagoreana (pre-copyright and post-copyright) the last edition published during Tagore's lifetime and also collected works of Rabindranath published in 27 volumes by Visva-Bharati were consulted as source material. *Books in Print from West Bengal* and *Book Fair Directory* 2002-2006 were consulted to know the publishers publishing Tagoreana after expiry of copyright [77]. Tagoreana published by different publishers after expiry of copyright also comes under purview of source material for this study. To study the use of punctuation marks, change of words, spelling error, font size, illustrations, compilation, price etc. Catalogue of Visva-Bharati Granthan Vibhaga (Publishing unit of Visva-Bharati in Calcutta) and also catalogue of all the publishers published Tagoreana after expiry of copyright were also considered as source material for this study as it helped to know the total number of publications by individual publishers.

One of the important components of Tagoreana is Tagore's huge number of letters. To study these letters from bibliometric point of view special attention had been given to seventeen volumes of Tagore's *Chithipatra* (letters) published by Visva-Bharati [78] as well as his English letters published in different books and periodicals on different occasions. Rabindranath's huge number of paintings and drawings also come under purview of Tagoreana. To study the paintings and drawings and also to consult original letters and manuscripts preserved in Rabindra Bhavana museum collection were consulted as source material [79].

Source material also includes Visva-Bharati Annual Report in general and Granthan Vibhaga Annual Report in particular to have an idea about market demand, popular titles, turns over of Tagoreana five years before and after expiry of copyright.

1.15 Delimitation of the Study

The purpose of this study is not to assess, interpret or criticize intellectual content of Tagoreana in the form of poetry, fiction, essays, letters, etc. on different literary aspects or themes like education, library, society, aesthetics, rural development etc. or to critically analyse the huge number of paintings drawn by Rabindranath. This study is directed to have an idea about the growth of Tagoreana with the help of statistical account and to know the position of Tagoreana after expiry of copyright in the year 2001. This study is further delimited to the publication of Tagoreana in Bengali language in India only five years before and after expiry of copyright (1997-2006).

1.16 Bibliographic Reference

The citation used in this study is numbered within square bracket in the text in numerical order and listed in the same order at the end of each chapter. The completeness and accuracy of bibliographical details of citation is based on IS: 2381 with minor modification of italicizing the title of the books in the following manner.

Books

Sequence:

Surname of the Author (First Name). *Title.* Edition. Year of Publication. Publisher; Place of Publication; Pagination.

Examples:

TAGORE (Rabindranath). *Siksha.* 2nd ed. 1973. Visva-Bharati Granthan Vibhaga; Calcutta; p. 18.

DUTTA (Krishna) and ROBINSON (Andrew). *Rabindranath Tagore: the myriad-minded man.* 1995. Bloomsbury; London; 493p.

Journal Articles

Sequence:

Surname of the Author (First Name). Title. *Name of the Periodical.* Volume Number; Issue Number; Year; Page.

Examples:

GHOSH (Nityapriyo). Publication of Tagoreana, with pleasure. *Desh.* 69, 12; 2002; 25-27.

RAY (Partha Pratim), BISWAS (Bidhan Ch) and SEN (BK). Knowledge communication in Tagore's model for rural development: an overview. *Annals of Library and Information Studies.* 52, 3; 2005; 94-102.

NOTES AND REFERENCES

1. TAGORE (Rabindranath). *On the edges of time.* 1958. Orient Longman; Calcutta; p. 2.
2. KRIPALANI (Krishna). *Rabindranath Tagore: a biography.* 1980. Visva-Bharati; Calcutta; p. 68.
3. SENGUPTA (Samir). *Rabindranather atmiyaswajan.* 2005. Sisu Sahitya Samsad; Kolkata; p. 157.
4. MUKHOPADHAYA (Prabhatkumar). *Life of Tagore.* 1975. Indian Book Company; New Delhi; p. 14. Translated from Bengali by Sisir Kumar Ghosh.
5. MUKHOPADHYAY (Prabhatkumar). *Rabindrajivankatha.*1988. Ananda Publishers; Calcutta; p. 4.
6. DUTTA (Bhabatosh). Tagore: a short biography. In CHAUDHURY (Bhabatosh). Ed. *Introduction to Tagore.* 1983. Visva-Bharati Granthan Vibhaga; Calcutta; pp. 56-57.
7. KRIPALANI (Krishna). *Rabindranath Tagore: a biography.* 1980. Visva-Bharati Granthan Vibhaga; Calcutta; pp. 18-19.
8. TAGORE (Rabindranath). *On the edges of time.* 1958. Orient Longman; Calcutta; p. 3.
9. *Ibid.* p. 6.
10. CHATTERJEE (Ramananda). Rabindranath Tagore. *Modern Review.* 50, 6; 1931; 675.
11. TAGORE (Rabindranath). *Reminiscences.* 1917. Macmillan; London; pp. 116-117. Translation of Rabindranath's Jivansmriti by Surendranath Tagore.

12. TAGORE (Rabindranath). *Santiniketan Brahmacharyasram*. 1358 (B.S.). Visva-Bharati; Santiniketan.
13. *Visva-Bharati and its institutions*. 1956. Visva-Bharati; Santiniketan; 1956. p. 42.
14. *Santiniketan: 1901-1951*. 1951. Visva-Bharati; Santiniketan.
15. Rural reconstruction programme at Sriniketan started in 1921 with the direct involvement of three great personalities—Tagore, with his vision and dreams; L.K. Elmhirst with his leadership, sympathy and love for poor villagers of Bengal and Mrs. Straight with her gift of money.
16. TAGORE (Rabindranath). *Vichitra prabandha*. 1907. Visva-Bharati Granthan Vibhaga; Calcutta; p. 149.
17. BAMANE (NJ). Legal implication to utilization of information technology products—intellectual property rights: Indian scenario and its future perspective. Paper presented in XX *IASLIC Conference*. 1995. Lucknow; pp. 145-150.
18. UK Copyright service. Fact sheet no. P-01. Available (Online) <http://www.copyrightservice.co.uk>, website visited on March 12, 2008.
19. KEDIA (Onkar) and PANDEY (Manoj). *Common mans guide to right and facilities*. 2002. Ministry of Information and Broadcasting; New Delhi; pp. 92-97.
20. FEATHER (John) and STRUGES (Paul). *International encyclopaedia of information and library science*. 2003. Routledge; London; pp. 109-111.
21. KAUR (Rajwant) and BHAGI (Rekha Goyal). Copyright in India: an overview. *International Library Movement (ILM)*, 27, 2; 2005; 61-77.
22. TAGORE (Rabindranath). *Vichitra prabandha*. 1907. Visva-Bharati Granthan Vibhaga; Calcutta; p. 149.
23. DUTTA (Krishna) and ROBINSON (Andrew). *Rabindranath Tagore: the myriad-minded man*. 1995. Bloomsbury; London; p. 3.
24. SEN (Pulinbehari). *Rabindra granthapanji*. 1973. Visva-Bharati Granthan Vibhaga; Calcutta; p. 287.
25. MUKHOPADHYAY (Prabhatkumar). *Rabindragrantha parichiti*. 1385 (B.S.). Visva-Bharati Research Publication; Santiniketan; p. 179.
26. THOMPSON (Edward). *Rabindranath Tagore: poet and dramatist*. 1979. *Rddhi*-India; Calcutta; p. 335.
27. KRIPALANI (Krishna). *Rabindranath Tagore: a biography*. 1980. Visva-Bharati Granthan Vibhaga; Calcutta; p. 492.
28. BANDYOPADHYAY (Somendranath). *Rabindra-chitrakala: Rabindrasahityer patabhumika*. 1982. Dey's Publishing; Calcutta; p. 330.
29. KUNDU (Ashokumar). *Rabindra dinapanji*. 1986. Banglabhasa Sahitya O Sanskriti Gabeshana Sansthan; Calcutta; p. 399.
30. MAJUMDER (Swapan). *Rabindra granthasuchi*. Vol. 1. Part 1. 1395 (B.S.). National Library; Calcutta; p. 394.
31. ROBINSON (Andrew). *The art of Rabindranath Tagore*. 1989. Rupa & Co.; Calcutta; p. 221.

32. PAUL (Prasanta Kumar). *Rabijibani.* 9 Vols. 1990. Ananda Publishers; Calcutta.
33. DATTA (Bimal Kumar). *Rabindra sahitye granthagar.* 1989. Bengal Library Association; Calcutta; p. 68.
34. MUKHOPADHYAY (Prabhatkumar). *Gitabitan: kalanukramik suchi.* 1399 (B.S.). Tagore Research Institute; Calcutta; p. 448.
35. MUKHOPADHYAY (Prabhatkumar). *Rabindrajibani o Rabindrasahitya-prabashak.* 4 Vols. 1994. Visva-Bharati Granthan Vibhaga; Calcutta.
36. MALLIK (BP), NARA (T) and BHATTACHARAYA (N). *Gitanjali: linguistic statistical analysis.* 1994. Indian Statistical Institute: Calcutta; p. 318.
37. DUTTA (Krishna) and ROBINSON (Andrew). 1995. *Rabindranath Tagore: the myriad-minded man.* 1995. Bloomsbury; London; p. 493.
38. MUKHOPADHYAY (Arunkumar). *Rabindra-samiksha.* 2005. Dey's Publishing; Kolkata; p. 144.
39. DAS (Anathnath). Visva-Bharati Granthan Vibhaga. In BASU (Arun Kumar). Ed. *Saraswat: a collection of profiles of some learned bodies of West Bengal.* 2008. Paschimbanga Bangla Akademi; Kolkata; pp. 317-334.
40. DAS (Anathnath). Publication of Rabindranath, copyright and copy left. *Desh.* 69, 12; 2002; 28-32.
41. GHOSH (Nityapriyo). Publication of Tagoreana, with pleasure. *Desh.* 69, 12; 2002; 25-27.
42. BASU CHOWDHURY (Alokranjan). Copyright free Rabindra creation: reaction of periodicals. *Rabindra Bhavana.* 26, 3; 2002; 19-29.
43. SAHA (Jadu). Problem and prospects of publication of translated works of Rabindranath after expiry of copyright. *Rabindra Bhavana.* 26, 4; 2002; 21-27.
44. RAY (Partha Pratim). Vision of library in Tagoreana: a bibliometric approach. *Granthagar.* 54, 6; 2004; 153-58.
45. RAY (Partha Pratim), BISWAS (Bidhan Ch) and SEN (BK). Tagore's vision of knowledge and its communication. *SRELS Journal of Information Management.* 44, 1; 2007; 3-14.
46. RAY (Partha Pratim), BISWAS (Bidhan Ch) and SEN (BK). Knowledge communication in Tagore's model for rural development: an overview. *Annals of Library and Information Studies.* 52, 3; 2005; 94-102.
47. *The encyclopaedia of social science*, Vol. 9. 1930. Macmillan; London.
48. OSTLE (Bemard) and MENSING (Richard W). *Statistics in research.* 1975. The Iowa State University; Ames, Iowa; p. 2.
49. *Ibid.* p. 2.
50. PEARSON (Karl). *The grammar of science.* 1957. Meridian Books; New York; pp. 10-12.
51. MANHEIM (Harry). *Sociological research: philosophy and methods.* 1977. The Dorsey Press; Illinois; p. 270.
52. SINGLETON (Royce A) and STRAITS (Bruce C). *Approaches to social research.* 1999. Oxford University Press; New York; p. 134.

53. BHATTACHARYAY (Amitrasudan). *Pathantar chayan: Rabindra upanyas. 1410 (B.S.).* Visva-Bharati Granthan Vibhaga; Calcutta; p. 272.
54. GHOSH (Debkumar). *Sonar tari: bishay pathantar.* 1987. Sahitya O Desh; Hooghly; p. 174.
55. LAWANI (SM). Bibliometrics: its theoretical foundations, methods and applications. *Libri.* 31, 4; 1981; 294-315.
56. SENGUPTA (I N). Bibliometrics: a bird's eye view. *IASLIC Bulletin.* 30, 4; 1985; 167-174.
57. PRITCHARD (A). Statistical bibliography or bibliometrics. *Journal of Documentation.* 24, 4; 1969; 348.
58. FAITHORNE (RA). Empirical hyperbolic distribution (Bradford Ziff-Model) for bibliometric description and production. *Journal of Documentation.* 25, 3; 1969; p. 317.
59. PRITCHARD (A). Statistical bibliography or bibliometrics. *Journal of Documentation.* 24, 4; 1969; 348.
60. DEVARAJAN (D). *Research in library and information science.* 2002. Ess Ess Publications; New Delhi; p. 97.
61. HULME (EW). *Statistical bibliography in relation to the growth of modern civilization.* 1923. Grafton; London; p. 44.
62. LOTKA (AJ). The frequency distribution of scientific productivity. *Journal of Washington Academy of Science.* 16, 12; 1926; 317-323.
63. ZIPF (GK) *Selected studies of the principle of relative frequency in language.* 1932. Harvard University Press; Cambridge; p. 156.
64. ZIPF (GK) *The psychobiology of language.* 1935. Houghton Mifflin; Boston; p. 217.
65. ZIPF (GK) *Human behaviour and the principle of least effort.* 1949. Addison-Wesley; Cambridge; p. 87.
66. MANDELBROT (Benoit). An informational theory of the statistical structure of language. In WILLS (Jackson) Ed. *Proceedings of the symposium on "application of communication theory".* 1953. Butterworth; London; pp. 486-502.
67. BRADFORD (SC). Sources of information on specific subjects. *Engineering.* 7, 13; 1934; 85-86.
68. MUKHOPADHYAY (Prabhatkumar). *Rabindrajibani O Rabindrasahitya-prabhashak.* 4 vols. 1970. Visva-Bharati Granthan Vibhaga; Calcutta.
69. KRIPALANI (Krishna). *Rabindranath: a biography.* 1980. Visva-Bharati Granthan Vibhaga; Calcutta; 491p.
70. PAL (Prasanta Kumar). *Rabijibani.* 9 vols. 1990-. Ananda Publisher; Calcutta.
71. HENN (Katherine). *Rabindranath Tagore: a biography.* 1985. Mathuchen; New Jersey; p. 348.
72. ROY (Kshitish). *Rabindranath Tagore: a life story.* 1990. New Delhi: Ministry of Information and Broadcasting; New Delhi; p. 319.
73. THOMPSON (Edward). *Rabindranath Tagore: poet and dramatist.* 1979. Rddhi-India; Calcutta; p. 335.

74. DUTTA (K) and ROBINSON (A). *Rabindranath Tagore: the myriad-minded man.* 1975. Bloomsbury; London; p. 493.
75. GHOSE (SK). *Rabindranath Tagore.* 1986. Sahitya Akademi; New Delhi; p. 131.
76. GHOSH (SN). *Rabindranath Tagore: his life and works.* 1947. Modern Book Agency; Calcutta; p. 286.
77. *Books in print from West Bengal and fair directory: 2002-2006.* Publishers and Booksellers Guild; Kolkata.
78. TAGORE (Rabindranath). *Chithipatra.* 17 Vols. 1942-. Visva-Bharati Granthan Vibhaga; Calcutta.
79. Rabindranath entered in the first house in present Uttarayan complex on 14/15 December, 1919. The house was made of mud, and had a hatched roof. The present changed structure of that house is Konark. At present the entire complex has five buildings (Udayan, Konark, Shyamali, Punascha and Udichi) made during Rabindranath's lifetime. Vichitra was constructed in the centenary year (1961) of Rabindranath as Tagore Research Centre (Rabindra Bhavana). All these buildings together are known as Uttarayan Complex.

2

Range and Sequential Order of Tagore's Publications

2.1 Introduction

Rabindranath composed his first poem at the age of eight and by the end of his life at the age of eighty, he has written twenty-five volumes of poetry, fifteen plays, ninety-five short stories, eleven novels, thirteen volumes of essays; initiated and edited various journals; prepared Bengali textbooks, penned thousands of letters; and crossing the age of seventy created more than two thousand paintings. All these writings and paintings come under the purview of Tagoreana. It starts with the publication of the first poem signed in his own name *Hindu Melar Upahar* (The Gift of Hindu Mela). The poet read this poem at the 9th annual conference of Hindumela on 12th February, 1875. The poem was of 22 stanzas with 88 lines. It was published in the *Prabashi Patrika* in 1338 (B.S.) Magh issue [1] and first verse narrative *Banaphul* (The Wild Flower) was published in *Gyanankur o Pratibimbo.* The last birth day of Rabindranath (7th May, 1941) is marked with the publication of three books, one in verse *Janmadine* (On my Birthday), one comprising short stories, *Galpasalpa* and the English version of *Chhelebela* (Boyhood days). There are few unsigned publications of Rabindranath, namely *Bharatbhumi,* published in *Bangadarshan* in January 1874; *Abhilash* a poem with 39 stanzas comprising 156 lines published in *Tattvabodhini Patrika* in 1874; *Prakirtir Khed* (Parts 1 and 2) 350-line poem published in *Tattvabodhini Patrika* (1876); *Pralap* (Parts 1 and 2) 216-line poem published in *Gyananakur o Pratibimbo* in 1876 [Agrahayan, 1282 (B.S.)]; *Pralap* (Part 3) with 96 lines, *Bhubanmohini Pratibha*, and *Abasar Sarojini* published in *Gyananakur o Pratibimbo* in 1976 [Baishak and Ashin-Kartik issue in 1283 (B.S.)]; *Delhi-Darbar* published in 1882 with certain changes, *Bhikharini*—a short story published in 1877 [Sraban-Bhadra 1284 (B.S.)]; *Meghnadbadh Kabya Samalochana* (Criticism of Meghnadbadh) and *Karuna* (Novel) in year 1877[2]. The first verse narrative *Banaphul* is a long narrative poem in eight cantos, running over 1600 lines. It is the story of a young girl Kamala who was brought up by her father in a solitary retreat in the Himalayas [3].

Tagore's long literary career has been classified by different scholars from different viewpoints of literary development. Chunkapura classified it as youth and early adulthood writings (1878-1900), *Gitanjali* period (1900-1912), the years of matured reflections (1912-1927) and the final years (1927-1941) [4]. Thompson classified development of Tagoreana as early life and poetry (1861-1886), The *Shileida* and *Sadhana* period (1887-1897), unrest and change (1898-1905), *Gitanjali* period (1905-1919) and finally, internationalism (1919-1941) [5]. Majumdar leaving aside the period of radiant dawn 1875-1880, before the rise of the effulgent sun, divided the literary life of the poet into four epochs. The first period covers seventeen years from 1881-1897, from the date of writing of *Bau Thakuranir Hat* to that of composing the *Lakshmir Pariksha*. The second period is that of full maturity extending from 1898 to 1913. The next thirteen years or third period from 1914 to 1926 may be called the age of rejuvenation of the poet and his revolt against the conventional society. The last period covering fifteen years, 1927 to 1941 is the age of glorious and picturesque sunset [6]. Tagore's biographer Prabhatkumar though not categorically distinguished writings of Tagore like others but pointed out different phases of life such as 'littérateur in the making', 'the flower blossoms', 'the humanitarian takes his stand'; 'the nationalist takes shape', 'the brotherhood of man', 'the diffusion of culture' [7]. Kripalani pointed out different phases as adolescence, youth, maturity, a man among men, a world citizen, world in one nest, old world and new, between two worlds [8]. It is obvious that the growth of Tagoreana with the passage of time reflected faithfully the diverse tendencies of his age. But at the same time these help to usher in a new epoch in Indian history. His works were at once the products of his age and the harbinger of a new era. Rabindranath undertook many tours within the country and abroad ranging from rural Bengal such as Kushtia, Pabna, Rajsahi (now in Bangladesh), to Asia and Western countries. Hence, Tagore wrote at different places and we can find influences of these places in his writings. For example Rabindranath wrote 47 short stories between 1881 and 1897. Of these incidents described in *Thakurdada* (Grandfather), *Manbhanjan* and *Ginni* took place in Calcutta. The place of occurrence of ten short stories, namely *Ek Ratri* (The Supreme Night), *Madhyabartini* (The Woman in the Middle), *Khoka Babur Pratyavartan* (My Lord, the baby), *Prayaschitta* (Expatiation), *Kankal* (The Skeleton), *Nishithe* (At the Dead of Night), *Apad* (The castaway), *Pratihimsa* (The Revenge), *Sampadaka* (The Editor) and *Vicharaka* (The Judge) is either some small town or mofussil. The remaining thirty-four stories relate to the life of rural Bengal especially of the districts of Kushtia, Pabna and Rajsahi [9].

2.2 Creative Writings in Bengali

The creative writings in Bengali publications in Tagoreana include all Bengali books written by Rabindranath Tagore and published during Tagore's lifetime as well as posthumous publications. It excludes *Gitabitan* (musical notation) and short stories as it had been dealt with separately under the heading 'Rabindrasangit' and 'Short Stories'. The year of publication has been considered as sequential order of contribution of Tagoreana in a particular year.

Year	Publication	No. of Publications
1878	*Kavi-Kahini* (Verse)	1
1880	*Banaphul* (Verse)	1
1881	*Valmiki Pratibha* (Musical Drama), *Bhagnahriday* (Drama, in verse), *Rudrachanda* (Drama, in verse), *Europe-Pravasir Patra* (Letters)	4
1882	*Sandhya Sangit* (Verse), *Kal-Mrigaya* (Musical drama)	2
1883	*Bau-Thakuranir Hat* (Novel), *Prabhat Sangit* (Verse), *Vividha Prasanga* (Essays).	3
1884	*Chhabi o Gan* (Verse), *Prakritir Pratisodh* (Drama, in Verse), *Nalini* (Drama), *Saisav Sangit* (Verse), *Bhanusimha Thakurer Padavali* (Poems and songs).	5
1885	*Ram Mohan Ray* (Verse), *Alochana* (Essays) *Rabichchhaya* (Songs)	3
1886	*Kadi o Kamal* (Verse)	1
1887	*Rajarshi* (Novel), *Chithipatra* (Essays)	2
1888	*Samalochana* (Essays), *Mayar Khela* (Musical drama)	2

1889	*Raja o Rani* (Drama, in verse)	1
1890	*Visarjan* (Drama, in verse), *Manasi* (Verse), *Mantri Avishak* (Address)	3
1891	*Europe-Yatrir Dayari* (Part 1) (Travel)	1
1892	*Chitrangada* (Drama, in verse), *Goday Galad* (Comedy)	2
1893	*Ganar Bahi o Valmiki Pratibha* (Musical drama), *Europe-Yatrir Dayari* (Part 2), (Travel)	2
1894	*Sonar Tari* (Verse), *Chhoto Galpa* (Short Stories), *Vichitra Galpa* (Part1 and 2)(Short stories), *Katha-Chatushtay* (Short stories), *Chitrangada* o *Viday Abhishap* (Drama, in verse)	5
1895	*Galpa-Dasak* (Short stories)	1
1896	*Nadi* (Verse), *Chitra* (Verse)	2
1897	*Baikunther Khata* (Comedy), *Panchabhut* (Essays)	2
1899	*Kanika* (Verse)	1
1900	*Katha* (Verse), *Kahini* (Verse), *Kalpana* (Verse-drama), *Kshanika* (Verse), *Galpaguchha* (Part1) (Short stories)	5
1901	*Naivedya* (Verse), *Upanishad Brahma* (Essays), *Galpaguchha* (Part 2)(Short stories)	3
1903	*Chokher Bali* (Novel), *Karmaphal* (Story), *Smaran* (Verse)	3
1905	*Atmasakti* (Essays), *Baul* (Songs)	2
1906	*Bharatvarsha* (Essays), *Kheya* (Verse), *Naukadubi* (Novel)	3
1907	*Vichitra Prabandha* (Essays), *Prachin Sahitya* (Essays), *Lokasahitya* (Essays), *Sahitya* (Essays), *Adhunik Sahitya* (Essays), *Hasya-Kautuk* (Comic plays), *Vyangakautuk* (Satirical plays and essays), *Charitapuja* (Essays), *Sabhapatir Avibhashan: Pabna Sammilani* (Presidential Address: Pabna)	9
1908	*Prajapatir Nirbandha* (Novel), *Raja Praja* (Essays) *Samuha* (Essays), *Svadesh* (Essays), *Samaj* (Essays), *Saradotsav* (Essays), *Siksha* (Essays) *Mukut* (Drama), *Katha o Kahini* (Verse)	9
1909	*Sabdatattva* (Essays), *Dharma* (Sermons),	6

	Prayaschitta (Drama), *Vidyasagar-Charit* (Essays), *Gan* (Songs). *Sisu* (Verse)	
1910	*Gora* (Novel), *Gitanjali* (Songs and poems), *Raja* (Drama), *Ingraji Sahaj Siksha* (How to Learn English), *Chhutir Pada* (Exercise)	5
1911	*Atthi Galpa* (Eight stories)	1
1912	*Dakghar* (Drama), *Galpa Chariti* (Stories), *Jivansmriti* (Autobiography), *Chhinnapatra* (Letters), *Achalayatan* (Drama), *Malini* (Drama, in Verse), *Chaitali* (Verse)	7
1914	*Giti-malya* (Songs), *Gitali* (Songs), *Utsarga* (Verse), *Gan* (Songs), *Dharmasangit* (Religious songs)	5
1916	*Phalguni* (Drama), *Ghare-Baire* (Novel), *Sanchay* (Essays), *Parichay* (Essays), *Chaturanga* (Novel), *Galpasaptak* (Short stories), *Balaka* (Verse)	7
1917	*Kartar Ichchai Karma* (Essays)	1
1918	*Guru* (Drama), *Palataka* (Verse)	2
1919	*Japan-Yatri* (Travel)	1
1920	*Arupratan* (Drama), *Payla Namber* (Short stories)	2
1921	*Rinsodh* (Drama)	1
1922	*Lipika* (Prose-poems, allegories, stories), *Muktadhara* (Drama), *Sisu Bholanath* (Verse)	3
1923	*Vasanta* (Musical drama)	1
1925	*Puravi* (Verse), *Grihapravesh* (Drama), *Pravahini* (Songs)	3
1926	*Chirakumar Sabha* (Comedy), *Sodh-bodh* (Comedy), *Natir Puja* (Drama), *Raktakarabi* (Drama), *Ritu Utsav* (Drama)	5
1927	*Lekhan* (Epigrams), *Rituranga* (Musical drama)	2
1928	*Sesh Raksha* (Drama)	1
1929	*Yatri* (Travel), *Paritran* (Drama), *Yogayog* (Novel), *Sesher Kavita* (Novel), *Tapati* (Drama), *Mahua* (Verse), *Pathprichay* (Children Book)	7
1930	*Bhanusimher Patravali* (Letters)	1
1931	*Nabin* (Musical drama), *Russiar Chithi* (Letters), *Sapmochan* (Musical drama), *Vanabani* (Verse and music), *Sahaj path* (Children Book,	7

	Part 1 and 2), (Children book), *Gitabitan* (Songs), *Sanchayita* (Verse)	
1932	*Parisesh* (Verse), *Kaler Yatra* (Drama), *Punascha* (Prose-poems), *Visvavidyalayer Rup* (Essays)	4
1933	*Dui Bon* (Novel), *Manusher Dharma* (Lectures), *Vichitrita* (Verse), *Chandalika* (Musical drama), *Taser Des* (Musical drama), *Bansari* (Drama), *Bharatpathik Rammohan Roy* (Essays and Address), *Sikshar Bikiran* (Address)	8
1934	*Malancha* (Novel), *Sravan-Gatha* (Musical drama), *Char Adhyay* (Novel)	3
1935	*Sesh Saptak* (Prose-poems), *Sur o Sangeet* (Letters), *Vithika* (Verse)	3
1936	*Nritya-Natya Chitrangada* (Dance-drama), *Patraput* (Prose-poems), *Chhanda* (Essays), *Japane-Parasye* (Travel), *Paschatta Bhrahman* (Travel), *Syamali* (Prose-poem), *Sahityer Pathe* (Essays), *Praktani* (Addresses). *Chhatrasamvashan* (Address to Students)	9
1937	*Khapchhada* (Non-sense rhymes), *Sey* (Stories), *Chhadar Chhabi* (Verse), *Visva-Parichay* (Essays), *Kalantar* (Essays)	5
1938	*Prantik* (Verse), *Chandalika Nritya-natya* (Dance-drama), *Pathe o Pather Prante* (Letters), *Senjuti* (Verse), *Banglabhasha Parichay* (Essays). *Banglakavya Parichay* (Essays)	6
1939	*Prahasini* (Verse), *Akash-pradip* (Verse), *Syama* (Dance-Drama), *Pather Sanchay* (Essays and letters)	4
1940	*Navajatak* (Verse), *Sanai* (Verse), *Chhelebela* (Autobiography), *Tin-Sangi* (Short stories), *Rogasajyay* (Verse), *Chitralipi* (Drawings and Paintings)	5
1941	*Arogya* (Verse), *Janmadine* (Verse), *Galpasalpa* (Stories and Poems), *Sabhyatar Samkat* (Address), *Asramer Rup o Vikas* (Essays).	5

The Bengali publications from 1878 to 1941 forming substantial part of Tagoreana may graphically be represented as follows:

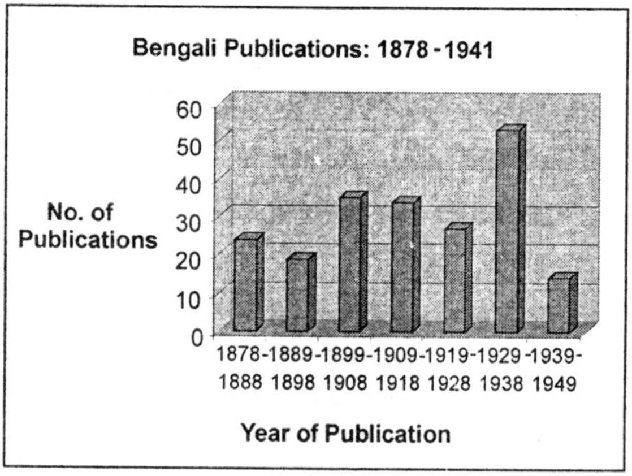

Posthumous Publications

1941	*Smriti* (Letters), *Chhada* (Verse), *Sesh Lekha* (Verse)	3
1942	*Chithipatra I, II, II* (Letters)	1
1943	*Atmaparichay* (Essays), *Sahityer Svarup* (Essays), *Chithipatra*-IV (Letters)	3
1945	*Sphulinga* (Verse), *Chithipatra-V* (Letters)	2
1948	*Mahatma Gandhi* (Addresses and essays), *Muktir Upay* (Comedy)	2
1951	*Visvabharati* (Essays), *Baikali* (Songs and poems), *Chitralipi* (Paintings)	3
1952	*Santiniketan Brahmacharyasram* (Addresses)	1
1954	*Samavayaniti* (Essays), *Chitravichitra* (Poems)	2
1955	*Itihas* (Essays)	1
1956	*Buddhadeva* (Essays and poems)	1
1957	*Chithipatra VI* (Letters)	1
1959	*Krishta* (Essays and poems)	1
1960	*Chithipatra-VII* (Letters), *Chhinapatravali* (Letters)	2
1962	*Palliprakriti* (Essays and letters)	1
1963	*Chithipatra-VIII* (Letters), *Svadesi Samaj* (Essays), *Parasya-Yatri* (Travels)	3
1964	*Chithipatra-IX* (Letters)	1
1965	*Rupantar* (Verse)	1
1966	*Sangit-Chinta* (Essays and letters)	1
1967	*Chithipatra-X* (Letters)	1

1968	*Maharshi Debendranath* (Essays, addresses, letters etc.)	1
1972	*Aurobindo Ghose* (Poem and essays)	1
1974	*Chithipatra-XI* (Letters), *Nataraj Riturangasala* (Musical drama)	2
1977	*Bankimchandra* (Essays, address and poem)	1
1979	*Malancha* (Dramatised version of the novel Malancha)	1

Posthumous publications published during 1941 to 1979 may graphically be represented as follows:

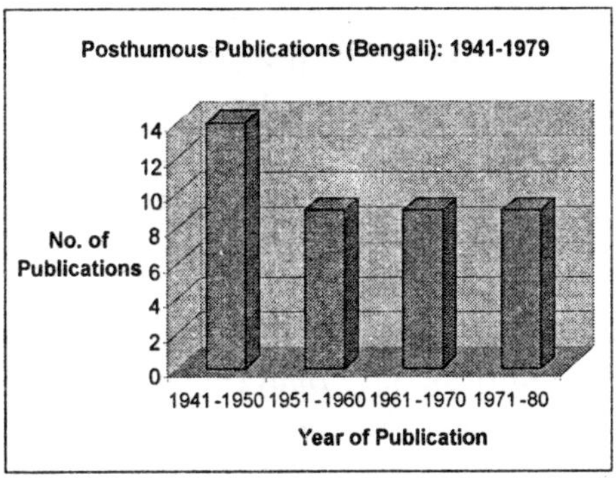

A comparative view of range and sequential order of Bengali publications in Tagoreana during life time of Tagore (1878-1941) and posthumously (1941-1979) may graphically be represented as follows:

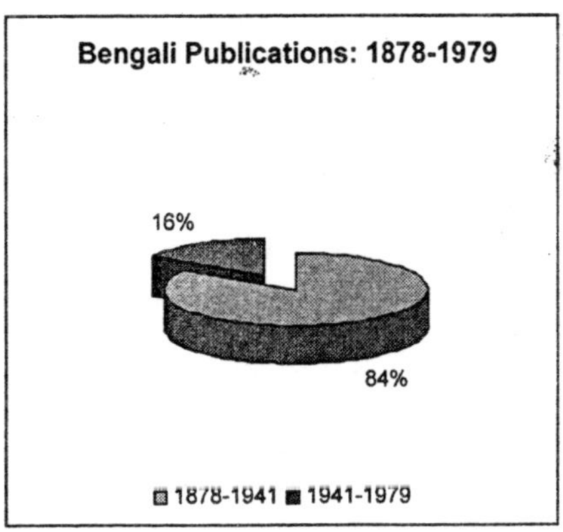

2.3 Essays and Other Works in English

Rabindranath's writings on English are mostly translations of his writings in Bengali. Only '*Poems of Kabir*' is the translations of poems written by Kabir.

Year	Publication	No. of Publication
1912	*Gitanjali* (Song Offerings)(Prose translation of poems)	1
1913	*Ghimpses of Bengal Life* (Short stories), *The Gardener* (Poems) (Prosetranslations of poems), *Sadhana* (Essays and letters), *The Crescent Moon* (Child poems) (Translation of poems), *Chitra* (Drama) (Translation of Chitrangada)	5
1914	*The King of the Dark Chamber* (Drama) (Translation of Raja) *One Hundred Poems of Kabir* (Translation of Kabir poems) *The Post Office* (Drama) (Translation of Dakghar)	3
1916	*Fruit-Gathering* (Poems), *The Hungry Stones and other Stories*, (Stories), *Stray Birds* (Epigrams)	3
1917	*My Reminiscences* (Autobiography), *Sacrifice and other Stories The Cycle of Spring* (Drama)(Translation of Phalguni), *Nationalism* (Lectures), *Personality* (Lectures)	5
1918	*Lover's Gift and Crossing* (Poems), *Mashi and other Stories* (Short Stories), *Stories from Tagore* (Stories), *The Parrot's Training* (Allegorical satire)	4
1919	*The Home and the World* (Novel), *The Fugitive* (Poems)	2
1921	*Greater India* (Essays), *The Wreck* (Novel), *Glimpses of Bengal* (Letters), *The Fugitive* (Poems), *Thought Relics* (Selected prose)	5
1922	*Creative Unity* (Essays and lectures), *Poems from Tagore* (An anthology of poems and songs)	2
1923	*The Visvabharati* (Essays)	1
1924	*Letters from Abroad* (Letters), *Gora* (Novel), *The Curse at Farewell* (Drama)	3
1925	*The Augustan Books of Modern Poetry* (Poems), *Talks in China* (Lectures), *Red Oleanders* (Drama), *Broken Ties and other Stories*	4
1928	*Fireflies* (Epigrams), *Lectures and addresses*, *Letters to*	4

	a Friend, *The Tagore Birthday Book* (Compilation of Tagore's work),	
1929	*Thoughts of Rabindranath Tagore* (Compilation of Tagore's work)	1
1931	*The Child* (Poem), *The Religion of Man* (Lectures)	2
1932	*The Golden Boat* (Poems), *Mahatmaji and the Depressed Humanity* (Address, Statements)	2
1935	*East and West* (Letters)	1
1936	*Collected Poems and Plays*	1
1937	*Man* (Lectures)	1
1940	*My Boyhood Days* (Autobiography)	1
1941	*Crisis in Civilization* (Essays)	1

The English publications in Tagoreana from 1912 to 1941 may graphically be represented as follows:

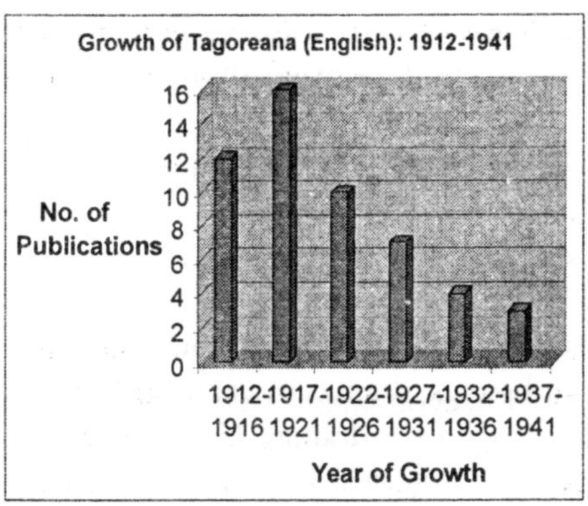

A comparison of Bengali and English publications of Tagoreana (1878-1979) may graphically be represented as follows:

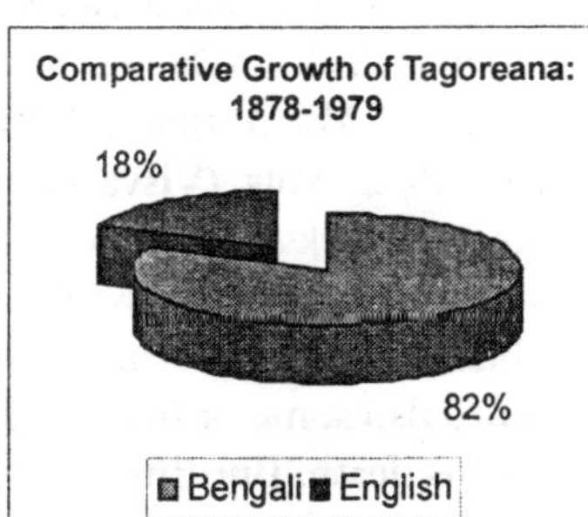

2.4 Publications of Collected Works

Year	Publication	No. of Publication
1896	*Kavya Granthavali* (Collected edition of poetical works which include dramas in verse and songs. *Malini* and *Chaitali* first published in this edition. Published by Satyaprasad Gangopadhyay)	1
1900-03	*Galpaguccha* 4. Vol. (Collection of short stories)	1
1903-04	*Kavya-Grantha*, 9 Vols. (Poems rearranged under new categories, also songs and dramas in verse *Smaran* and *Sisu* were first published under the editorship of Mohit Chandra Sen, by Majumder Library)	1
1904	*Rabindra Granthavali.* (Collection of short stories, novels, dramas and essays. Published by Hitavadi Sabha)	1
1907-09	*Gadya-Granthavali.* 16 Vols. (Collection of prose writings, essays, humorous dramas, two comedies, and a novel)	1
1909-16	*Santiniketan* (Parts 1-17)(Sermons)	1
1910-18	*Gitalipi-. 6 Vols.*(Songs)	1
1818-21	*Gitalekha 3 Vols.* (Songs)	1
1922	*Nabagitika 2 Vols.* (Songs)	1
1915-16	*Kavyagrantha,* 10 Vols.(Collection of poetical works, verse and songs, dramas in verse and prose-drama)	1
1926	*Ritu-Utsav* (Season-dramas. Collection contains *Sesh varshan*, (*Saradotsav, Vasanta, Sundar and Phalguni*)	1
1926-30	*Gitamalika,* 2 Vols. (Songs)	1
1931-32	*Gitabitan*, 3 Vols. (Songs)	1
1938	*Patradhara.* 3 Vols. Calcutta: Visva-Bharati Granthalaya. Letters. Vol. 1. *Chhinnapatra*, Vol. 2. *Bhanusinghar Patrabali*, Vol. 3. *Pathe o Pather Prante*	1
1939-65	*Rabindra-rachanavali,* 27 Vols. (Visva-Bharati published collected works of Rabindranath that contains most of Rabindranath's writings—prose, poetry, etc published in book form during Tagore's lifetime, also some of his writings published after his death. But this collection	1

	excludes letters and songs not occurring in dramas or collection of poems)	
1940-41	*Rabindra-Rachanavalii: Achalita Sangraha.* 2 Vols. (Published by Visva-Bharati as additional volumes to the Rabindra-Rachanavali. The second volume includes textbooks written by Rabindranath)	1
1942-	*Chithipatra.* 17 Vols. 1942- (Letters written by Rabindranath Tagore, Vol. 17 published in the year 1998)	1
1961-67	*Rabindra Rachanavali,* 15 Vols. (West Bengal Government Publication. Re-arranged edition on the occasion of Tagore Centenary)	1
1967	*Gitabitan,* 3 Vols. (Visva-Bharati edition comprises most of Tagore's songs, musical drama, and dance dramas)	1

Anthologies

1905	*Svadesh* (Patriotic poems and songs)	1
1909	*Chayanika* (Poems and songs)	1
1925	*Samkalan* (Prose writings other than fictions)	1
1931	*Sanchayita* (Poems, songs and verse dramas)	1

2.5 Short Stories of Rabindranath

The art of short story writing has in recent times received a great deal of attention in literary circle. But when Rabindranath started writing short stories the practice had not been fully established. Through its brevity, the short story subjected the writer to a discipline and for a period Rabindranath welcomed this discipline for his objective writing. A study of Rabindranath's short stories in the chronological order would help study pattern and change in joint family life, outside family ties, social structure etc. and also change of elements of dialogue from third person narratives to dialogue-based writings. As a result of this change the speakers took the readers nearer their heart.

Sl. No.	**Short Story**	**Publication**
1.	Bhikharini	*Bharati*,1878 (Shravan-Bhadra, 1284)

2.	Karuna	*Bharati*, 1879 (Bhadra 1285)
3.	Ghater Katha	*Bharati*, 1884 (Kartick, 1291)
4.	Rajpather Katha	*Nabajiban*, 1884 (Agrahayana, 1291)
5.	Mukut	*Balak*, 1885 (Baisakh, 1292)
6.	Dena Paona	*Hitavadi*, 1891 (Jaishthya, 1298)
7.	Postmaster	*Hitavadi*, 1891 (Jaishthya, 1298).
8.	Ginni	*Hitavadi*, 1891 (Jaishthya, 1298)
9.	Ramkanaier Nirbuddhit	*Hitavadi*, 1891 (Jaishthya, 1298)
10.	Vyabadhan	*Hitavadi*, 1891 (Asadh, 1298)
11.	Taraprasanner Kuti	*Hitavadi*, 1891 (Asadh, 1298)
12.	Khata	*Hitavadi*, 1891 (Asadh, 1298)
13.	Khoka Babur Pratyabartan	*Sadhana*, 1891 (Agrahayana 1298)
14.	Sampatti Samarpan	*Sadhana*, 1891 (Pous, 1298)
15.	Dalia	*Sadhana*, 1891 (Magh, 1298)
16.	Kankal	*Sadhana*, 1891 (Phalgun, 1298)
17.	Muktir Upaya	*Sadhana*, 1891 (Chaitra, 1298)
18.	Tyaga	*Sadhana*, 1892 (Baisakh, 1299)
19.	Ek Ratri	*Sadhana*, 1892 (Jaishthya, 1299)
20.	Ekta Ashade Galpa	*Sadhana*, 1892 (Asadh, 1299)
21.	Jivita o Mrita	*Sadhana*, 1892 (Shravan, 1299)
22.	Swarna Mrigaya	*Sadhana*, 1892 (Bhadra-Asvin, 1299)
23.	Ritimata Novel	*Sadhana*, 1892 (Bhadra-Asvin, 1299)
24.	Jaya Parajaya	*Sadhana*, 1892 (Kartick, 1299)
25.	Cabuliwala	*Sadhana*, 1892 (Agrahayana, 1299)
26.	Chhuti	*Sadhana*, 1892 (Pous, 1299)
27.	Subha	*Sadhana*, 1892 (Magh, 1299)
28.	Mahamaya	*Sadhana*, 1892 (Phalgun, 1299)
29.	Dan Pratidan	*Sadhana*, 1892 (Chaitra, 1300)
30.	Sampadaka	*Sadhana*, 1893 (Baisakh, 1300)
31.	Madhyabartini	*Sadhana*, 1893 (Jaishthya, 1300)
32.	Asambhav Katha	*Sadhana*, 1893 (Asadh, 1300)
33.	Shasti	*Sadhana*, 1893 (Bhadra, 1300)
34.	Ekti Kshudra Puratan Galpa	*Sadhana*, 1893 (Bhadra, 1300)
35.	Samapti	*Sadhana*, 1893 (Bhadra, 1300)
36.	Samasya Puran	*Sadhana*, 1893 (Agrahayana, 1300)
37.	Anadhikar Pravesh	*Sadhana*, 1894 (Shravan, 1301)
38.	Megh o Raudra	*Sadhana*, 1894 (Asvin-Kartick, 1301)

39.	Prayaschitta	*Sadhana*, 1894 (Agrahayana, 1301)
40.	Vicharak	*Sadhana*, 1894 (Pous, 1301)
41.	Nishithe	*Sadhana*, 1894 (Magh, 1301)
42.	Apad	*Sadhana*, 1894 (Phalgun, 1301)
43.	Didi	*Sadhana*, 1894 (Chaitra, 1301)
44.	Manbhanjan	*Sadhana*, 1895 (Baisakh, 1302)
45.	Thakurda	*Sadhana*, 1895 (Jaishthya, 1302)
46.	Pratihimsa	*Sadhana*, 1895 (Asadh, 1302)
47.	Kshudhita Pashan	*Sadhana*, 1895 (Shravan, 1302)
48.	Atithi	*Sadhana,* 1895 (Bhadra-Kartick, 1302)
49.	Ichchhapuran	*Sakha o Sathi*, 1895 (Asvin, 1302)
50.	Durasha	*Bharati*, 1898 (Baisakh, 1305)
51.	Putra Yajna	*Bharati*, 1898 (Jaishthya, 1305)
52.	Detective	*Bharati*, 1898 (Asadh, 1305)
53.	Adhyapaka	*Bharati*, 1898 (Bhadra, 1305)
54.	Rajatika	*Bharati*, 1898 (Asvin, 1305)
55.	Manihara	*Bharati*, 1898 (Agrahayana, 1305)
56.	Dristidan	*Bharati*, 1898 (Pous, 1305)
57.	Sadar o Andar	*Pradeep*, 1900 (Asadh, 1307)
58.	Uddhara	*Bharati*, 1900 (Shravan, 1307)
59.	Durbuddhi	*Bharati*, 1900 (Bhadra, 1307)
60.	Fail	Bharati, 1900 (Asvin 1307)
61.	Subhadristi	*Pradeep*, 1900 (Asvin, 1307)
62.	Yajneswarer Yajna	Not Published in any Journal
63.	Ulukharer Vipad	-do-
64.	Pratibeshini	-do-
65.	Nasta-Nir	*Bharati*, 1901 (Baisakh-Agrahayana 1308)
66.	Darpaharan	*Bangadarshan*, 1902 (Phalgun, 1309)
67.	Malyadan	*Bangadarshan*, 1902 (Chaitra, 1309)
68.	Karmaphal	Not Published in any Journal
69.	Gupta Dhan	*Bangabhasha*, 1904 (Kartick, 1311)
70.	Master Mashai	*Prabashi*, 1907 (Asadh-Shravan, 1314)
71.	Rashmanir Chhele	*Bharati*, 1911 (Asvin, 1318)
72.	Panraksha	*Bharati*, 1911 (Pous, 1318)
73.	Haldar Goshthi	*Sabujpatra*, 1914 (Baisakh, 1321)
74.	Haimanti	*Sabujpatra*, 1914 (Jaishthya, 1321)
75.	Bostami	*Sabujpatra*, 1914 (Asadh, 1321)
76.	Streer Patra	*Sabujpatra*, 1914 (Asadh, 1321)
77.	Bhai Phonta	*Sabujpatra*, 1914 (Bhadra, 1321)

78.	Sesher Ratri	*Sabujpatra*, 1914 (Asvin, 1321)
79.	Aparichita	*Sabujpatra*, 1914 (Kartick, 1321)
80.	Tapasvini	*Sabujpatra*, 1917 (Jaishthya, 1324)
81.	Payala Number	*Sabujpatra*, 1917 (Asadh, 1324)
82.	Patra o Patri	*Sabujpatra*, 1917 (Pous, 1324)
83.	Namanjur Galpa	*Prabasi*, 1925 (Agrahayana, 1332)
84.	Sanskar	*Prabasi*, 1928 (Asadh, 1335)
85.	Balai	*Prabasi*, 1929 (Agrahayana, 1335)
86.	Chitrakar	*Prabasi*, 1929 (Kartick, 1336)
87.	Chorai Dhan	*Chotogalpa*, 1933 (Kartick, 1340)
88.	Rabibar	*Anandabazar* (Puja Sankha)1939, (Asvin, 1346)
89.	Shesh Katha	*Sanibarar Chithi*, 1939 (Phalgun, 1346)
90.	Chotogalpa	*Desh*, 1939 (Agrahayana, 1346)
91.	Laboratory	*Anandabazar* (Puja Sankha)1940, (Asvin, 1347)
92.	Badnam	*Prabasi*, 1941 (Asadh, 1348)
93.	Pragati Samhar	*Anandabazar* (Puja Sankha)1941, (Asvin, 1348)
94.	Shesh Purashkar	*Visvabharati Patrika*1942 (Shravan, 1349)
95.	Musalmanir Galpa	*Ritupatra*, 1955 (Asadh, 1362)

The publication of short stories in Tagoreana from 1878 to 1955 may graphically be represented as follows:

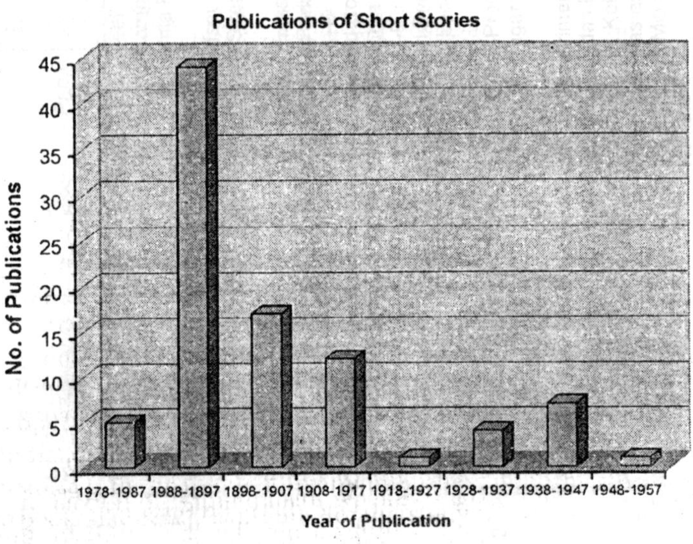

2.6 Tagore: The Phenomenal Letter-writer

Rabindranath wrote huge number of letters during his lifetime not only to communicate messages to persons for specific purpose but also to describe nature, idea on society, education, etc. These writings form a substantial part of Togareana. Tagore's letters written to his niece Indira Devi Chaudhurani published in *Chhinapatravali* written during 1885-1895 are not just letters but finer prose where from the true picture of poet Rabindranath as well as imaginative Rabindranath can be drawn. These letters may help to know Tagore's imaginative thinking to construct his biography, to establish his relationship with different people, period of letter correspondence, mode of relationship, etc. Most of the letters were first published in different journals and were in the personal collection of different people to whom the poet wrote. Only after the establishment of Rabindra Bhavana, Visva-Bharati took initiatives to collect them and later on published in the book entitled *Chithipatra* [10]. Many letters may still be in the custody of individuals. There are 4098 Rabindra-patravali (letters) published in *Chithipatra.* The chronological order of writings of letters being a substantial part of Tagoreana can be found from the table 2.1.

Rabindranath wrote letters to his family members, relatives, Santiniketan-associates, political personalities like Subhas Chandra Bose, Mahatma Gandhi, literary colleagues. The poet also expressed his ideas about religion, education, society, politics, etc. in his numerous letters. An alphabetical listing of recipients of Rabindra-patra (letters of Rabindranath) with the dates of the first and the last letter might be of help for further study in this respect.

It is clear that Rabindranath wrote a huge number of letters but his letters should not be regarded as material only for a study of his rare and many-faceted mind. It is wrong to think that they are fascinating only because they come from the pen of one whose superlative achievements in other forms of literature and in other spheres of activity have made him world famous. They are interesting in themselves, for more often than not they are not perfect specimen of the epistolary art. It is a joy to read them because whatever their subject, and whatever the mood that inspires them—buoyant or serene, humorous or pensive—they are always supremely well-written.

Table 2.1: Sequential Order of Letters in Tagoreana

Year	Jan	Feb.	March	April	May	June	July	Aug.	Sept.	Oct.	Nov.	Dec.	Total
1878										5			5
1879													7(7)
1880	1												1
1881													1(1)
1882							1						1
1883	3		6									3	12
1884	1	1											12(10)
1885							1		1	3		2	11(4)
1886	2			1	2		2						35(28)
1887		1		1			1		2	2			7
1888				2		1							4(1)
1889				1		1						1	4(1)
1890	3				2	2		1	2	2		1	13
1891	9	8	1			10	2	4	3	5	1	1	45(1)
1892	3	1	1	2	11	12	7	2	1		1	10	55(4)
1893		9	5	4	6	3	9	4	2	1			43
1894		2	6	1		6	10	16	11	16	5	5	78
1895	1	9	11	7	1	5	6	6	5	8	5	9	73
1896			1							1			2
1897								1					2(1)
1898						2	2				1		4

(Contd.)

Year	Jan	Feb.	March	April	May	June	July	Aug.	Sept.	Oct.	Nov.	Dec.	Total
1899				1	1	6	5	5	7	2	3	3	36(3)
1900		1	1	1	2	4	8	16	7	4	3	9	56
1901	4	3	17	10	10	6	7	7	4	2	3		74(1)
1902	1	6	2	14	8	1	3	2	2	3	4	4	50
1903	6	4	11	6	7	5	6	15	1	10	3	5	84(5)
1904	3	2	5	5	7	6	5	7	4	6	7		58(1)
1905			2	3	4	2	4	3		4	1	2	26(1)
1906	1	2	3	5	4	6	3			6	3	1	34
1907		1	1	5	8	2	4	4	6	10	5	15	63(2)
1908	14	17	10	8	6	3	9	3	6	3	7	4	90
1909	2		4	10	3		6	2	4	8	5	6	52(2)
1910	3	2	2	10	8	3	10	6	10	9	7	4	77(3)
1911	7	3	4	10	17	13	6	7	12	17	23	3	125(3)
1912	8	12	18	7	11	11	1	9	11	14	13	15	130
1913	21	16	10	11	20	5	4	2	2	5	12	5	115(2)
1914	4	6	9	9	7	5	8	2	5	4	1	4	70(6)
1915	4	10	10	4		4	6	5	4	4	5	5	66(5)
1916	9	13	4	13	8	3	4	6	7	7			74
1917			4	10	5	6	2	9	5	11	13	2	70(3)
1918	5	11	3	8	7	1	9	7	9	10	8	11	89
1919	3	3	2	12	12	4	6	5	2	8	10	5	74(2)
1920	6	5	2	1	2	2	3	7	4	2	2	4	40

(Contd.)

Year	Jan.	Feb.	March	April	May	June	July	Aug.	Sept.	Oct.	Nov.	Dec.	Total
1921	1	1	4	4	6	1	2	2	13	7	6	3	54(4)
1922	5	5	11	7	10	5	3	2	7	3	4		64(2)
1923	1	2	5	3	2	2	2	2	8	6	5	2	41(1)
1924	2	3	3	4	2			2	7	2	1	7	34(1)
1925	2		3	9	8	4	3	1	5	9	4	8	57(1)
1926	5		1	7	8	3	4		1	5	1	14	52(3)
1927	16	5	14	9	10	6	14	14	13	9	19	12	144(3)
1928	7	18	4	6	8	5	13	17	20	23	12	5	138
1929	5	4	14	1		1	15	12	15	15	19	8	109
1930	7	13	2	5	9	5	7	7	7	20	5	1	88
1931	1	8	10	21	25	26	22	19	14	23	12	14	197(2)
1932	13	10	8	2		12	9	11	7	19	14	8	114(1)
1933	3	3	4	8	5	10	11	7	10	11	13	2	87
1934	10	1	11	22	7	5	12	15	6	18	6	6	119
1935	19	2	18	16	17	21	11	12	14	23	8	7	168
1936	10	6	4	14	5	9	12	6	15	28	5	9	123
1937	9	4	13	9	17	5	12	12	4	20	12	5	124(2)
1938	13	12	12	11	33	14	10	12	19	21	12	11	180
1939	9	8	14	9	11	9	9	5	12	19	7	3	117(2)
1940	11	8	9	7	16	7	6	6	5	3	2	4	84
1941	3	2	3	8	10	9	1						36

* Number within bracket in the total column indicates letter written in the corresponding year without any reference to the month or date

Sl. No.	Name	Date of writing First-Last Letter	No. of Letters
		A	
1.	*Abala Basu*	4.06.1901-24.11.1937	07
2.	*Abaninath Ray*	20.12.1915-11.06.1939	09
3.	*Abanindranath Tagore*	24.08.1916-29.06.1941	06
4.	*Abdul Oudud*	28.04.1919	01
5.	*Achintakumar Sengupta*	17.10.1928	01
6.	*Ahgornath Chattopadhyay*	23.02.1909	01
7.	*Ajindranath Tagore*	6.03.1940	01
8	*Ajit Kumar Chakraborty*	28.03.1903-10.10.1913	50
9.	*Akshoy Kumar Bhattacharya*	5.10.1934	01
10.	*Akshoy Kumar Maitra*	1.9.1902-18.12.1913	02
11.	*Alakananda (Swami)*	Feb.1929	01
12.	*Altaf Chowdhury*	30.04.1934	01
13.	*Amal Home*	5.12.1909-10.11.1940	50
14.	*Amita Tagore*	4.05.1939-18.12.1940	03
15.	*Amiya Chakravarty*	22.06.1922-22.12.1940	81
16.	*Amiyakumar Ghosh*	July 1918	01
17.	*Anadikumar Dastidar*	5.08.1920-28.10.1923	03
18.	*Anangamohan Ray*	12.07.1910	01
19.	*Anangamohini Devi*	2.08.1911	01
20.	*Anathnath Basu*	10.03.1919	01
21.	*Anderson, J.D.*	18.02.1914-2.07.1914	02
22.	*Annadasankar Ray*	2.01.1930-8.05.1940	03
23.	*Anupama Bandyopadhyay*	5.03.1920	01

24.	*Arabindomohan Basu*	19.11.1908-1910	02
25.	*Arun Chandra Sen*	19.8.1929	01
26.	*Asha Devi*	28.02.1930-2.10.1930	02
27.	*Ashalata Devi*	1.05.1933	01
28.	*Ashutosh Mukhopadhaya*	20.10.1921-26.06.1923	02
29.	*Asit Kumar Haldar*	9.12.1912-15.09.1939	291
30.	*Atul Ghosh*	25.11.1906	01
31.	*Atul Prasad Sen*	1897-22.07.1932	10
32.	*Atul Sen*	13.11.1915-4.3.1916	11

B

33.	*Balai Chand Mukhopadhyay*	16.04.1937-Nov.1939	17
34.	*Balendranath Tagore*	Aug.1891-1891	03
35.	*Bankim Chandra Ray*	July 1913-17.04.1919	08
36.	*Basanta Kumar Gupta*	23.03.1901-13.03.1902	07
37.	*Basanti Bagchi*	27.06.1931-29.10.1939	32
38.	*Bengal Chemical Employees*	Nov.1940	01
39.	*Bhakti Devi*	5.09.1930-13.10.1930	02
40.	*Bhupendrachandra Chakraborty*	22.12.1920-31.10.1934	02
41.	*Bhupendrachandra Rakshit*	24.11.1920	01
42.	*Bhupendranath Sanyal*	27.09.1904-1917	81
43.	*Bhupeschandra Ray*	1.08.1908-27.03.1916.	02
44.	*Bidhan Chandra Ray*	8.03.1934	01
45.	*Bidhushekar Shastri*	12.05.1908-25.06.1938	14
46.	*Biharilal Goswami*	1907	01
47.	*Biharilal Gupta*	10.10.1913	01
48.	*Bijan Behari Bhattacharyya*	30.09.1935-16.11.1938	02

49.	*Bijay Chandra Majumder*	12.09.1902-23.11.1919	04
50.	*Bijaykrishna Ghosh*	10.03.1922-30.03.1922	03
51.	*Bijaylal Chattopadhyay*	10.10.1918-4.02.1939	07
52.	*Bijayranjan Sen*	19.05.1938	01
53.	*Bimalakanta Raychowdhury*	13.11.1927-10.05.1940	12
54.	*Bimalnarayan Chowdhury*	1.08.1932	01
55.	*Binayendranath Sen*	24.02.1902-29.05.1906	03
56.	*Bipin Behari Gupta*	20.11.1911-19.06.1913	03
57.	*Bir Bikram Dev Manikya Bahadur*	8.01.1939-14.05.1941	02
58.	*Birchandra Manikya*	05.05.1886	01
59.	*Birendra Krishna Manikya*	27.01.1920-2.02.1920	02
60.	*Birendrakishore Raychowdhury*	19.08.1931-23.08.1931	02
61.	*Bisu Mukhopadhyay*	23.06.1941	01
62.	*Bomkesh Mustafi*	11.03.1905	01
63.	*Brajendra Kishore Devbarma*	3.08.1901-3.12.1926	29
64.	*Brajendranath Sil*	31.10.1921-25.2.1936	02
65.	*Bratindranath Tagore*	7.08.1924-10.05.1925	02
66.	*Brindabanchandra Bhattacharyya*	6.04.1919-29.03.1937	06
67.	*Buddhadev Basu*	29.08.1938-May 1940	11

C

68.	*Chaitanya Library*	Feb.1891	01
69.	*Chanchala Devi*	30.01.1932-28.10.1939	09
70.	*Chandranath Basu*	6.07.1891	01
71.	*Charuchandra Bandyopadhyay*	28.09.1909-13.05.1938	35

72.	*Charuchandra Dutta*	29.08.1936	01
73.	*Chittaranjan Bandyopadhyay*	23.10.1931	01
		D	
74.	*Dakshinaranjan Mitra-Majumder*	14.04.1908-18.10.1908	02
75.	*Debendranath Mukhopadhyay*	27.07.1929-19.11.1929	02
76.	*Debkumar Chowdhury*	26.01.1933	01
77.	*Debprasad Ghosh*	12.06.1937	02
78.	*Debrani Devi*	22.10.1935-14.04.1941	11
79.	*Dhirendrakrishna Debbarma*	26.03.1925-21.05.1934	11
80.	*Dhirendramohan Sen*	15.07.1935	01
81.	*Dhirendranath Mukhopadhaya*	29.10.1910-1922	12
82.	*Dhurjati Prasad Mukhopadhaya*	8.10.1917-13.07.1935	17
83.	*Dijendralal Ray*	6.05.1905	01
84.	*Dijendranath Datta*	12.02.1940	01
85.	*Dijendranath Maitra*	2.12.1909-14.04.1916	20
86.	*Dilipkumar Roy*	11.11.1923-Feb.1939	64
87.	*Dinendranath Tagore*	22.05.1816-6.10.1927	05
88.	*Dineshchandra Sen*	23.06.1898-10.01.1910	46
89.	*Dwarakanath Datta*	16.04.1927	01
90.	*Dwijendranath Tagore*	6.07.1920	01
		E	
91.	*Editor, Anandabazar Patrika*	19.08.1936	01
92.	*Editor, Bharati*	1879	01
93.	*Editor, Chattogram Sammiliini*	16.03.1909	01

94.	*Editor, Desh*	June 1936	01
95.	*Editor, Prabasi*	6.05.1928-9.7.1939	03
96.	*Editor, Swaraj Patrika*	19.12.1927	01
97.	*Editor, Vichitra*	25.09.1936	01

G

98.	*Gagenendranath Tagore*	Nov.1898-26.10.1928	04
99.	*Girijanath Chakraborty*	24.08.1914	01
100.	*Gita Bandyopadhyay*	24.10.1938	01
101.	*Gourhari Sen*	31.12.1909	01
102.	*Gurhari Mitra*	7.10.1936	01
103.	*Gurudas Bandyopadhyay*	Dec.1892	01
104.	*Gurugopal Ghosh*	27.03.1910-15.04.1911	05
105.	*Gurusaday Dutta*	1932	01

H

106.	*Haimanti Devi*	28.12.1938	01
107.	*Haricharan Bandyopadhyay*	27.09.1926	01
108.	*Harihar Seth*	18.03.1937	01
109.	*Haritkrishna Deb*	13.05.1933-11.05.1938	02
110.	*Hemantabala Devi*	8.02.1931-10.05.1940	265
111.	*Hembala Sen*	6.10.1927-28.10.1930	05
112.	*Hemendrakumar Ray*	9.03.1936	01
113.	*Hemendraprasad Ghosh*	18.09.1935	01
114.	*Hemlata Tagore*	10.10.1911-1913	20
115.	*Hijlir Rajbandi*	22.01.1932	01
116.	*Hitendramohan Nandi*	27.05.1911-Jan 1920	10

I

117.	*Indira Devi*	14.07.1938	01

118.	*Indira Devi Chaudhuri*	16.09.1887-13.5.1941	339
119.	*Indulekha Chowdhury*	29.10.1910	01

J

120.	*Jadunath Sarkar*	8.05.1910-26.04.1934	16
121.	*Jagadananda Roy*	5.06.1908-28.02.1930	43
122.	*Jagatmohan Sen*	21.11.1933	01
123.	*Jagdishchandra Bose*	26.06.2899-13.11.1928	37
124.	*Jamini Ray*	25.05.1941-7.06.1944	02
125.	*Janakinath Ray*	2.07.1906-29.04.1911	04
126.	*Jibanmay Ray*	5.11.1931-13.02.1933	02
127.	*Jnanadanandini Devi*	3.09.1911	01
128.	*Jnanchandra Bandyopadhyay*	22.08.1917-23.08.1922	02
129.	*Jnanendranath Ghosh*	30.03.1909-4.09.1923	14
130.	*Jnanendralal Bhaduri*	6.07.1934	01
131.	*Jnanendranath Chattopadhyay*	19.12.1908-25.04.1913	07
132.	*Jogenchandra Debbarma*	9.11.1922	01
133.	*Jogendranath Ray*	6.05.1914	01
134.	*Jogindranath Basu*	16.04.1907	01
135.	*Jotindramohan Tagore*	16.10.1905-14.04.1907	02
136.	*Jotindranath Mukhopadhyaya*	2.01.1911-23.05.1911	03
137.	*Jugalkishore Sarkar*	16.10.1929	01
138.	*Jyotirindranath Tagore*	1879-March 1914	07

K

139.	*Kadambari Devi*	Oct.1878-10.05.1931	09
140.	*Kadambini Devi*	1.10.1903-10.05.1931	95

141.	*Kalidas Basu*	22.10.1910-7.06.1913	02
142.	*Kalidas Nag*	26.03.1917-25.07.1936	25
143.	*Kalimohan Ghose*	2.10.1930	01
144.	*Kalyani Bhattacharyya*	3.12.1932	01
145.	*Kanjilal Ghosh*	13.11.1902	01
146.	*Kedarnath Bandyopadhyay*	7.12.1925-22.04.1937	07
147.	*Khirodchandra Raychowdhury*	Aug.1892-April 1893	02
148.	*Kiranbala Sen*	10.01.1918-6.06.1930	02
149.	*Kishorekanta Bagchi*	30.07.1938-20.10.1938	02
150.	*Kishorimohan Santra*	9.05.1938	01
151.	*Krishnadayal Basu*	21.09.1925	01
152.	*Kshitimohan Sen*	17.10.1921	01
153.	*Kshitishchandra Datta*	1.03.1922	01
154.	*Kumudini Basu*	20.04.1907-5.07.1909	03

L

155.	*Labanyalekha Chakraborty*	27.01.1910-27.04.1919	03
156.	*Lalitkumar Bandyopadhya*	19.11.1911-23.12.1911	02
157.	*Lokendranath Palit*	March 1892-Sept.1892	04

M

158.	*M.A. Ajan*	25.03.1934	01
159.	*Madhurilata Devi*	19.031912-3.03.1913	05
160.	*Maitreyi Devi*	13.11.1927-30.06.1941	38
161.	*Mamata Dasgupta*	8.09.1925-14.01.2927	03
162.	*Manoranjan Bandyopadhyaya*	25.05.1902-14.06.1940	103
163.	*Manoranjan Chowdhury*	5.11.1909-12.02.1916	18
164.	*Meghnad Saha*	11.11.1938	01
165.	*Mira Devi*	5.02.1907-14.04.1938	83
166.	*Mohanlal Gangyopadhyay*	10.06.1931	01

167.	*Mohim Tagore*	12.04.1899-16.06.1906	10
168.	*Mohinimohan Mukhopadhyay*	27.05.1937	01
169.	*Mohitchandra Sen*	12.01.1902-16.05.1905	53
170.	*Monika Mahalanobis*	8.12.1931-16.11.1932	02
171.	*Monilal Gangyopadhyaya*	14.09.1911-13.09.1924	40
172.	*Monilal Ray*	8.12.1932	01
173.	*Monindranath Bandyopadhyaya*	16.11.1902	01
174.	*Monomohan Sen*	24.10.1940	01
175.	*Mrinalini Devi*	Jan. 1890-Nov.1901	36
176.	*Mrinalini Sen*	12.04.1917	01
177.	*Murari Bhaduri*	26.11.1929	01

N

178.	*Nabendusundar Bandyopadhyaya*	19.06.1932-21.08.1936	02
179.	*Nabinchandra Sen*	9.08.1894-10.08.1900	05
180.	*Nagendranath Gangyopadhyaya*	22.05.1907-8.06.1925	40
181.	*Nagendranath Gupta*	July 1885	01
182.	*Nalinchandra Ganguly*	28.7.1930	01
183.	*Nalini Devi*	14.04.1911-22.08.1911	02
184.	*Nandagopal Sengupta*	22.12.1937-24.06.1941	13
185.	*Nandalal Bose*	25.04.1914-3.12.1940	06
186.	*Nandita Devi*	4.12.1924-May 1941	20
187.	*Nandita Kripalini*	26.12.1934-11.06.1939	10
188.	*Narendra Deb*	11.05.1931-9.05.1938	02
189.	*Narendrachandra Debberma*	30.09.1921	01
190.	*Narendranath Nandi*	22.05.1912-1.01.1931	06
191.	*Nareshchandra Sengupta*	29.11.1927-21.04.1931	04
192.	*Nepalchandra Ray*	26.10.1911-16.04.1934	25
193.	*Nikhilchandra Bagchi*	12.10.1938	01

194.	*Nilima Das*	26.02.1912-2.11.1932	03
195.	*Nirjharani Sarkar*	6.05.1908-15.10.1936	24
196.	*Nirmal Kumar Mahalanobis*	22.04.1925-8.6.1941	506
197.	*Nirmalchandra De*	2.06.1911	01
198.	*Nirmalchandra Mallick*	17.05.1937	01
199.	*Nirmalchandra Sen*	16.02.1932	01
200.	*Nishikanta Raychowdhury*	13.01.1940	01
201.	*Nitendranath Gangyopadhyaya*	24.10.1930-12.07.1932	09

P

202.	*P.K. Ray*	28.04.1910	01
203.	*Padminimohan Neogi*	21.07.1910-13.09.1910	02
204.	*Parimal Goswami*	17.02.1908-20.06.1931	02
205.	*Parimohan Sengupta*	13.03.1931-1939	02
206.	*Parul Devi*	1.06.1935-12.11.1935	03
207.	*Pashupati Bhattacharaya*	10.09.1923	01
208.	*Pearson, W.W.*	6.04.1913-6.08.1913	03
209.	*Phanibhushan Adhikari*	3.05.1931-7.10.1936	03
210.	*Prabhat Chandra Gupta*	20.02.1937-17.05.1938	03
211.	*Prabhatkumar Muhkopadhyaya* (Writer)	24.11.1895-27.07.1914	11
212.	*Prabhatkumar Mukhopadhyaya* (Tagore's Biographer)	11.10.1911-14.04.1936	04
213.	*Prabodh Chandra Sen*	23.08.1932	01
214.	*Prabodh Kumar Sanyal*	5.11.1933-3.04.1938	03

215.	*Prabodhendunath Tagore*	4.07.1936	01
216.	*Prafullachandra Ray*	4.12.1925	01
217.	*Prafullakumar Sarkar*	15.01.1928	01
218.	*Prafullanath Tagore*	8.08.1934-17.08.1934	02
219.	*Pramadaranjan Ghosh*	19.04.1921	01
220.	*Pramatha Choudhuri*	21.05.1890-22.07.1940	137
221.	*Pramathnath Bisi*	29.04.1936	01
222.	*Pramathnath Tarkabhushan*	20.05.1922	01
223.	*Premendra Mitra*	19.03.1939-8.04.1939	02
224.	*Pranab Bahubalindra*	4.02.1935	01
225.	*Prasantachandra Mahalanobis.*	25.09.1930-1.10.1930	02
226.	*Pratima Devi*	7.07.1910-30.07.1941	73
227.	*Pritthisingh Nahar*	4.08.1928-14.10.1932	02
228.	*Priyonath Sen*	1881-1915	199
229.	*Pulinbehari Sen*	20.11.1937	01
230.	*Puspa Devi*	27.01.1940	01

R

231.	*Rebatimohan Barman*	22.01.1932	01
232.	*Radha Kishore Manikya*	27.03.1900-29.12.1906	14
233.	*Radhananda Debsarma*	16.01.1940	01
234.	*Radharaman Kar*	7.02.1902-	02
235.	*Radharani Devi*	2.08.1924-21.06.1938	18
236.	*Rajanikanta Sen*	30.06.1910	01
237.	*Rajnarayan Basu*	11.10.1895	01
238.	*Rajsekhar Basu*	11.02.1931	01
239.	*Rama Devi*	29.05.1933	01
240.	*Rama Kar*	7.03.1929	01
241.	*Ramananda Chattopadhyaya*	25.06.1910-24.06.1941	120
242.	*Ramanuj Acharyagoswami*	24.01.1932	01

243.	*Ramendrasundar Trivedi*	19.07.1897-21.03.1917	27
244.	*Rameshchandra Majumder*	16.12.1925-Jan 1926	06
245.	*Ranu Mookerjii*	19.08.1917-21.04.1927	63
246.	*Rathindranath Tagore*	14.05.1903-24.04.1940	111
247.	*Reba Ray*	8.11.1927-30.10.1931	03
248.	*Rukminibabu*	1885	01

S

249.	*Sabita Bhattacharyya*	29.03.1935-18.04.1935	03
250.	*Sachindranath Adhikari*	19.05.1938	01
251.	*Sachindranath Chattopadhyay*	1918	01
252.	*Sahana Devi*	10.01.1927-4.09.1938	07
253.	*Sailendranath Ghosh*	11.03.1931-14.10.1936	03
254.	*Saileshchandra Debbarma*	17.04.1927-29.10.1939	07
255.	*Samarendranath Tagore*	2.09.1916-7.10.1924	03
256.	*Sanjay Bhattacharyya*	22.05.1935-10.05.1940	04
257.	*Sanjukta Das*	4.03.1922-4.06.1941	30
258.	*Santa Devi*	21.01.1925-12.10.1937	16
259.	*Santidev Ghosh*	21.01.1941-21.03.1941	02
260.	*Santoshchandra Mazumder*	17.08.1910-19.05.1926	21
261.	*Saradacharan Datta*	23.08.1910-9.12.1918	05
262.	*Sarajkumari Devi*	20.07.1909	01
263.	*Sarasilal Sarkar*	9.04.1928-11.10.1931	03
264.	*Saratchandra Chattopadhaya*	10.02.1927-11.10.1936	07
265.	*Saratchandra Ray*	19.12.1907	01
266.	*Sarju Debbarma*	26.10.1928	01
267.	*Sarju Devi*	3.12.1919	01
268.	*Sasadhar Singha*	15.05.1934	01

269.	*Satishchandra Roy* (Adhyapak, Santiniketan)	March 1903-14.12.1903	04
270.	*Satishchandra Roy* (Tripura)	27.10.1922-1922	03
271.	*Satyabhusan Datta*	11.01.1922	01
272.	*Satyabhusan Sen*	3.01.1930-June 1931	02
273.	*Satyaprasad Gangyopadhyay*	Aug.1091-15.04.1916	02
274.	*Satyendranath Datta*	15.01.1913-1914	03
275.	*Satyendranath Tagore*	11.01.1922	01
276.	*Shyamdas Lahiri*	8.11.1932	03
277.	*Sibnath Shastri*	23.07.1898	01
278.	*Sipra Sarkar*	7.09.1937	01
279.	*Sisirkumar Maitra*	18.09.1921-3.04.1937	07
280.	*Sita Devi*	26.12.1927	01
281.	*Sitalchandra Ray*	14.10.1920	01
282.	*Snehalata Sen*	2.07.1906-8.02.1931	09
283.	*Sobhana Devi*	11.05.1923	01
284.	*Soumendra Chandra Debbarma*	12.10.1913-29.10.1921	04
285.	*Srischandra Mazumder*	16.10.1885-15.09.1908	44
286.	*Subhas Chandra Bose*	16.04.1931-12.12.1939	14
287.	*Subodhchandra Mazumder*	25.01.1903-10.03.1928	13
288.	*Sucharu Devi*	17.10.1906-22.01.1936	07
289.	*Sudhakanta Roychowdhury*	27.05.1911-13.10.1940	15
290.	*Sudharani Das*	16.04.1934	01
291.	*Sudhenduranjan Homeray*	14.03.1924	01
292.	*Sudhindranath Datta*	11.07.1928-16.06.1939	26
293.	*Sudhirkumar Bandyopadhyay*	18.06.1932	01
294.	*Suhridkumar Mukhopadhyay*	12.06.1910-9.10.1931	08
295.	*Sujitkumar Mahalanobis*	22.02.1928	01

296.	*Sukumar Chattopadhyay*	11.05.1938-20.01.1940	04
297.	*Suniti Chattopadhyay*	25.11.1927-4.05.1940	06
298.	*Suniti Devi*	18.08.1919-8.12.1929	03
299.	*Surendranath Dasgupta*	20.11.1910-Oct.1937	17
300.	*Surendranath Kar*	6.05.1921-8.10.1930	06
301.	*Surendranath Maitra*	14.12.1936	01
302.	*Surendranath Tagore*	2.09.1916	01
303.	*Sureshchandra Chakraborty*	14.04.1924	01
304.	*Suriti Devi*	21.11.1911-13.05.1928	08
305.	*Sushil Chandra Mitra*	20.06.1931-21.07.1932	02
306.	*Sushil Kumar Gupta*	21.09.1910-26.04.1911	04
307.	*Swarnakumari Devi*	3.09.1912-April 1925	03
		T	
308.	*Tanu Devi*	12.02.1930	01
309.	*Thakurdas Mukhopadhyay*	15.03.1895-1903	07
310.	*Tejeshchandra Sen*	23.10.1926	01
		U	
311.	*Uma Gupta*	1927	01
312.	*Uma Mitra*	11.05.1938	01
313.	*Umeshchandra Batyabal*	1.04.1894	01
314.	*Unknown*	Oct. 1878-12.09.1938	30
315.	*Upendranath Gangyopadhyay*	20.02.1930	01

An in-depth study of letters written by Rabindranath indicates that many characters of his short stories like Giribala of '*Megh o Raudra*', '*Postmaster*', Mrinmayi of '*Samapti*' or Phatik of '*Chhuti*' make their first appearance in letters. Not only that many well-known poems have their first draft as it were in letters. Example of such delightful prose counterpart of poems can be cited from the poems of *Chaitali* and *Chitra* as *'Noon'*, *'Morning'*, *'The River Icchamati'*, *'Farewell Padma'*, *'Full Moon'* etc. To see a great personality like Rabindranath giving shape to an idea in two different media at about the same time is a fascinating experience for it seems to give us a glimpse of the very process of literary creations [11].

2.7 Rabindrasangit

Tagore's first collection of songs *Rabichchhaya* was published in 1292 (B.S.). It has been stated in the introduction that, "this volume includes almost all the songs composed by Rabindrababu up to the last date of the year 1291" [12]. Later on, in the year 1300 (B.S.) a book of songs entitled *Ganer Bahi o Valmiki Pratibha* was published including songs of the dance drama *Valmiki Pratibha* [13]. In the year 1303 (B.S.) Tagore's first *Kabya Granthavali* was published which included *Gan* (Song) and *Brahmasangit*. Under the editorship of Mohit Chandra Sen, collected works of Rabindranath was published organizing it on the basis of the theme; *Gan* was included in volume 8 in the year 1310 (B.S.) [14].

Later on *Gan* was published by Jogendranath Sarkar of City Book Society in the year 1315 (B.S.). There were 528 songs in this book. In the next year (1909) second edition of *Gan* was published by Indian Publishing House. This edition tried to collect and publish all the songs of Rabindranath which numbered 727. It was declared in the introduction of *Gan* published in 1316 (B.S.) that "this book published all the best songs of Poet starting from his boyhood days up to date but failed to achieve complete success" [15]. The publisher had to give this statement because at the beginning of first decades of Twentieth Century research on Tagoreana was not started on scientific basis. This edition organized the songs on the basis of theme or subject such as season, nature, etc.

Indian Publishing House, Calcutta published collected works of Rabindranath Tagore in the year 1915-16. *Gan* finds its place in tenth volume [16]. But it was once again an incomplete effort. Besides that individual volume was not available for sale. After the establishment of Santiniketan Press in the year 1323 (B.S.) publication of *Rabindrasangit* started with notation such as *Gitapanchasika* (Asvin, 1325), *Baitalik* (Chaitra, 1325), *Gitabithika* (Baisakh, 1326), *Ketaki* (Shravan, 1326), *Shefali* (Bhadra, 1326), *Kabyagiti* (Pous, 1326), etc. [17].

In the year 1338 (B.S.) on the occasion of celebration of seventy years of the Poet, a collection of Rabindrasangit was published under the title *Gitabitan*. The first and second volume published in Asvin of 1338 (B.S.) and the third volume in Shravana of 1339 (B.S.). The volumes were published by Jagadananda Ray, a teacher of Santiniketan, from Visva-Bharati Granthalaya, 210 Cornwallis Street, Calcutta. The editorial responsibility for this publication was vested on Sudhirchandra Kar, and Adhyapak Amiyachandra Chakraborty was adviser to the editor. In the first edition of *Gitabitan* the songs were organized on the basis of date of publication and not on the basis of themes. In the introduction Adhyapak Kar wrote "Volume two and three includes 1128 songs from adolescent to songs of *Basanta* dance drama. 148 songs were not included as per the direction of the Poet" [18]. The first and second volume of *Gitabitan* includes songs of Rabindranath up to 1300 (B.S.). The songs were organized on the basis of the themes as Tagore thought arrangement on the basis of themes only will be appropriate.

Chronological listing of books containing songs would help to know range and sequential order of songs written by Rabindranath.

Books on Songs in Tagoreana

Age	Title	Year of Publication	No. of Songs
19	*Valmiki Pratibha*	1881	27
20	*Bhagnahriday*	1881	11
20	*Rudrachanda*	1881	02
21	*Kal-Mrigaya*	1882	39
23	*Bau-Thakuranir Hat*	1884	11
23	*Prakritir Pratisodh*	1884	10
23	*Nalini*	1884	04
23	*Saisav Sangit*	1884	11
23	*Bhanusimha Thakurer Padavali*	1884	22
23	*Chhabi o Gan*	1884	02
24	*Rabichchhaya*	1885	201
25	*Kadi o Komal*	1886	11
25	*Valmiki Pratibha – 2nd Ed.*	1886	53
	(25 songs of first edition, 7 songs of *Kalmrigya* and 21 new songs)		
26	*Rajarshi*	1887	02
27	*Mayar Khela*	1888	63
28	*Raja o Rani*	1889	09
29	*Visarjan*	1890	06

29	*Manasi*	1890	04
31	*Chitrangada*	1892	47
31	*Goday Galad*	1892	01
32	*Ganar Bahi o Valmiki Pratibha*	1893	423
	(Contains: 218 songs of *Ganer Bahi*, 55 songs of *Valmiki Pratibha* and 150 songs of *Brahmasangit*)		
33	*Megh o Raudra*	1894	01
33	*Sonar Tari*	1894	03
35	*Chitra*	1896	09
35	*Kabyagranthavali*	1896	480
	(Contains: 16 songs of *Kaishorak*, 20 *Bhanusimghar Padavali*, 2 *Chhabi o Gan*, 9 *Prakritir Pratisodh*, 10 *Kadi o Kamal*, 1 *Manasi*, 8 *Raja o Rani*, 1 *Chaitali*, 5 *Visarjan*, 3 *Sonar Tari*, 9 *Chitra*, 54 *Valmiki Pratibha*, 61 *Mayar Khela*, 119 *Gan*, 162 *Brahmasangit*)		
39	*Kalpana*	1900	16
39	*Kshanika*	1900	04
39	*Naivedya*	1901	17
41	*Kabyagrantha*	1903	428
	(Total songs 442, but 14 songs printed twice)		
43	*Rabindragranthavali* (Hitavadi Ed)	1904	421
	(Contains: *Ganer Bahi* 218, *Valmiki Pratibha* 54, *Brahmasangit* 149)		
44	*Baul*	1905	20
45	*Kheya*	1906	08
46	*Bini Paisar Bhoj*	1907	01
46	*Bashikaran*	1907	02
47	*Prajapatir Nirbandha*	1908	25
47	*Gan*	1908	528
	(Contains: Various songs 132, *Mayar Khela* 63, *Valmiki Pratibha* 52, *National songs* 13, *Baul* 20, *Brahmasangit* 248)		
47	*Saradutsav*	1908	10
48	*Prayaschitta*	1909	23
	(Includes 5 songs from *Bau-Thakuranir Hat*)		
48	*Gan*	1909	727
48	*Sisu*	1909	01
49	*Gitanjali*	1910	85
49	*Gitalipi—Vol. 1*	1910	18
49	*Gitalipi—Vol. 2*	1910	17
49	*Gitalipi—Vol. 3*	1910	15
49	*Raja*	1910	25

50	*Gitalipi—Vol. 4*	1911	15
50	*Gitalipi—Vol. 5*	1911	16
51	*Achalayatan*	1912	23
53	*Utsarga*	1914	01
53	*Gan*	1914	395
	(Contains: 52 songs of *Valmiki Pratibha*, 63 *Mayar Khela*, 246 *Gan and* 34 *National Songs*)		
53	*Dharmasangit*	1914	325
	(Renaming of the *Gan* including all the Brahmasangit)		
53	*Giti-malya*	1914	87
53	*Gitali*	1914	66
54	*Kavyagrantha Vol. 10*	1916	492
	(Contains: *Valmiki Pratibha* 52, *Mayar Khela* 33, Various Sangit 120, *Dharmasangit* 220, *National songs* 30, *Marriage Songs* 7)		
54	*Phalguni*	1916	30
55	*Ghare-Baire*	1916	04
55	*Balaka*	1916	04
55	*Chaturanga*	1916	01
55	*Sesher Ratri*	1916	01
57	*Guru*	1918	07
57	*Gitalekha—Vol. 1*	1918	29
57	*Gitalipi—Vol. 6*	1918	13
57	*Gitapanchasika*	1918	50
57	*Baitalik*	1918	36
58	*Gitalekha—Vol. 2*	1919	28
58	*Gitabithika*	1919	22
58	*Ketaki*	1919	31
	(Includes one Vidyabatir Pad)		
58	*Shefali*	1919	28
59	*Kavyagiti*	1920	23
59	*Arupratan*	1920	39
60	*Varshamangal*	1921	17
60	*Gitalekha—Vol. 3*	1921	24
60	*Rinsodh*	1921	07
61	*Muktadhara*	1922	14
61	*Varshamangal*	1922	18
61	*Lipika*	1922	01
61	*Nabagitika—Vol. 1*	1922	34
61	*Nabagitika—Vol. 2*	1922	59
62	*Vasanta*	1923	23

64	*Puravi*	1925	01
64	*Grihapravesh*	1925	09
64	*Pravahini*	1925	235
65	*Chirakumar Sabha*	1926	32
65	*Sodh-bodh*	1926	03
65	*Ritu-Utsav*	1926	108
	(Contains: *Seshbarshan* 24, *Saradutsav* 10, *Basanta* 23, *Sundar* 24, *Phalguni* 27)		
65	*Natir Puja*	1926	11
65	*Raktakarabi*	1926	08
65	*Gitamalika—Vol. 1*	1926	52
66	*Rituranga*	1927	29
67	*Sesh Raksha*	1928	09
68	*Paritran*	1929	21
68	*Tapati*	1929	10
68	*Mahua*	1929	12
69	*Gitamalika—Vol. 2*	1930	50
70	*Navin*	1931	21
70	*Sapmochan*	1931	23
70	*Gitabitan—Vol. 1*	1931	1128
71	*Gitabitan—Vol. 3*	1932	357
71	*Gitoutsav*	1932	03
71	*Parisodh*	1932	30
72	*Tasher Des*	1933	22
73	*Shravan-Gantha*	1934	22
73	*Char Adhyay*	1934	01
74	*Vithika*	1935	04
75	*Nritya-natya Chitrangada*	1936	47
75	*Arupratan*	1936	25
77	*Chandalika Nritya-natya*	1938	51
77	*Muktir Upay*	1938	02
78	*Syama*	1939	52
79	*Sanai*	1940	23
80	*Badnam*	1941	01
80	*Seshlekha*	1941	02

Rabindranath wrote many dance dramas where songs from his numerous writings or specially written for a particular dance drama, were included. In dance dramas *Nritya Natya Chitrangada, Chandalika* and *Syama* there are 150 songs. Similarly in the dance dramas *Navin,*

Varshamangal, Saradutsav, Vasanta, Sundar and *Phalguni* there are 126 songs. In the dance dramas *Valmiki Pratibha, Kal-Mrigaya, Mayar Khela, Prakritir Pratisodh* there are 165 songs. The number of songs used in different dramas can be observed from the following:

Songs in Dramas

Sl. No.	**Drama**	**No. of Songs**
1.	*Raja o Rani*	09
2.	*Visarjan*	06
3.	*Goday Galad*	01
4.	*Prayaschitta*	23
5.	*Raja*	25
6.	*Achalayatan*	23
7.	*Guru*	07
8.	*Arupratan (1920 ed.)*	39
9.	*Rinsodh*	07
10.	*Muktadhara*	14
11.	*Grihapravesh*	09
12.	*Chirakumar Sabha*	32
13.	*Sodh-bodh*	03
14.	*Natir Puja*	11
15.	*Raktakarabi*	08
16.	*Sesh Raksha*	09
17.	*Paritran*	21
18.	*Tapati*	10
19.	*Sapmochan*	23
20.	*Parisodh*	30
21.	*Taser Des*	22
22.	*Arupratan (1936)*	25

Total number of songs given against the books cannot be counted as the total number of songs written by Rabindranath as many songs were repeated in various books. Moreover, the number of songs increased in different editions of the same book. For example, the first edition (1881) of *Valmiki Pratibha* contained 27 songs but the number increased to 53 in the second edition (1886). The first and second volume of *Gitabitan* containing 1500 songs was printed in Bhadra, 1346 (B.S.), but published after his death. The third volume was published in 1357 (B.S.) by Visva-Bharati Granthan Vibhaga after the demise of Rabindranath. According to the index of the new edition (Magh 1379 B.S.) of third volume, the total number of songs is 732. Out of the songs in three volumes of *Gitabitan,* notation of 1890 songs could be found in 60 volumes of *Swarabitan* (book of notation). For example *Bhanusimha Thakurer Padavali* contains 22 songs but one could find notation of 10 songs only. Tagore adopted notation to many lyric poems and included in *Gitabitan.* Still there are many *gitadharmi* (having the characteristics of songs) poems of Tagore which require notation [19].

Table 2.2: Year-wise Break-up of Rabindrasangit

Year (Bangiya Sakabda within Bracket)	Age of Rabindranath	Number of Songs	Cumulative Total
1875 (1281)	13	1	1
1875 (1282)	14	1	2
1877-78 (1284)	16	9	11
1878 (1285)	17	10	21
1879-80 (1286)	18	16	37
1880-81 (1287)	19	45	82
1881-82 (1288)	20	32	114
1882-83 (1289)	21	47	161
1883-84 (1290)	22	56	217
1884-85 (1291)	23	91	308
1885-86 (1292)	24	45	353
1886-87 (1293)	25	47	400
1887-88 (1294)	26	19	419
1888-89 (1295-96)	27	60	479
1889-90 (1296-97)	28	11	490
1890 (1297)	29	6	496
1892 (1298)	30	2	498
1892-93 (1299)	31	13	511
1893-94 (1300)	32	27	538
1894-95 (1301)	33	9	547
1895-96 (1302-03)	34	33	580
1896-97 (1303-04)	35	23	603
1897-98 (1304)	36	30	633
1899 (1305)	37	6	639
1900 (1306)	38	24	663
1900-01 (1307)	39	50	713

(Contd.)

Table 2.2: (*Contd.*)

Year (Bangiya Sakabda within Bracket)	Age of Rabindranath	Number of Songs	Cumulative Total
1901-02 (1308)	40	13	726
1902-03 (1309)	41	14	740
1903-04 (1310)	42	5	745
1904-05 (1311)	43	10	755
1905-06 (1312)	44	37	792
1906-07	45	7	799
1907-08 (1314)	46	9	808
1908-09 (1315)	47	19	827
1909-10 (1316-17)	48	76	903
1910-11 (1317)	49	66	969
1911-12 (1318-19)	50	45	1014
1912 (1319)	51	2	1016
1913-14 (1320-21)	52	64	1080
1914-15 (1321-22)	53	114	1194
1915-16 (1322-23)	54	25	1219
1916-17 (1323-24)	55	1	1220
1917-18 (1324-25)	56	14	1234
1918-19 (1325-26)	57	33	1267
1919-20 (1326-27)	58	19	1286
1921-22 (1328-29)	60	57	1343
1922-23 (1329-30)	61	97	1440
1923-24 (1330-31)	62	31	1471
1924-25 (1331-32)	63	33	1504
1925-26 (1332-33)	64	99	1603
1926-27 (1333-34)	65	61	1664
1927-28 (1334-35)	66	46	1710
1928-29 (1335-36)	67	8	1718
1929-30 (1336-37)	68	38	1756
1930-31 (1337-38)	69	26	1782
1932-33 (1339-40)	71	8	1790
1933-34 (1340-41)	72	38	1828

(*Contd.*)

Table 2.2: (*Contd.*)

Year (Bangiya akabda within Bracket)	Age of Rabindranath	Number of Songs	Cumulative Total
1934-35 (1341-42)	73	10	1838
1935-36 (1342-43)	74	64	1902
1936-37 (1343-44)	75	49	1951
1937-38 (1344-45)	76	84	2039
1938-39 (1345-46)	77	84	2123
1939-40 (1345-46)	78	46	2169
1940 (1347)	79	7	2176
1941 (1348)	80	2	2178

Source: Gitabitan.

The above table indicates that Rabindranath started writing songs in 1875 well before writing the verse *Kavi-Kahini* in 1878. It is also clear that Tagore wrote highest number of songs (N= 91) at the age of 23 in the year 1884-85 (1291 B.S.) and continued writing songs till death. A literary analysis of songs would reveal that *Rabindrasangit* (music written by Rabindranath) covers different aspects like *prem* (love), *puja* (prayer), *prakriti* (description of nature), etc.

The above year-wise break-up table indicating the output of Rabindrasangit with the passage of time can graphically be represented as follows:

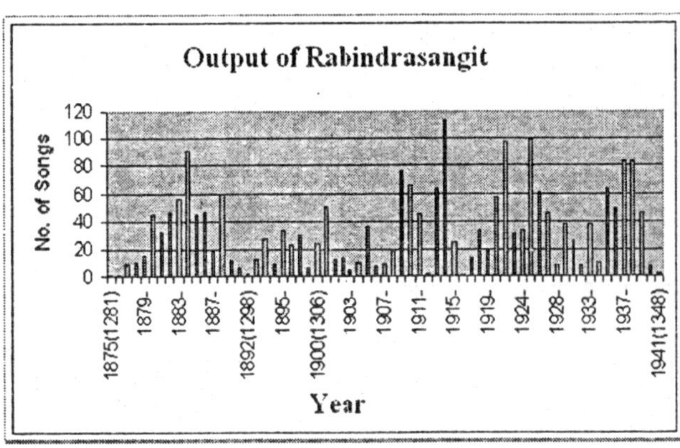

2.8 Conclusion

It is very difficult to have a total picture of books in Tagoreana or to indicate year-wise literary output, as many of them were first published in the form of booklet/address/pamphlet and later published as a book or included as a part of a book. Particularly in *Swaralipi* (Notation) many writings were treated as books such as *Nrityanatya Syama*. For that reason only an individual *Swarabitan* has been treated as a separate book for depicting the growth of Tagoreana. Moreover, in the case of literature what matters is the depth of knowledge; wisdom expressed in writings not the numbers. The romantic touches reflected in the novels of Rabindranath come from *His* rapport with the beauty and mystery in nature deeply rooted in social, family and individual life. It is desirable to see the novels as a part of changing social history—reflection of society. In his short stories also problems relating to personal, familial, social, etc. are not denied but presented in an aesthetically valid universe. These reflections can never be measured with mere statistical indicators. Even it becomes difficult to categorise his writings. For example, Rabindranath's poetry is so vast, varied and voluminous that it is very difficult to schematize. Before he was eighteen, he had published nearly seven thousand lines of verse [20]. One critic, historian Niharranjan Ray had tried with a six-fold pattern of growth: Germination and Early Blossoms (1872-88), Fruits of Maturity (1888-1900), Fruits of Offerings (1901-1913), The Nest and the Sky (1914-25), New Flowers and Fruits (1926-37) and The Sunset Glow (1937-41). But the metaphor breaks down at least in two occasions. When the same critic tells us that in *Sandhya Sangit* (Evening Songs, 1882) Tagore had come of age. It is difficult to disagree. He admits no grand generalization will hold, no poet is mature at twenty-one [21].

While considering the range of Tagoreana one should not forget that Rabindranath not only expressed his vision on society, education, rural development, religion, in his numerous writings but also tried to give it a concrete shape with the establishment of his experimental school at *Santiniketan* and rural reconstruction programme at *Sriniketan*. He wished to "*bring to the village health and knowledge, wealth and peace in which to live, wealth of time in which to work and to rest and enjoy*" [22]. Reform of education and regeneration of villages were the major tasks of his life. To quote Rabindranath "*in my institution I tried to make provisions for three aspects of freedom—freedom of mind, freedom of heart and freedom of will. I have deep rooted conviction that through freedom can man attain fullness of growth"* [23].

Rabindranath faced a number of deaths of his kith and kin in his life time such as mother Sarada Devi (10.3.1875), bauthan (wife of Jyotirindranath), Kadambini Devi (19.4.1884), elder brother Hemendranath Tagore (5.6.1984), nephew Balendranath (22.8.1899), wife Mrinalini Devi (23.11.1902), second daughter Renuka (19.9.1903), associate of Santiniketan Satishchandra Ray (1.2.1904), father Debendranath Tagore (9.1.1905), son Shamindranath (Nov., 1907), daughter Madhurilata (13.5.1918), elder sister Saratkumari (11.4.1920), elder brother Satyendranath (9.1.1923), close associate of Santiniketan Pearson (24.9.1923), elder brother Jyotirindranath (4.3.1925), elder brother Dwijendranath (18.1.1926), grandson Nitindranath (29.7.1932), Santiniketan associate C.F. Andrew (5.4.1940), nephew Surendranath (3.5.1940) to name a few [24]. But if we consider the rise of *Sun* with the first writing *Kavi-Kahini* in the year 1878 and *Sunset* (demise of Rabindranath) in 1941, then it can be concluded that sorrow caused by the death of family members or close associates could not stop his mighty pen. The Poet's son Rathindranath wrote in this respect "vicissitudes of life, pain and afflictions never upset the equanimity of my father's mind. His inward peace was not disturbed by any calamity, however painful. Some inner resources gave him the power to face and rise above misfortunes of the most painful nature" [25]. Thus, to conclude, to believe him, his life and works form a parable of the play of the *Finite* and *Infinite* (*Seema-Aseemer Pala*). It is impossible to judge to which he was more loyal, to the sky or the nest, the wings or the roots.

NOTES AND REFERENCES

1. BANDYOPADHYAYA (Brajendranath). *Rabindra grantha-parichay (1878-1943)*. 1349 (B.S.). Sahitya-Niketan; Calcutta; p. 28.
2. MUKHOPADHYAYA (Prabhatkumar). *Rabindragrantha parichiti*. 1385 (B.S.). Visva-Bharati Research Publication; Santiniketan; pp. 2-4.
3. KRIPALANI (Krishna). *Rabindranath Tagore: a biography*. 1980. Visva-Bharati Granthan Vibhaga; Calcutta; p. 66.

4. CHUNKAPURA (Jose). *The God of Rabindranath Tagore: a study of the evolution of his understanding of God.* 2002. Visva-Bharati Granthan Vibhaga; Calcutta; 351p.
5. THOMPSON (Edward). *Rabindranath Tagore: poet and dramatist.* 1979. Rddhi-India; Calcutta; 335p.
6. MAJUMDAR (Bimanbehari). *Heroines of Tagore: a study in the transformation of Indian society 1875-1941.*1968. Firma K.L. Mukhopadhyay; Calcutta; p. 15.
7. MUKHOPADHYAYA (Prabhatkumar). *Life of Tagore.* 1975. Indian Book Company; New Delhi; p. 208. Tr. from Bengali by Sisirkumar Ghosh.
8. KRIPALANI (Krishna). *Rabindranath Tagore: a biography.* 1980. Visva-Bharati Granthan Vibhaga; Calcutta; p. 491.
9. MAJUMDAR (Bimanbehari). *Heroines of Tagore: a study in the transformation of Indian society 1875-1941.* 1968. Firma K.L. Mukhopadhyay; Calcutta; pp. 15-16.
10. TAGORE (Rabindranath). *Chithipatra.* 19 Vols. 1942-. Visva-Bharati Granthan Vibhaga; Calcutta.
11. MITRA (Somnath). The letters of Rabindranath Tagore. In *Rabindranath Tagore: a centenary volume 1861-1961.* 1986. Sahitya Akademi; New Delhi; pp. 163-171.
12. TAGORE (Rabindranath). *Rabichchhaya.* 1292 (B.S.). Jogendranarayan Mitra; Calcutta; p. 1.
13. TAGORE (Rabindranath). *Ganar bahi o valmiki pratibha.* 1330 (B.S.). Adi Brahma Samaj; Calcutta; p. 407.
14. TAGORE (Rabindranath). *Kavya-grantha.* Vol. 8. Majumder Library; Calcutta; p. 338.
15. TAGORE (Rabindranath). *Gan.* 1316 (B.S.). Indian Press; Allahabad; p. 412.
16. TAGORE (Rabindranath). *Gan.* 1321 (B.S.). Indian Publishing House; Calcutta; p. 168.
17. MUKHOPADHAYAYA (Prabhatkumar). *Gitabitan: kalanukramick suchi.* 1399 (B.S.). Tagore Research Institute; Calcutta; p. 26.
18. TAGORE (Rabindranath). *Gitabitan.* 3 Vols. 1338 (B.S.). Visva-Bharati Granthan Vibhaga; p. 864.
19. MUKHOPADHAYAYA (Prabhatkumar). *Gitabitan: kalanukramick suchi.* 1399 (B.S.). Tagore Research Institute; Calcutta; p. 31.
20. THOMPSON (Edward). *Rabindranath Tagore: poet and dramatist.* 1979. Rddhi-India; Calcutta; p. 30.
21. GHOSE (Sisirkumar). *Rabindranath Tagore.* 1998. Sahitya Akademi; New Delhi; p. 32.
22. TAGORE (Rabindranath). *City and village.* 1976. Visva-Bharati Granthan Vibhaga; Calcutta; p. 48.
23. TAGORE (Rabindranath). *My school.* 1916. Visva-Bharati Bulletin; Santiniketan; p. 5.

24. KUNDU (Ashok Kumar). *Rabindra-dinopanji*. 1986. Banglabhasha Sahityo o Samskriti Gabeshana Samsthan; Calcutta; 399p.

25. TAGORE (Rathindranath). Father as I know him. In *Rabindranath Tagore: a centenary volume 1861-1961*. 1986. Sahitya Akademi; New Delhi; p. 48.

3

Tagoreana: A Bibliometric Study

3.1 Introduction

The writings of Rabindranath Tagore are universal in expression and temper but rooted in oriental culture. His writings on literature, music, art, education, rural development, history, co-operative ideas, etc. in one hand and on the other his activities on experimental school at Santiniketan, rural reconstruction programme at Sriniketan, all turned into gold with the passage of time. This is true in case of Tagore's vision of library in his writings as well as its implementation at Santiniketan.

It is possible to conduct bibliometric study on any aspect of Tagorean concept such as education, history or on a particular book may be conducted. In this work a selective bibliometric study on Tagore's writings on library, drawings and paintings and *Gitanjali* has been conducted. Tagore's numerous writings on 'library' touches every aspect of library science right from collection, development, documentation, conservation, to the effective use of collection. Tagore's vision was to establish Visva-Bharati as a centre of universal culture and research *'Yatra visvam bhavatyakenidam'* (where the world makes its home in a single nest). The objective of development of education and library is clearly expressed in the trust deed made by Maharshi Devendranath Tagore, father of Rabindranath Tagore in the year 1888 which reads as follows: "*in pursuance of the need of enhancement of the quality of living in the Ashram the trustees were empowered to establish a Brahmavidyalaya at Santiniketan and a library*" [1]. Thus the concept of library was from the very beginning a constituent of the Santiniketan Ashram. Tagore wrote "*The collection of our revered father's books was kept in one of the three rooms. We first looked after the proper preservation of books and manuscripts. What occupied our thoughts thereafter was where we could fix students' residence"* [2]. Tagore's writings and growth of Visva-Bharati and its library are linked with the growth of his life as he wrote *"the growth of this school was the growth of my life and not of a mere carrying out of my doctrines, its ideals changed with the maturity like a ripening fruit that not only grows in its bulk and deepens in its colour, but undergoes change in the very quality of its inner pulp"*[3].

3.2 Vision of Library in Tagoreana

Tagore's writings on book and library cover both philosophical and functional aspect of library science. In two essays, namely "*Library*" [4] and "*Librarir Mukhyo Kartabyo*" [5], Rabindranath expressed his philosophical and functional vision of a library. The first one covers the philosophical aspects where Tagore described library as a place where sounds of ocean of thousand years stopped like a sleeping child, flow of language; currents are imprisoned by the chain of black words. People get a chance to move in any direction of knowledge. Rabindranath describes library as a place where man encompasses his freedom in a small place. In the functional aspect he advised librarians to be free from bias of the number of accumulating as "*once he starts to gather and store, he becomes distracted with the obsession of number, and tends to overlook the purpose of his accumulating.*" "*The part of its contents which is for the purpose of extensive accumulation has its usefulness, but the other part which is for constant and varied use, gives its significance*"[6]. In respect of documentation Rabindranath suggested "*it is necessary that its contents should be clearly and specifically brought to notice. Otherwise it is very difficult for the ordinary man to find his way about them, and the library is left as a city of vast accommodation that lacks means of communication*"[7]. Rabindranath in his poem has mentioned that books may be kept in precious racks with good care, but without proper use it is meaningless [8].

For developing readership in a library Rabindranath reminds that the readers make the library is not the whole truth; but library also makes readers. For this, library has to go beyond the traditional form of invitation "*Here is my catalogue, come and select for yourself*". "*But in the usual catalogue there is no introduction, no invitation, and no spirit of welcome. That library alone can be called hospitable, which shows an eagerness to invite readers to the feast at its disposal, it is such hospitability that makes a library big not its size*" [9]. As to the role of a librarian Rabindranath suggests "the worth of a librarian I would gauge by his power of attracting and looking after such circle, of acting as the intermediary for an intimacy of relationship between the reader and the library" [10]. Regarding librarian's duty Rabindranath reminds *"...as to the books, the librarian's duty should not be confined to those that he can gather, but he must also keep himself acquainted with all those others that are published from time to time, subject by subject"*[11].

Tagore in his numerous writings mentioned the role of a library in the development of a society and methods of knowledge communication citing examples from *Sruti* and *Tapabon* [12] and medium of writing from the period of ancient India, i.e. Ashok's inscription [13] even with proper example from Greece and Persia [14]. For development of reading habit among school students Rabindranath suggested for rapid reading literature books in English, Sanskrit along with traditional step by step teaching methods in these subjects [15]. For this rapid reading on many subjects, library is the only place. Pramathanath Bisi recaptured his memory of Rabindranath's opinion about library that people can never be truly educated from colleges and teachers, on the other hand he should be the teacher of his own and library is the proper place of education as he learns many things only from huge reading in a library [16]. For development of personal reading Rabindranath also mentioned in his poem that one college student prepares a list of gifts for his beloved one where 'recent fiction' and book of poem 'printed on antique paper' gets its place [17]. The same kind of reference can also be cited from his famous novel *Naukadubi* where Akshay presented books to Hemnalini as gift [18].

A good book is a good friend that helps to know many unknown things, character building and also helps to increase creativity. Besides, it provides many information as it is not possible to go everywhere to observe everything. This concept has been reflected in a poem *Janmadine* [19]. Enhancement of knowledge helps to achieve greater mental satisfaction as well as pleasure [20]. The role of a book as a friend with whom one can exchange ideas has been reflected in a letter of Rabindranath where he mentioned *Amiel's Journal* as an intimate friend [21]. Rabindranath was a voracious reader who became deeply involved with the character of the books he read as he mentioned in describing the episode of *Ramayana* reading in *Jivansmriti* [22]. A good book has a long-term impact on reader's mind like classical song. It has also been reflected in Rabindranath's poetry [23] as well as letters [24]. Good books help to generate new ideas to write new things as Rabindranath has mentioned being impressed by a book entitled *Chineman Letter.* Rabindranath wrote an essay on this [25]. Actually Rabindranath's literary culture starts with habit of reading as he mentioned in *Jivansmriti* [26].

Rabindranath in his writings also warns against being too much bookish which may create hindrance in the development of imagination and power of expression. Children may loose the power of free mixing by too much reading. He knows the character of books but not the man in his locality. Even this may lead to develop some ideas which have no connection with reality [27]. Rabindranath gave example of this type of detachment. By studying ethnology one tries to learn many things but forgets to be familiar with the neighbour. We consider a book as a real big thing but forget the real people who are described in the book [28].

The success of a library depends on reader satisfaction in pursuit of information or knowledge. Librarians have to be very careful regarding reader's requirement, likeness, reading habit, in a word, reader's psychology. Rabindranath in his numerous writings mentioned these aspects. Truth centred on humanity gets reflected in literature. Only permanent truth can give more satisfaction to readers [29]. The reading habit of different reader varies. Some want to study alone in a lonely place [30]. Married women used to keep books under a pillow to keep them safe from their kids. This is also mentioned in a poem of *Kshanika* [31]. In a poem called *Sisu* Rabindranath has also drawn a picture of *Ramayana* reading in the noon [32]. Such example is also found in the fiction *Chokher Bali* where Binodini is requested to read *Santisatak* for Pishima [33]. The change of reading material from *Ramayana* to modern literature and its likings, and also the picture of a good library of Abinash have been narrated in *Sesher Kavita* [34]. For reader's satisfaction a library should collect best books covering all aspects of reader's requirement. Rabindranath in a letter mentioned this aspect [35].

One of the most important functions of a library is conservation of library collection to keep the documents safe from harm or loss, damage, destruction or decay, and maintain it in reasonably sound condition for present and future use. Rabindranath in his two poems *Kiter Bichar* and *Granthakit* [36] describes the nature of *kit* (worm) and how they destroy book. In the objectives and functions of Santiniketan Brahmacharyasram it is stated that the responsibility of cleaning the library, rooms and garden should be vested to students. Clear instruction was given to collect borrowed books from the guests [37]. In a letter to Subodh Chandra Majumder, Rabindranath's care for book is reflected. Where Rabindranath wrote '*I mailed two books Religious Systems and Origin of Aryans. Keep them in the library. Dust the library and give naphthalene*' [38].

3.3 Library in Tagoreana: A Bibliometric Study

To conduct the bibliometric study on the concept of library in Tagoreana two major methods are followed:

1. *Literature Survey*—Survey is an account of some research examination or enquiry, which has been done by scientific or organized method. Literature survey is the search for documents including books, journal articles, dissertations, theses etc. on the subject under research [39]. For literature survey on the subject under study collected works of Rabindranath Tagore [40] as well as all other published and unpublished writings of Tagore and also other probable primary and secondary sources were consulted.

2. *Bibliometric Technique*—For bibliometric study, bibliometric technique 'as the quantitative treatment of the properties of recorded discourse and behaviour pertaining to it' [41] was followed. With the help of descriptive bibliometrics, the number of publications in a given year, in different literary form etc. was constructed.

Table 3.1: Number of Publications on Library

Year of Publication	*Number*
1888-1893	2
1893-1898	1
1898-1903	2
1903-1908	3
1908-1913	1
1913-1918	1
1918-1923	1
1923-1928	29
1928-1933	31
1933-1938	2
Total	**76**

Table 3.2: Year-wise Distribution of Publications on Library

Year of Publication	*Number*
1933	22
1931	15
1928	10
1925	7
1923	6
Total	**60**

Table 3.3: Publication on Library in Different Literary Forms

Journal articles	*Letters*	*Addresses*	*Essays*	*Poems*	*Autobiographies*	*Total*
5	12	21	5	29	4	46

Tagore's literary career may be classified as youth and early childhood writings (1878-1900), *Gitanjali* period (1900-1912), the years of matured reflections (1912-1927) and the final years (1927-1941) [42]. Thus from Table 3.1 it is observed that Rabindranath expressed his vision on library throughout his literary career (1883-1938).

The highest number of writings (N=22) were published in the year 1933, which is 28.95 per cent of total writings on the subject. Rabindranath expressed his vision about library more according to number of publications within 1928-1933 which is 61.84 per cent of total writings. Tagore's presidential address on "*library*" on All India Library Congress 1928 may have some impact on his later writings. He also wrote on functional aspects of library "*Librarir Mukhyo Kartabyo*" (main responsibility of library) in this period. On 76 occasions Rabindranath mentioned the concept of '*Library*' in Tagoreana in all literary forms like letters, addresses, essays, poems etc. But he wrote mostly on the subject in the form of poems (N = 29, which is 38.16% of total writings) as Rabindranath is predominately a poet.

Rabindranath was eager to develop the library system of India. When he went to Russia he observed the role of a library in academic set up of that country. For the purpose of development of libraries in India, he even compared their system with that of India. He mentioned "*their museum is not passive like our library at Santiniketan but active*" [43]. Today with the advent of education library movement and services has *reached to a point* of development. But one should not forget Rabindranath's remarks—*"Establishment of libraries has spread in villages and towns of Bengal. Care should be taken, so that these efforts do not confine to recreation only but can spread culture in public domain"* [44].

With this objective of disseminating knowledge to rural mass, Rabindranath started mobile library service.

3.4 Mobile Library Services "Chalantika" in Tagorean Concept

The rural library service concept was developed and initiated with the very inception of Sriniketan experiment of rural reconstruction in 1922. Tagore believed that *"for the fundamental purpose of education it is not merely to enrich ourselves through the fullness of knowledge, but also to establish the bond of love and friendship between man and man"* [45]. For that he suggests *"the higher educational institutions should assimilate knowledge from all sources and disseminate it for benefit of the masses in order to strengthen their own foundation"* [46]. The same has clearly been stated in one of the objectives of Sriniketan which reads as follows: "to carry the knowledge and experience gained in the class-room and farm to the village"[47].

Rural library services in the form of mobile library services named *"Chalantika"* started in the year 1925 with an initial collection of 200 books. In the year 1927 Satish Chandra Muhkopadhyay (5.6.1865-18.4.1948) donated 70 books to *Chalantika* [48]. The following table indicates the increase of collection and augmentation of its use by the rural masses in the initial years of its establishment.

Table 3.4: Collection and its Use through Chalantika: 1929-1934

Year	*No. of Books*	*Books Issued*
1929	450	729
1930	385 and 5 Periodicals	709
1931	400	600
1932	461	950
1933	512	1474
1934	1087	2457

Source: Visva-Bharati Annual Report: 1929-34.

In the year 1925, 1937 and 1940 the number of books was 200, 1200 and 1504 respectively. In the year 1939, the number of books issued was 2793[49]. At the initial stage there were only two mobile library branches at Bolpur and Goalpara in Birbhum district. The collection was mainly of fiction, biography, epigraphy, agriculture, health, nursing and children's books. School teachers help in supplying books to the villagers. Pamphlets on agricultural problems, health care, primary education, and rural reconstruction were published by the institute and circulated through mobile library. For establishing contact with the world of knowledge, a fortnightly journal named *Dese Videse* was published by the institute. For attracting people towards the library, regular lectures on various local problems and magic lantern show were organized. In the year 1929, twenty-six lectures were delivered in nineteen villages, with a total attendance of 6,000 people [50]. Tagore believed "*knowledge associated with joy and satisfaction increases our power of learning, consequently our power of reception, apprehension, thinking and judgment develop easily and naturally*" [51]. Tagore laid the foundation of rural library services in the form of *Chalantika* which has now bloomed with the services through 38 rural libraries and eight children libraries scattered in eight gram panchayats of two development blocks of Bolpur-Santiniketan and Illambazar of Birbhum district of West Bengal. The number of enrolled readers as on March 2006, were 4083 (Male 2395, Female 1688) and the number of books issued were 22579 [52].

Tagore's writings on library and establishment of his experimental school and its library at Santiniketan are based on his educational philosophy of "*freedom of mind, freedom of heart and freedom of will*" [53]. His idea of a library was alike with his idea of rural development as he states "*reform of education and regeneration of villages are the major task of my life*" [54]. Tagore gave stress on rural library services as he felt "*a natural bond between education in the schools and colleges and the country outside them is immensely necessary*" [55]. This is necessary to fulfil the objectives of education as "*the highest education is that which does not give us information but makes our life in harmony with all existence*" [56]. A library as the storehouse of recorded knowledge has a tremendous role to play. But to ensure fullest use of its resources Tagore suggests, "*it is necessary that its contents should clearly and specifically brought to notice*" of readers with human touch because "*the library by itself imposes a responsibility—the responsibility relating to riches. In so far as the library contains books, it attains fulfilment only through having those books read. It will not remain inactive; may it play an active role by issuing a call.* Because "*Jannastam yanna deeyate*" [57].

3.5 Paintings and Drawings in Tagoreana: A Bibliometric Study

Rabindranath started sketching the manuscript of his writings at the time of writing *Puravi* in the year 1924 which can be described as the origin of Tagore paintings [58] though according to available data his first painting is dated 15th March, 1929. Up to 1940 Rabindranath had produced more than 2000 paintings and drawings [59]. Victoria Ocampo, while she was nursing the poet back to his health in her villa in Buenos Aires in Argentina in 1924, was impressed upon by seeing the radical imagination of sketch and lines in his notebook and encouraged Rabindranath for drawing and painting. Later she organized an exhibition of Tagore paintings at Paris [60].

In 1930 a series of exhibitions of Rabindranath's art work was organized in Europe. Reviews in general of the exhibition of 1930 were complementary. Critiques expressed surprise at the unexpected beauty of the works with imagination. But before that Rabindranath was not confident about his paintings. He wrote to William Rothenstein "*My pictures certainly possess psychological interest being products of untutored figures and untrained mind. I am sure, they do not reveal a strangeness born of my utter inexperience and individual limitations*" [61]. Rabindranath had no formal training in art besides the cultural ambience of the family. But according to Rabindranath "*the only training which I had from my young days was the training in rhythm in thought, the rhythm in sound. I had come to know that rhythm gives reality to that which is desultory, which is insignificant in itself. And therefore, when the scratches in my manuscript cried, like sinners, for salvation, and assailed my eyes with the ugliness of their irrelevance, I often took more time in rescuing them into a merciless finality of rhythm than in carrying on what was my obvious task*"[62].

This understanding of rhythm is the reason behind success in art, which Rabindranath started enjoying later on. He expressed this feeling in a letter to Rothenstein in 1937 " *I have been havoc in the complacent and stagnant world of Indian art and my people are puzzled for they do not know what judgment to pronounce upon my picture. But I must say enjoying hugely my role as a painter*" [63]. This was also recognized by European reviewers like Henri Bidou, as they were impressed with Tagore's naïve 'automatic' self-taught quality, especially as they were aware of his high quality formal 'mimetic' literary output. Art critique Coomaraswamy was convinced that Rabindranath had expunged all previous literary experience to produce a truly naïve art, like a child, inventing his own technique [64]. Besides the vision of rhythm and childlike quality Rabindranath had two other elements, unpredictability and dream imagination. This is expressed by Rabindranath in 1930—"*People often ask me about the meaning of my pictures. I remain silent even as they are. It is for them to express not to explain...*" [65].

A bibliometric study of 1573 drawings and paintings of Rabindranath available in Rabindra Bhavana at Santiniketan is made on different aspects such as theme, medium used, signature, place and date of drawing, titles given by him. This would provide an idea about Tagore as a painter.

Table 3.5: Theme of the Paintings in Tagoreana

Sl. No.	*Theme*	*No. of Paintings*	*Percentage*
1.	Figures	496	31.532
2	Human face	219	13.922
3.	Head study	206	13.096
4.	Landscape	173	10.998
5.	Animal	63	4.005
6.	Bird	62	3.941
7.	Design	58	3.687
8.	Composition	54	3.433
9.	Illustration for books etc. (30 for the book *Khapchhada*)	49	3.115
10.	Mask	40	2.543
11.	Different forms	40	2.543
12.	Sketch	29	1.844
13.	Flower study	26	1.653
14.	Nude study (Female 11, Male 4)	15	0.954
15.	Portrait	14	0.890
16.	Flower	8	0.509
17.	Couple	8	0.509
18.	Fish	4	0.254
19.	Fish and a cat	1	0.063
20.	Plant study	1	0.063
21.	Two pine trees	1	0.063
22.	Tree	1	0.063
23.	Croton leaf	1	0.063
24.	Steam engine	1	0.063
25.	Animal head	1	0.063
26.	Hut	1	0.063
27.	Wild face	1	0.063
	Total	1573	100.000

The broad categorization of Tagore's paintings made on the basis of descriptive catalogue of Rabindra Bhavana and experts' opinion reveals that Rabindranath drew on 27 themes. A detailed analytical study of the themes is made hereunder:

Table 3.6: Paintings of Figures in Tagoreana

Sl. No.	Theme	No. of Painting	Percentage
1	Human figure	249	50.201
2.	Standing figure	71	14.315
3.	Figure-seated	34	6.855
4.	Bearded man	22	4.435
5.	Dancing figure	15	3.024
6.	Man with a raised hand	12	2.419
7.	An old man with a stick	06	1.210
8.	Man with a cap	04	0.806
9.	Figure on a coach	04	0.806
10.	Figure with animal head	3	0.605
11.	Couple	3	0.605
12.	Man with a torch	3	0.605
13.	Man–knelling	3	0.605
14.	Old man with a mirror	3	0.605
15.	Woman under a tree	3	0.605
16.	Woman and a child	2	0.403
17.	Man with a girl	2	0.403
18.	Woman with a veena	2	0.403
19.	An old man riding on a bird	2	0.403
20.	Mother and a child	2	0.403
21.	Lady with a mirror in hand	1	0.201
22.	Lady with a lamp	1	0.201
23.	Lady with a flower	1	0.201
24.	Female figure with a pot on shoulder	1	0.201
25.	A walking man	1	0.201
26.	Man with a musical instrument	1	0.201
27.	Woman absorbed in painting	1	0.201
28.	Woman seating with a picture in hand	1	0.201
29.	Man in a long robe	1	0.201
30.	Running figure	1	0.201
31.	Lovers	1	0.201
32.	Woman in woods	1	0.201
33.	An old man blending	1	0.201
34.	Lady with a pot	1	0.201
35.	Woman and rain	1	0.201
36.	A man standing with a sword	1	0.201
37.	An old man standing	1	0.201
38.	Men in armour	1	0.201
39.	A couple with a camel	1	0.201
40.	Woman on an animal	1	0.201
41.	Woman on a cot	1	0.201
42.	Man playing a drum	1	0.201
43.	Man with spectacles	1	0.201

(Contd.)

Table 3.6: (*Contd.*)

Sl. No.	*Theme*	*No. of Painting*	*Percentage*
44.	A man seated by waterside	1	0.201
45.	A man with a goat	1	0.201
46.	Woman standing at window	1	0.201
47.	Two men fighting	1	0.201
48.	Man with a cock	1	0.201
49.	One man blessing other	1	0.201
50.	Man with a pole	1	0.201
51.	Study of a boy in profile	1	0.201
52.	Man with a helmet	1	0.201
53.	Woman heavily ornamented	1	0.201
54.	Woman in black dress	1	0.201
55.	Woman behind a hillock	1	0.201
56.	Woman on a sofa	1	0.201
57.	Woman with closed eyes	1	0.201
58.	An old man and a child	1	0.201
59.	Female figure with a bird	1	0.201
60.	Wild figure	1	0.201
61.	Two figures and a poem	1	0.201
62.	Man and woman	1	0.201
63.	Man in the back of a bird in flight	1	0.201
64.	Boy with a stick	1	0.201
65.	Woman-bathing	1	0.201
66.	Woman in a boat	1	0.201
67.	Boat and a man	1	0.201
68.	Bull and a man	1	0.201
69.	Woman carrying a picture	1	0.201
70.	Man with a dog	1	0.201
71.	Woman nursing a sick person	1	0.201
	Total	**496**	**100.00**

Table 3.7: Paintings of Human Faces in Tagoreana

Sl. No.	*Theme*	*No. of Paintings*	*Percentage*
1.	Human face (male and female)	200	91.324
2.	Bearded face	10	4.566
3.	Face study	3	1.370
4.	Human face-design	2	0.913
5.	Face of a man with a cap	2	0.913
6.	Human face and a fish	1	0.457
7.	Mask like face	1	0.457
	Total	**219**	**100.00**

Table 3.8: Paintings of Animals in Tagoreana

Sl. No.	*Theme*	*No. of Paintings*	*Percentage*
1.	Animal-fantasy	17	26.984
2.	Animal like figure	14	22.222
3.	Dog	10	15.873
4.	Cow	3	4.762
5.	Animal head	3	4.762
6.	Fox	2	3.175
7.	Elephant	2	3.175
8.	Jackal—illustration for "Sey"	2	3.175
9.	Deer	1	1.587
10.	Crocodile	1	1.587
11.	Camel like figure	1	1.587
12.	Two serpents	1	1.587
13.	Two alligators	1	1.587
14.	Two animals—one rodent and one bird	1	1.587
15.	Animal in a forest	1	1.587
16.	Animal inside a bowl	1	1.587
17.	Animal face	1	1.587
18.	Rabbit	1	1.587
	Total	**63**	**100.00**

Table 3.9: Paintings of Birds in Tagoreana

Sl. No.	*Theme*	*No. of Paintings*	*Percentage*
1.	Birds (form and shape)	36	58.065
2.	Bird-design	8	12.903
3.	Bird in flight	3	4.839
4.	Birds and animals	3	4.839
5.	Bird-fantasy	2	3.226
6.	Owl	2	3.226
7.	Birds on the sea waves	1	1.613
8.	Birds on a geometric form	1	1.613
9.	Bird and a bearded man	1	1.613
10.	Birds and reptiles	1	1.613
11.	Two peacocks	1	1.613
12.	Duck	1	1.613
13.	Cock	1	1.613
14.	Crane	1	1.613
	Total	**62**	**100.00**

Table 3.10: Drawing of Designs in Tagoreana

Sl. No.	*Theme*	*No. of Paintings*	*Percentage*
1.	Bearded man	16	27.586
2.	Design	15	25.862
3.	Design of a sitting figure	5	8.620
4.	Water pot	3	5.172
5.	Architectural design with a face	3	5.172
6.	Design of a man	3	5.172
7.	Animal	2	3.448
8.	Human figure inside a design	2	3.448
9.	Design resembling a face	2	3.448
10.	Human head	1	1.724
11.	Tray	1	1.724
12.	Dancing figure with a design	1	1.724
13.	Fish-design	1	1.724
14.	Design over a poem	1	1.724
15.	Design of a oval shaped horse	1	1.724
16.	Design with Bengali script	1	1.724
	Total	58	100.000

Table 3.11: Paintings of Compositions in Tagoreana

Sl. No.	*Themes*	*No. of paintings*	*Percentage*
1.	Figure composition	43	79.630
2.	Man and a boy	1	1.852
3.	Two figures with a child	1	1.852
4.	Worship of a primitive idol	1	1.852
5.	Male figure riding on a crocodile	1	1.852
6.	Donkey in a forest	1	1.852
7.	Composition—Chandraloke	1	1.852
8.	Composition with a woman face	1	1.852
9.	Colour composition	1	1.852
10.	Man and a boat	1	1.852
11.	Composition with birds	1	1.852
12.	Composition with architecture	1	1.852
	Total	**54**	**100.00**

Table 3.12: Illustrations for Khapchhada

Sl. No.	*Theme*	*No. of Paintings*	*Percentage*
1.	Face of woman/man	5	16.667
2.	Figure-standing	2	6.667
3.	Head	2	6.667
4.	Matilal Nandi	1	3.333
5.	Narahari Sharma	1	3.333
6.	Kabi-adhunik	1	3.333
7.	Two figures	1	3.333
8.	Leg being brushed	1	3.333
9.	Rannar Sab Thik	1	3.333
10.	Badsa	1	3.333
11.	M.Sc.	1	3.333
12.	Chhoto Bau	1	3.333
13.	Sindhkata	1	3.333
14.	Potter Khudu	1	3.333
15.	Baneswar	1	3.333
15a.	Mukh dheke	1	3.333
16.	Neyamat Darji	1	3.333
17.	Daktar	1	3.333
18.	Man with a raised hand	1	3.333
19.	Smiling face	1	3.333
20.	Damodar Seth	1	3.333
21.	Girl with a earring	1	3.333
22.	Pencho	1	3.333
23.	Adhkhana-Bel	1	3.333
	Total	**30**	**100.00**

Table 3.13: Different Forms of Paintings in Tagoreana

Sl. No.	*Themes*	*No. of Paintings*	*Percentage*
1.	Zoomorphic form	15	37.500
2.	Animal form	9	22.500
3.	Geometric form	6	15.000
4.	Reptile	3	7.500
5.	Angular form	3	7.500
6.	Snake like form – fantasy	1	2.500
7.	Silhouette form	1	2.500
8.	Composite form	1	2.500
9.	Two forms	1	2.500
	Total	**40**	**100.00**

Table 3.14: Different Types of Sketch in Tagoreana

Sl. No.	Themes	No. of Paintings	Percentage
1.	Coloured sketch	12	41.379
2.	Woman-sketch	4	13.793
3.	A woman at the door	2	6.897
4.	Two human figures	2	6.897
5.	Sketch	1	3.448
6.	An old man	1	3.448
7.	A man with a cap	1	3.448
8.	Man with a turban	1	3.448
9.	Five faces	1	3.448
10.	Taimurlong—sketch of a boy	1	3.448
11.	Woman in a net	1	3.448
12.	Khudiram—sketch of a boy	1	3.448
13.	Sketch—incomplete	1	3.448
	Total	**29**	**100.00**

Table 3.15: Portrait in Tagoreana

Sl. No.	Themes	No. of Paintings	Percentage
1.	Portrait of a woman	7	50.000
2.	Self portrait	4	28.571
3.	Portrait of a man	2	14.286
4.	Turbaned head	1	7.1430
	Total	**14**	**100.00**

From the above tables (3.5 to 3.15) an idea about 27 different themes of Rabindranath's paintings can be obtained. By analyzing the themes it can be noticed that at least on 177 different sub-themes Rabindranath created paintings which cover animals, birds, design, sketch, composition, forms and illustrations.

Rabindranath used various media for his paintings. He used pen ink, waterproof ink, crayon, water colour, pastel colour and pencil in different combinations. The varieties of combinations are shown as in Table 3.16 to 3.22.

From the tables (3.16 to 3.22), varieties of medium used by Rabindranath for his paintings can be traced. Actually Rabindranath used to combine different mediums in his drawings and paintings instead of using a single medium. For example, Tagore used exclusively pen ink in 466 (71.145%) paintings out of 655 paintings where pen ink was used. It can be noticed that Rabindranath used pen ink with 21 combinations, waterproof ink with 30 combinations, crayon with 5 combinations, water colour with 9 combinations and pastel and pencil with 8 and 4 combinations respectively.

Table 3.16: Use of Pen Ink, and Pen Ink with other Mediums in Paintings

Sl. No.	*Colour Combination*	*No. of Paintings*	*Percentage*
1.	Pen ink	466	71.145
2.	Pen ink with reed pen and brush	44	6.718
3.	Pen ink and water colour	31	4.733
4.	Pen ink and poster colour	29	4.427
5.	Pen ink and crayon	21	3.206
6.	Pen ink, water colour and waterproof ink	11	1.679
7.	Pen ink and brush work	11	1.679
8.	Pen ink with pencil underlining	9	1.374
9.	Pen ink with reed pen	7	1.069
10.	Pen ink and pastel colour	6	0.916
11.	Pen ink, crayon and pastel	5	0.763
12.	Pen ink, water colour and poster colour	4	0.611
13.	Pen ink, poster colour and pastel	2	0.305
14.	Pen ink, poster colour and crayon	2	0.305
15.	Pen ink and gold ink	1	0.153
16.	Pen ink, poster white with brush	1	0.153
17.	Pen ink, water colour, poster colour and pastel	1	0.153
18.	Pen ink, poster colour and water colour	1	0.153
19.	Pen ink, waterproof ink with brush	1	0.153
20.	Pen ink, water colour and golden colour	1	0.153
21.	Pen ink and vegetable colour	1	0.153
	Total	**655**	**100.00**

Table 3.17: Use of Waterproof Ink and Waterproof Ink with other Mediums in Paintings

Sl. No.	*Colour Combination*	*No. of Paintings*	*Percentage*
1.	Waterproof ink	218	30.748
2.	Waterproof ink and pen ink	216	30.465
3.	Waterproof ink and poster colour	102	14.386
4.	Waterproof ink, pen ink and poster colour	63	8.886
5.	Waterproof ink, pen ink, brush and pen work	24	3.385
6.	Waterproof ink and water colour	20	2.820
7.	Waterproof ink and crayon	9	1.269
8.	Waterproof ink and pastel	8	1.128
9.	Waterproof ink, poster colour and pastel	4	0.564
10.	Waterproof ink, poster colour and crayon	4	0.564
11.	Waterproof ink, poster colour and water colour	4	0.564
12.	Waterproof ink and gauche	4	0.564
13.	Waterproof ink, brush and reed handling	3	0.423
14.	Waterproof ink and brush work	3	0.423
15.	Waterproof ink, pen ink and crayon	3	0.423
16.	Waterproof ink and pen ink with reed pen	3	0.423
17.	Waterproof ink with ink and wash handling	2	0.282
18.	Waterproof ink, pen ink, poster and pastel	2	0.282
19.	Waterproof ink, pen ink and pastel	2	0.282
20.	Waterproof ink, pen ink with gold dust with glue	2	0.282
21.	Waterproof ink and pencil	2	0.282
22.	Waterproof ink, poster colour, crayon and pen ink	2	0.282
23.	Waterproof ink with varnish	2	0.282
24.	Waterproof ink with pen and brush	1	0.141
25.	Waterproof ink, poster colour, pen ink with brush and pen	1	0.141
26.	Waterproof ink, pen ink, water colour and pastel	1	0.141
27.	Waterproof ink, water colour and pastel	1	0.141
28.	Waterproof ink, water colour, pen ink and poster colour	1	0.141
29.	Waterproof ink over charcoal drawing	1	0.141
30.	Waterproof ink, water colour with crayon	1	0.141
	Total	**709**	**100.00**

Table 3.18: Use of Crayon and Crayon with other Mediums in Paintings

Sl. No.	Colour Combination	No. of Paintings	Percentage
1.	Crayon	52	64.198
2.	Crayon and pastel colour	24	29.630
3.	Crayon and pencil	3	3.704
4.	Crayon and water colour	1	1.235
5.	Crayon, pastel and waterproof ink	1	1.235
	Total	**81**	**100.00**

Table 3.19: Use of Water Colour and Water Colour with Other Mediums in Paintings

Sl. No.	Colour Combination	No. of Paintings	Percentage
1.	Water colour	16	37.209
2.	Water colour and pen ink	11	25.581
3.	Water colour and poster colour	4	9.302
4.	Water colour and waterproof ink	4	9.302
5.	Water colour, ink and brush work	3	6.977
6.	Water colour and pastel	2	4.651
7.	Water colour and brush handling	1	2.326
8.	Water colour, waterproof ink and crayon	1	2.326
9.	Water colour, pen ink with crayon	1	2.326
	Total	**43**	**100.00**

Table 3.20: Use of Pastel and Pastel with Other Mediums in Paintings

Sl. No.	Colour Combination	No. of Paintings	Percentage
1.	Pastel and pen ink	11	40.741
2.	Pastel	8	29.630
3.	Pastel, waterproof ink and poster colour	2	7.407
4.	Pastel and pencil	2	7.407
5.	Pastel, pen ink and pencil	1	3.703
6.	Pastel, pen wash with water colour	1	3.703
7.	Pastel and poster colour	1	3.703
8.	Pastel, crayon, pen and water colour	1	3.703
	Total	**27**	**100.00**

Table 3.21: Use of Pencil and Pencil with Other Mediums in Paintings

Sl. No.	Colour Combination	No. of Paintings	Percentage
1.	Pencil	31	88.571
2.	Pencil with pastel and crayon	2	5.714
3.	Pencil, poster colour and waterproof ink	1	2.857
4.	Pencil, crayon and pen ink	1	2.857
	Total	**35**	**100.00**

Table 3.22: Use of Other Mediums in Paintings

Sl. No	Colour Combination	No. of Paintings	Percentage
1.	Poster colour	13	56.522
2.	Etching print	5	21.739
3.	Etching print Gouche (5 on paper and 1 on silk)	4	17.391
4.	Vegetable colour	1	4.348
	Total	**23**	**100.00**

Rabindranath used various canvases for paintings and drawings which can be traced out from the following tables (3.23 to 3.36).

Table 3.23: Canvas used in Paintings of Tagoreana

Sl. No.	Painted on	No. of Paintings	Percentage
1	Plain paper	1524	96.884
2	Other than plain paper	49	3.115
	Total	**1573**	**100.00**

Table 3.24: Works on Different Canvases Other than Paper in Paintings of Tagoreana

Sl. No.	Painted on	No. of Paintings	Percentage
1.	Printed on Visva-Bharati News [66]	12	24.490
2.	Card	9	18.367
3.	Silk	6	12.245
4.	Wood	5	10.204
5.	Wooden box	5	10.204
6.	Wooden board	4	8.163
7.	Varnished paper	2	4.082
8.	Pasted card	2	4.082
9.	Glazed paper	1	2.041
10.	Exercise book	1	2.041
11.	Backside of a letter	1	2.041
12.	Pasted paper	1	2.041
	Total	**49**	**100.00**

Table 3.25: Paintings on Visva-Bharati News

Sl. No.	*Medium*	*No. of Paintings*	*Percentage*
1.	Pen ink and water colour	5	41.667
2.	Pen ink and poster colour	2	16.667
3.	Pen ink and pastel	2	16.667
4.	Pen ink	1	8.333
5.	Pastel and water colour	1	8.333
6.	Pastel, crayon, pencil, pen and water colour	1	8.333
	Total (12 sketches)	**12**	**100.00**

Table 3.26: Paintings on Card

Sl. No.	*Theme*	*Medium*	*No. of Paintings*	*Percentage*
1.	Head study	1 Pen ink, 1 lead pencil	2	22.222
2.	Face	Pen ink	2	22.222
3.	Bearded man	Pen ink	1	11.111
4.	Male figure	Pen ink	1	11.111
5.	Female figure	Pen ink	1	11.111
6.	Woman on a sofa	Pen ink	1	11.111
7.	Chitralipi	Water colour	1	11.111
	Total		**9**	**100.00**

Table 3.27: Paintings on Silk

Sl. No.	*Theme*	*Medium*	*No. of Paintings*	*Percentage*
1.	Head study-woman	1 Gouche colour, 1 water proof ink, 1 water colour	3	50.000
2.	Animal	Water proof ink	1	16.667
3.	Landscape	Pastel and pen ink	1	16.667
4.	Dancing girl	Crayon and pen	1	16.667
	Total		**6**	**100.00**

Table 3.28: Paintings on Wood

Sl. No.	*Theme*	*Medium*	*No. of Paintings*	*Percentage*
1.	Seated woman	Pen ink and waterproof ink	2	40.000
2.	Owl	Pen ink and water colour	1	20.000
3.	Man playing	Pen ink and water colour	1	20.000
4.	Mask like figure	Poster colour, waterproof ink, pen ink	1	20.000
	Total		**5**	**100.00**

Table 3.29: Paintings on Wooden Box

Sl. No.	*Theme*	*Medium*	*No. of Paintings*	*Percentage*
1.	Bird	Pen ink and waterproof ink	2	40.000
2.	Face of a bearded man	Pen ink and waterproof ink	1	20.000
3.	Face in profile	Pen ink, waterproof and water colour ink	1	20.000
4.	Composition with architecture	Water colour and waterproof ink	1	20.000
	Total		**5**	**100.00**

Table 3.30: Paintings on Wooden Board

Sl. No.	*Theme*	*Medium*	*No. of Paintings*	*Percentage*
1.	Landscape	Pen ink, waterproof ink and poster colour	1	25.000
2.	Bearded man	Waterproof ink, pen ink and poster colour	1	25.000
3.	Standing figure	Waterproof ink, pen ink and poster colour	1	25.000
4.	Tree	Water colour, waterproof ink and pen ink	1	25.000
	Total		**4**	**100.00**

Table 3.31: Paintings on Varnished Paper

Sl. No.	*Theme*	*Medium*	*No. of Paintings*	*Percentage*
1.	Face of a woman	Water colour and waterproof ink	1	50.000
2.	Head study-profile	Water colour and waterproof ink	1	50.000
	Total		**2**	**100.00**

Table 3.32: Paintings on Pasted Card

Sl. No.	*Theme*	*Medium*	*No. of Paintings*	*Percentage*
1.	Face of a woman	Pen ink	1	50.000
2.	Mask like face	Pen ink	1	50.000
	Total		**2**	**100.00**

Table 3.33: Paintings on Glazed Paper

Sl. No.	*Theme*	*Medium*	*No. of Paintings*	*Percentage*
1	Narabudbud	Waterproof ink	1	100.00

Table 3.34: Painting in Exercise Book

Sl. No.	*Theme*	*Medium*	*No. of Paintings*	*Percentage*
1.	Design over a poem	Pen ink	1	100.00

Table 3.35: Painting on Backside of a Paper

Sl. No.	*Theme*	*Medium*	*No. of Paintings*	*Percentage*
1	Flower	Pen ink	1	100.00

Table 3.36: Painting on Pasted Paper

Sl. No.	*Theme*	*Medium*	*No. of Paintings*	*Percentage*
1	Flower study	Pen ink and water colour	1	100.00

It can be observed that Rabindranath mostly used paper as a medium in 1524 paintings out of 1573 paintings but for the remaining 49 paintings under study he used 12 other different mediums including Visva-Bharati News. The theme of paintings drawn on canvas other than paper includes human figure, bird, composition, tree, flower, landscape, etc.

To authenticate his drawings and paintings Rabindranath used to put his different types of signature in different languages on it. An account of signature used by Rabindranath on his paintings and drawings is given in Tables 3. 37 to 3.41.

Table 3.37: Signature of Rabindranath Tagore on Paintings

Sl. No.	*Signature*	*No. of Paintings*	*Percentage*
1.	Signed	958	60.903
2.	Unsigned	615	39.097
	Total	**1573**	**100.00**

Table 3.38: Signature of Rabindranath Tagore in Different Languages on Paintings

Sl. No.	*Signature*	*No. of Paintings*	*Percentage*
1.	Bengali	903	94.259
2.	English	53	5.532
3.	Bengali and English both	02	0.209
	Total	958	100.00

Table 3.39: Different Types of Bengali Signatures of Rabindranath Tagore on Paintings

Sl. No.	*Signature*	*No. of Paintings*	*Percentage*
1.	"Rabindra"	571	63.234
2.	"Sri Rabindra"	299	33.112
3.	"Rabindranath"	13	1.440
4.	"Sri Rabindranath Thakur"	9	0.997
5.	"Rabindranath Thakur"	5	0.554
6.	"Rabindra" and also "Ra Tha"	1	0.111
7.	"Sri Rabindra" and "Rabindra"	1	0.111
8.	"Ra Tha"	1	0.111
9.	"Rabi Dada"	1	0.111
10.	"Ra Tha" and "Sri Rabindranath Tagore"	1	0.111
11.	"Sri Rabindra" and "Rabindranath Tagore"	1	0.111
	Total	**903**	**100.00**

Table 3.40: Different Types of English Signatures of Rabindranath Tagore on Paintings

Sl. No.	*Signature*	*No. of Paintings*	*Percentage*
1.	"Rabindranath"	24	45.283
2.	"Rabindra"	18	33.962
3.	"Rabindranath Tagore"	09	16.981
4.	"Sri Rabindra"	02	3.774
	Total	**53**	**100.00**

Table 3.41: Combination of English and Bengali Signatures of Rabindranath Tagore on Paintings

Sl. No.	*Signature*	*No. of Paintings*	*Percentage*
1.	"Sri Rabindranath Tagore" in Bengali script and "Rabindranath Tagore" in Roman Script	1	50.000
2.	"Rabindra" in Bengali Script and "Rabindranath" in Roman Script	1	50.000
	Total	**2**	**100.00**

It may be observed from the tables (3.37 to 3.41) that Rabindranath put his signatures in 958 occasions predominantly as Rabindra (63.234%) and in Bengali (94.259%).

Rabindranath extensively travelled throughout the world besides India. Rabindranath used to write name of the place and date in his writings. But in the case of paintings, place of paintings has not been mentioned always as can be noticed from the following tables (3.42 to 3.47).

Table 3.42: Place of Painting

Sl. No.	*Place*	*No. of Paintings*	*Percentage*
1.	Not mentioned	1525	96.949
2.	Mentioned	48	3.051
	Total	**1573**	**100.00**

Table 3.43: Place of Paintings Mentioned in Tagoreana

Sl. No.	*Place*	*No. of Paintings*	*Percentage*
1.	Indian	29	60.417
2.	Foreign	19	39.583
	Total	**48**	**100.00**

Table 3.44: Indian Places of Paintings Mentioned in Tagoreana

Sl. No.	*Place*	*No. of Paintings*	*Percentage*
1.	Adihar	11	37.932
2.	Santiniketan	7	24.138
3.	Hyderabad	5	17.242
4.	Mongpu	1	3.448
5.	Darjeeling	1	3.448
6.	Chandannagar	1	3.448
7.	Jorasanko	1	3.448
8.	Kalimpong	1	3.448
9.	Delhi	1	3.448
	Total	**29**	**100.00**

Table 3.45: Foreign Places of Paintings Mentioned in Tagoreana

Sl. No.	*Place*	*No. of Paintings*	*Percentage*
1.	Moscow	7	36.842
2.	Lahore	5	26.316
3.	S.S. Taiyomary (San Francisco)	3	15.790
4.	Baghdad	1	5.263
5.	Sanghai	1	5.263
6.	Tehran	1	5.263
7.	S.S. Angers	1	5.263
	Total	**19**	**100.00**

Table 3.46: Dates of Paintings where Place Mentioned: India

Sl. No.	*Place*	*Dates of Paintings*	*No. of Paintings*
1.	Adihar	19.10.1934, 22.10.1934, 23.10.1934, 25.10.1934, 26.20.1934, 29.10.1934, 30.10.1934, Nov.1934	11
2.	Santiniketan	22.5.1931, 17.11.1933, 20.8.1934, Nov.1934, 20.12.1934, 6.4.1935, 6.9.1935	7
3.	Hyderabad	12.12.1933, 18.12.1933(2), 23.12.1933, 24.12.1933	5
4.	Mongpu	17.6.1939	1
5.	Darjeeling	Nov.1931	1
6.	Chandannagar	3.11.1933	1
7.	Jorasanko	30.12.1933	1
8.	Delhi	3.11.1936	1
9.	Kalimpong	Sept. 1940	1
	Total		**29**

Note : Number within bracket indicates number of paintings in a day

Table 3.47: Dates of Paintings where Place Mentioned: Foreign

Sl. No.	Place	Dates of Paintings	No. of Paintings
1.	Moscow	15.9.1930(4), 16.9.1930, 19.9.1930, Sept.1930	7
2.	Lahore	24.2.1935(2), 25.2.1935(2), 27.1.1935	5
3.	S.S. Taiyomaru	21.4.1929, 26.4.1929, one no date	3
4.	Baghdad	12.5.1932	1
5.	Sanghai	17.3.1929	1
6.	Tehran	6.5.1932	1
7.	S.S. Angers	6.10.1929	1
	Total		**19**

Note: Number within brackets indicate number of paintings in a day.

A quick look into the Tables (3.42 to 3.47) reveals that Rabindranath mentioned place of paintings only on 48 occasions (i.e. in 3.051% of his paintings) which are predominantly India (29 places, i.e. 60.417%.). But in all the paintings with dates, place of drawing is also mentioned.

Dates on writings help observe a chronological development of writings or ideas. But paintings in Tagoreana lacks date in 1100 cases (i.e. 69.930 % of Tagore's paintings) as identified from Tables 3.48 to 3.50.

Table 3.48: Date of Paintings

Sl. No.	Date	No. of Paintings	Percentage
1.	Date not mentioned	1100	69.930
2.	Date mentioned	473	30.070
	Total	**1573**	**100.00**

Table 3.49: Year-wise Production of Dated Paintings

Sl. No.	Year	No. of Paintings	Percentage
1.	1929	6	1.418
2.	1930	8	1.891
3.	1931	11	2.600
4.	1932	25	5.910
5.	1933	20	4.728
6.	1934	57	13.475
7.	1935	61	14.421
8.	1936	65	15.366
9.	1937	53	12.520
10.	1938	48	11.348
11.	1939	60	14.184
12.	1940	9	2.177
	Total	**423**	**100.00**

Table 3.50: Date-wise Production of Dated Paintings

Sl. No.	Year	Date of Paintings	No.
1.	1929	15.3, 21.3, 21.4, 25.4, 26.4, 1929	6
2.	1930	15.9.(3), 16.9, 18.9, 19.9, Sept.(2)	8
3.	1931	13.1.(2), 10.3, March, 2.5, 19.5, May (2), June, Nov., 1931	11
4.	1932	Jan., 1.2, 2.3.(3), 5.3, 6.3, March (6), April, 6.5, 12.5, May, 1932(8)	25
5.	1933	March, 15.9, 1.11, 2.11, 3.11.(2), 17.11, 18.11.(2), 31.11, 7.12, 8.12, 12.12, 15.12, 18.2.(2), 2.12, 24.12, 31.12(2)	20
6.	1934	6.1.(3), 12.1.(3), 13.1.(2), 6.1.(4), 21.1.(2), 22.1, 24.1, 27.1, 30.1, 7.4, 9.4, May, 20.6, 3.7, 19.7, 7.10, 10.10, 15.10, 16.10.(3), 19.10, 22.10, 23.10, 24.10.(2), 25.10.(5), 26.10, 27.10, 28.10, 29.10.(2), 30.10.(2), 31.10, 10.11, 12.11, 27.11, Nov.(3), 20.2, Dec.(2)	57
7.	1935	31.1.(2), 1.2, 17.2, 18.2, 22.2, 24.2, 25.2.(2), 27.2.(3), 17.3, 6.4, 10.4.(2), 14.4.(2), 18.4, April, 4.5, 5.5.(2), 5.6, 13.6, 23.6.(2), 9.7.(2), 20.7, 24.7.(2), 28.7, 9.8, 19.8.(2), 22.8.(2), 25.8, 28.8, Aug, 6.9, 21.9, 14.10.(3), 15.10, 30.10, 31.10, 2.11, 4.11, 7.11.(5), 8.11, 10.11, 14.11, 6.12, 1935.	61
8.	1936	Jan., 1.3, 3.3, 3.4, 5.4.(2), 16.4, 24.4.(2), 11.5, 14.5.(2), 15.5.(3), 16.5.(2), 18.5, 19.5.(2), 20.5.(2), 21.5.(3), 20.6.(4), 26.6.(2), 28.6.(6), 30.6, June, 20.7, 1.8, 3.8.(3), 16.8.(2), 23.8, 10.10, 17.10, 20.10.(2), 3.11, 5.11.(2), 6.11, 7.11.(3), 11.11, 1936(6)	65
9.	1937	1.3, 20.3, 29.3, 5.4, 6.4, 8.4, 9.4.(2), 10.4, 15.4, 23.6, 27.6, 13.9, 21.9.(2), 22.9.(3), 25.9.(2), 26.9, 27.9.(2), 3.10.(2), 5.10, 9.10.(3), 10.10.(2), 19.10, 20.10, 23.10, 6.11.(3), 7.11.(2), 8.11.(2), 9.11.(3), 10.11, 15.11, 6.12.(3), 16.12, 1937(3)	53
10.	1938	22.1, 9.2.(2), 25.2.(4), March (3), 3.4, 5.4.(2), 7.4.(2), 17.4, 24.4, 27.4, 25.6, 1.10, 15.10, 2.11.(2), 7.11.(4), Nov., 20.12, 1938(19)	48
11.	1939	15.1, 22.1, 29.1, 19.2.(2), 20.2.(2), 21.2, 22.2.(4), 26.2.(2), 2.3, 21.3.(2), 5.6, 13.6, 15.6, 16.6.(2), 17.6, 20.6, 22.6, 23.6, 20.7.(4), 26.7, 8.11, 9.11, 11.11, 13.11, 16.11, Nov.(2), 3.12, 1939(21)	60
12.	1940	5.4, 12.4, 16.4, 5.5, 10.5, 13.6, Sept., 5.9, 3.11.	9

Note: Number within brackets indicate number of paintings in a date month etc.

It may be recorded from the available dates that the first painting was drawn on 15th March, 1929 and last one on 3rd November 1939. But as Rabindranath put date only in 473 paintings (i.e. 30% of total paintings) it would not be possible to determine the chronology of paintings in Tagoreana.

Rabindranath gave titles to his drawings and paintings only in 46 occasions as indicated in Table 3.51.

Table 3.51: Titles of Paintings Given by Rabindranath

Sl. No.	Title	Theme	Size in CM	Date
1.	"Suo Rani Duo Rani"	Flower study	21.5 × 33	
2.	"Jantur juju"		42 × 9.5	17.11.1937
3.	"Chandraloke"	Composition	25 × 31.5	March 1931
4.	"Chandar Khata"	Zoomorphic form	14.6 × 23	
5.	"Galpa-Salpa"	Group of figures	21 × 29	Sept. 1940
6.	"Chitralipi"		13.2 × 20.5	
7.	"Baibahik"	Standing figure	17 × 20	
8.	"Consoler"		20.5 × 35.5	
9.	"Pollaram"	Man with a stick	21.5 × 36.4	
10.	"Nara bud bud"		18.5 × 23	
11.	"Hasi"	Head of an animal	11 × 19	
12.	"Gandi Sang-dung"	Zoomorphic form	17 × 21	
13.	"Sandhan"	Animal form	11.2 × 14.5	
14.	"Minati"	Dog	12.8 × 18.8	
15.	"Bholanath"	Figure	13.5 × 22	
16.	"Utkata-danti"		14 × 25	7.11.1936
17.	"Pandeji"	Head study	13 × 17.5	
18.	"Byasta"	Human figure	14 × 19	
19.	"Strir bon"	Female figure	13 × 18.5	
20.	"Eskul Arano"	Face of a boy	14.3 × 17	
21.	"Mejo Bau"	Female figure	17 × 21	
22.	"Neyamat Darji"	Face of a man	11 × 19.5	

(Contd.)

Table 3.51: *(Contd.)*

Sl. No.	Title	Theme	Size in CM	Date
23.	"Pachamba"	Female figure	11.2 × 19	
24.	"Benu"	Figure	13.5 × 23.2	
25.	"Sakal Atta"	Reclined figure	13 × 16.5	
26.	"Mokter"	Illustration for "Se"	13 × 18.2	
27.	"Adhkhana Bel"	Illustration for "Khapchhada"	12 × 17.5	
28.	"Khudiram"	Sketch of a boy	12 × 21.5	
29.	"Damodar Seth"	Man in profile—illustration for "Khapchhada"	11 × 20	6.11.1936
30.	"Pencho"	Illustration for "Khapchhada"	12.5 × 19.5	
31.	"Matilal Nandi"	Illustration for "Khapchhada"	10.6 × 15.7	
32.	"Narahari Sharma"	Illustration for "Khapchhada"	7.5 × 14.5	
33.	"Kabi Adhunik"	Illustration for "Khapchhada"	16 × 21	Bhadra, 1343
34.	"Rannar sab thik"	Illustration for "Khapchada"	12 × 16	
35.	"Badsa"	Illustration for "Khapchhada"	16 × 19.5	
36.	"M.Sc."	Illustration for "Khapchada"	8 × 13	
37.	"Chhoto Bau"	Illustration for "Khapchhada"	16 × 19.5	
38.	"Sindh kata"	Illustration for "Khapchhada"	16 × 20.2	
39.	"Paltar khudu"	Illustration for "Khapchhada"	16 × 20	
40.	"Baneshwar"	Illustration for "Khapchhada"	16 × 20	
41.	"Mukh dheke"	Illustration for "Khapchhada"	16 × 20	
42.	"Neyamat darji"	Illustration for "Khapchhada"	16 × 20	
43.	"Daktar"	Illustration for "Khapchhada"	16 × 20	
44.	"Siraj"		16.2 × 25	
45.	"Alu"		17.3 × 23	
46.	"Aluke"	Mask like face	22 × 30	16.4.40

It is surprising to note that Rabindranath, as a painter, was first recognized in the West, mainly after his exhibitions in Paris in the year 1930. A list of exhibitions during Tagore's lifetime would justify this statement.

Table 3.52: Exhibitions of Paintings and Drawings of Rabindranath during his Lifetime

Sl. No.	*Year*	*Gallery*	*Place*	*Country*
1.	1930, May	Galerie Pigalle	Paris	France
2.	1930 June	City Art Gallery	Birmingham	U.K.
3.	1930 June	India Society	London	U.K.
4.	1930 July	Moeller's Gallery	Berlin	Germany
5.	1930 July	Art Club of Saxony	Dresden	Germany
6.	1930 July	Gallery Caspari	Munich	Germany
7.	1930 August	Charlottenburg Picture Gallery	Copenhagen	Denmark
8.	1930 August-September	Geneva	Geneva	Switzerland
9.	1930 September	State Museum of New Western Art	Moscow	U.S.S.R.
10.	1930 October	Doll and Richards Gallery	Boston	U.S.A.
11.	1930 October	Museum of Fine Arts	Boston	U.S.A.
12.	1930 December	Fifty-Sixth Street Galleries	New York	U.S.A.
13.	1930 December	Newman Galleries	Philadelphia	U.S.A.
14.	1931 December	Town Hall	Calcutta	India
15.	1932 February	Government School of Art	Calcutta	India
16.	1933 November	Town Hall	Bombay	India
17.	1934 May	Colombo	Colombo	Ceylon
18.	1934 October	Congress House	Madras	India
19.	1938 December	Calmann Gallery	London	U.K.
20.	1939 February	Bangiya Sahitya Parishad	Calcutta	India

Source: Rabindra-Chitrakala: Rabindrasahityer Patabhumika.

From the above tables it is clear that Rabindranath authored a good number of drawings and paintings in a short span of 12 years (15.3.1929-3.11.1940) on different themes, with various colour combinations. Rabindranath's paintings include figures in different shapes and forms, human face, head study, landscape, birds, animals, nudes, etc. Every subject has its own childlike imaginary rhythmic speciality. Regarding the head study, observation of sculptor Marguerite Milward after Paris exhibition is worth mentioning. "Perhaps the heads attract me the most, faces of every shape, sometimes only eyes that haunt and follow me out of the dark. Here is a portrait perhaps, very soft and flat in colour, a shape of hair, oval face and smiling mouth. A dream indeed weird and beautiful" [67]. We may quote Vossische Zeitung's observation on Berlin exhibition dated 16.7.1930, "New visions were seized in his pictures that descend to the depth, to the origin, of which the reality of the world is only a feeble copy, reflected light. Animals play a great part in them, but not those from the zoo, but those who alarm us in black nightmares. The way Tagore coloured these monkeys, tigers, vultures and marauders, displays the educated sensitive taste of oldest culture; radish brownish yellowish tones that are full of coloured life often contrast with the black background that plays an important part—it is the night of dream. We meet with dark harmonies of the deep mystery, from where the objects often emerge with light outlines"[68].

As a medium of painting Rabindranath used mainly ink (41.513 %). But a single or various combinations of pen ink, waterproof ink, water colour, crayon, poster colour, pastel, pencil, vegetable colour, etc. used mainly on paper (96.88%). Whatever medium Rabindranath used "his colours are scattered through nature" [69]. Regarding role of lines with different mediums in paintings Rabindranath had deep feelings as he narrated in his speech in London India Society. "*It interests me deeply to watch how lines find their life and character, as their connection with each other develops in varied cadences, and how they begin to speak in gesticulations. I can imagine the universe to be a universe of lines*" [70].

Rabindranath signed in 903 paintings (60.903%) in different languages (predominantly in Bengali), (N=903), i.e. 94.26 per cent, different combinations and in different types and styles. Out of signed paintings he signed "*Rabindra*" in Bengali in 571 paintings (63.23%) and "*Sri Rabindra*" in 299 (33.11%) paintings. According to Tagore biographer Prabhatkumar, Rabindranath stopped writing "*Sri*" in August 1932. But he used to write "*Sri Rabindra*" in paintings. Later on Rabindranath stopped writing "*Sri*" in his paintings also [71]. This statement can be justified as according to available dates Rabindranath produced most of the paintings after 1932.

Rabindranath signed in majority of his paintings (60.903%) but gave dates only to 473 paintings (30.070%). This creates a great hindrance in generating a chronological index of paintings in Tagoreana. But one interesting finding comes from the available dates that Rabindranath painted two to three paintings in a day quite a number of times, even four (6.1.1934, 7.11.1938, 20.7.1939) and five pictures in a day in two occasions (25.10.1934, 7.11.1935) and six paintings once (28.6.1938).

During the study of paintings it was also observed that Rabindranath used various sizes of canvas for his paintings. The largest size of painting is 70.5×78 cm, the largest breadth of painting is 60.8×90.4 cm. Similarly, the smallest size and breadth of paintings are 8×3 cm, minimum length 3.5×48.5 cm. Maximum number of paintings (N=37) is in the size of 25.5×35.5 cm.

It is very difficult to explain why at the age of sixty-seven Rabindranath started painting as a non-verbal medium of expression. Many guesses are there, such as declining reputation, conflicting ideologies, fear of death, etc. The statistical analysis shows the variety of colour, theme, size, date, etc. of Tagore paintings and drawings, but mere statistical analysis cannot reveal the inner insight of painting. We may note Nandalal Bose's observation in this respect "majority of the artists begin the creative processes with the subject or idea... But Rabindranath, it seems, often begins creating even before the subject has taken any conscious form in his mind. This might easily lead one to suppose that mere craftsmanship or mere architectural design or the mere effect of colours were his end, but when the picture is complete we discover all the essential constituents of a work of art in it, all blended in one subject and pervaded by that rhythm of life which the hand of genius alone can impart. That is why his paintings are always real, though rarely realistic" [72]. Actually it is not realistic but "his art is mainly symbolic—whether it is poetry, or music, or dance, or painting... Even the portraits were the symbols of abstract qualities" [73]. Yeast's opinion on Tagoreana can be applicable to Rabindranath's paintings and drawings also "Most persons write so that if you were to detach a sentence from its context, it would have no meaning. With Tagore's writing, however, it is just the other way round. Almost any sentence will stand by itself—almost any clause. The more you study his compositions, the more significant do they become. They grow upon you" [74]. A more realistic view may be "his artistic language and skills were limited, but within those limitations he created a very personal form of modernism with the power to disturb and astonish" [75].

3.6 Gitanjali (Song Offerings): A Bibliometric Study

Gitanjali in Bengali was published in September 1910 with 157 songs and poems. Out of these 20 songs were previously published in *Sarodutsav* in 1908 and *Gan* in 1909. The remaining 137 poems and songs were written in 90 days in between August 1909 to August 1910 [10th Bhadra, 1316 to 29th Sravan, 1317 (B.S.)] [76]. Rabindranath Tagore himself took the task of the translation of *Gitanjali (Song Offerings)* when he sailed for England on 27th May, 1912. There he handed over the poems to William Rothenstein whom he met earlier in Calcutta in the year 1911. Moved by the poems Rothenstein in turn gave the poems to W.B. Yeats to read. The literary and artistic circle of Yeats decided to publish the poems after Yeats made a selection of them and wished to write an introduction to it. That is how *Gitanjali* was first published by India Society of London on 1st November, 1912. It was written in the half title page of the publication that "seven hundred and fifty copies of this edition have been printed for the INDIA SOCIETY of which two hundred and fifty copies only are for sale" [77]. Regarding this Rabindranath wrote to Kshitimohan Sen "*... I feel he must be happy with my writing and wants others to share that happiness. It is something like our taking delight in the lotus we offer him because he delights in it. I feel he has brought me from East to West...*" [78]. Rabindranath got Nobel Prize for literature on 13th November, 1913 for *Gitanjali (Song Offerings)*. The recommendation within Swedish Academy came from another winner of Nobel Prize Werner von Heidenstam. He wrote that he had read no lyric writing to equal Tagore's in the previous twenty years or more. "They gave me hours of intense enjoyment; it was like drinking the water of a fresh, clear spring... There is nothing in his work that is controversial and offensive, nothing vain, worldly and petty, and if ever a poet may be said to possess the qualities that make him entitled to the Nobel Prize, it is he" [79]. The Daily Mail (November 14, 1913; p. 7, Col. 13) under the heading Nobel Prize for an Indian Poet quotes W.B. Yeats "I know of no man in my life time who has done anything in the English language equal to Mr. Tagore's lyrics" [80].

The next edition of *Gitanjali* was published in the next year (March 1913) by Macmillan and Company, London. The number of poems in Bengali and English *Gitanjali* are not the same. In Bengali there were 157 poems, but in English it was 103. The poems were first published in different *kavyagrantha* (collection of poems) or in different journals. At the end of the Indian edition of India Society or Macmillan there was a statement: "These translations are of poems contained in three books—*Naivedya, Kheya* and *Gitanjali* – to be had at the Indian Publishing House, 22 Cornwallis Street, Calcutta; and of a few poems which have appeared in periodicals" [81]. But this information is not complete as the poems were collected from ten books (Table 3.53).

Even a comparative study of *Gitanjali* published by India Society, London and Macmillan edition besides punctuation, change can be noticed such as in poem number 52 one can observe in India Society Edition:

...no more coyness and sweetness of demeanor... (Page 47)
But the same line in Macmillan edition has changed as:
...no more shy and soft demeanor.

These changes have been made comparing it from manuscript and according to Yeats' suggestions. Even there were some mistakes in the first line of the content of India Society publication, (the correct line is given in the bracket) such as:

Prisoner, tell me, who it was (31);(Prisoner, tell me, who was it);
Let only that little remain of me (34);(Let only that little be left of me);
Hast thou not heard his silent steps? (45);(Have you not heard his silent steps?);
When first they came out, the warriors (85);(When the warriors came out first);
When I give up the helm, then the time has come (99). (When I give up the helm, I know that the time has come);

Even by scientific comparison of original Bengali poems and English translation one can find,

(i) In the English translation number 61 of "*Khoka*" of "*Sisu*" last two stanzas were deleted.
(ii) In the second line of translation number 71"amar" has been translated as "thy" but actually it is "tomar".
(iii) The translated poem number 95 comprises two poems; complete poem number 89 of "*Naivedya*" and last stanza of 90th poem in Bengali,

(iv) Only first part of the poem "*Utsarga*" has been translated in the English translation number 102.

For bibliometric study of *Gitanjali*, bilingual edition of *Gitanjali*, published by Rabindra Bhavana was consulted as the source document as Bengali poems of this edition has been taken from the last publication (1349 B.S.) of *Gitanjali* during Tagore's life time and as it is bilingual edition, so a comparative study is possible [82]. Editions of India Society and Macmillan were also consulted. *Gitabitan* [83] and all the volumes of *Swarabitan* [84] were also consulted to find out how many poems of *Gitanjali* are songs and are included in the volume on *Swarabitan* (Book of notations).

Actually *Gitanjali* submitted for Nobel prize is a collection of 103 poems from ten other 'books of poems' published earlier. Table 3.53 indicates the poems taken from different 'books of poems' and their years of publication.

Table 3.53: Poems of Gitanjali from Different Books of Poems

Sl. No.	*Book*	*Year of Publication*	*No. of Poems*
1	*Chaitali*	1912	1
2.	*Kalpana*	1900	1
3.	*Naivedya*	1901	15
4.	*Smaran*	1903	1
5.	*Sisu*	1903	3
6.	*Utsarga*	1903	1
7.	*Kheya*	1906	11
8.	*Gitanjali*	1910	53
9.	*Achalayatan*	1912	1
10.	*Giti-malya [85](collected from manuscript for Gitanjali, before publication as book in 1914)*	1914	16
	Total		**103**

Poems of *Gitanjali* were written at different places even on the train, though majority of the poems were written at Bolpur-Santiniketan (18 poems out of 52 poems where place of writing is mentioned).

Table 3.54: Place of Writing Poems of *Gitanjali*

Sl. No.	Place	No. of Poems	%
1	Bolpur	11	10.680
2	Santiniketan	7	6.796
3	Silaidaha	13	12.621
4	Calcutta	11	10.680
5	Almorah	2	1.942
6	Hampstead	2	1.942
7	Kaya/Korai	1	0.970
8	Tindhariya	1	0.970
9	"Padma" on Boat	1	0.970
10	Railway/E.I.R.	1	0.970
11	Giridih	1	0.970
12	Jainpur/Gorai	1	0.970
13	Not Mentioned	51	49.515
	Total	**103**	**100.00**

Rabindranath did not mention the place of writing in 51 poems of *Gitanjali*. The above Table (3.54) indicated the name and number of poems of the original Kavyagrantha.

Table 3.55: Poems where Place of Writing not Mentioned

Sl. No.	Kavyagrantha	No. of Poems	Serial No. of Poems in Gitanjali	%
1.	*Gitanjali*	29	2(78), 3(22), 6(87), 9(105), 10(107), 15(31), 17(150), 28(144), 29(142), 30(103), 34(138), 38(88), 39(58), 46(34), 49(56), 58(134), 30(59), 63(3), 65(101), 66(148), 74(26), 77(92), 79(28), 83(10), 84(25), 96(157), 97(68), 132(101), 103(147)	56.863
2	*Naivedya*	15	4(75), 25(98), 35(72), 36(99), 40(86), 43(33), 67(81), 69(26), 73(30), 75(44), 76(1), 79(28), 82(39), 86(18), 95(89&90)	29.411
3	*Kheya*	1	54	1.961
4	*Achalayatan*	1	57	1.961
5	*Sisu*	1	62	1.961
6	*Swaran*	1	87	1.961
7	*Kalpana*	1	88	1.961
8	*Chaitali*	1	92(6)	1.961
9	*Utsarga*	1	102(6)	1.961
	Total	**51**		**100.0**

Note: In the column of serial number of poems there are two numbers: first one indicates the number of *Gitanjali* and the second one within first brackets indicates the poem number in original Kavyagrantha ('books of poems').

From Table 3.55 it is clear that most of the poems where place of writing is not mentioned are from original Bengali version of *Gitanjali* which contained 157 poems, out of which 53 poems were selected for English version of *Gitanjali* submitted for Nobel Prize. In case of poem number 95 of *Gitanjali* (English version) two poems of original kavyagrantha *Naivedya* (number 89 and 90) were combined together.

But in all the poems of *Gitanjali* dates of 103 poems are available as indicated in Table 3.56.

Table 3.56: Dates of Writing of Poems of *Gitanjali*

Sl. No.	*Year*	*Year, Date*	*No. of Poems*
1.	1895	2nd April	1
2.	1901	1901(1)	1
3.	1902	1902(15)	15
4.	1903	1903(1)	1
5.	1904	1904 (3), July/Aug, 23rd Aug	5
6.	1906-07	11th Aug, 14th Aug, 13th Sept, 15th Jan, 21st March, 24th March, 25th March.	7
7.	1907	17th June, 25th June	2
8.	1908	28th June	1
9.	1909	1909(1)	1
10.	1910-11	7th April, June/July (3), July/Aug, 28th Aug, 30th Aug.(2), 31st Aug, 3rd Sept.(3), 5th Sept, 14th Sept, 18th Oct, 28th Dec. 10th April, 11th April	18
11.	1911	26th April, 18th May, 1st June, 2nd June, 11th June, 13th June, 14th June, 18th June (2), 20th June, 28th June (2), 30th June, 4th July, 10th July, 11th July, 12th July, 13th July, 16th July (2), 18th July, 19th July, 26th July, 28th July, 1st Aug, 7th Aug, 8th Aug (2), 9th Aug, 10th Aug, 11th Aug (2), 15th Aug.	33
12.	1912	Aug/Sept, 23rd March, 1st April (2), 2nd April, 8th April, 9th April, 10th April (2), 11th April, 13th April, 14th April	12
13.	1913	20th April, 21st April (2), 23rd April, 24th June, 26th June	6
	Total		**103**

Note: The number within brackets indicate number of poems written in that particular year, month.

From the above table it is clear that most of the poems (69 out of 103) were written in the years 1910-13 just before the submission of *Gitanjali* to Nobel Committee, on the other hand some poems were written long before even in the year of 1895.

Length of the poems of *Gitanjali* would help to have an idea about total number of lines and its percentage thereof.

Table 3.57: Length of Poems of *Gitanjali*

Sl. No.	*No. of Lines*	*Poem Nos. in Gitanjali*	*No. of Poems*	*Total Lines*	*%*
1.	72	48	1	72	3.270
2.	60	51, 52	2	120	5.450
3.	50	50, 61	2	100	4.541
4.	48	41	1	48	2.180
5.	46	102	1	46	2.089
6.	40	47, 60, 66	3	120	5.450
7.	36	54, 64, 78	3	108	4.905
8.	33	80	1	33	1.499
9.	32	71	1	32	1.453
10.	30	27	1	30	1.362
11.	28	31, 88, 91	3	84	3.815
12.	27	79	1	27	1.226
13.	25	55	1	25	1.135
14.	24	11, 12	2	48	2.180
15.	22	13, 103	2	44	1.998
16.	21	44, 70	2	42	1.907
17.	20	6, 8, 9, 14, 17, 18, 47, 49, 62, 62, 74, 85, 86, 89, 96	15	300	13.624
18.	19	95	1	19	0.863
19.	18	10, 56, 59	3	54	2.452
20.	16	1, 2, 5, 7, 15, 19, 20, 21, 22, 24, 26, 28, 30, 32, 33, 38, 39, 42, 46, 53, 65, 76, 77, 83, 84, 90, 94, 97, 99, 100	30	480	21.798
21.	15	25, 72, 73, 101	4	60	2.725
22.	14	4, 16, 23, 34, 35, 36, 40, 43, 58, 67, 68, 69, 75, 81, 82, 87, 92	17	238	10.808
23	12	3, 29, 37, 57, 93, 98	6	72	3.270
	Total		**103**	**2202**	**100.00**

From Table 3.57 it is clear that 30 poems (21.798%) are of 16 lines and 17 poems (10.808%) are of 15 lines.

Use of double or triple words in sentences as well as repetition of single word in lines indicates the literary stress on that word that is indicated in Tables 3.58 and 3.59 respectively. For example it can be observed from Table 3.58 that in poem number 10 of *Gitanjali* the word *Sobar* (for all) has been used four times to indicate 'the poorest, and lowliest, and lost' or in poem number 91 the word *Moron* (death) has been used four times as the poet prayed for the *'last fulfilment of life, death, my death, come and whisper to me'*[86].

Table 3.58: Double/Triple Words Used in a Sentence or Part of a Sentence in *Gitanjali*

Sl. No.	*Poem No.*	*Sentences*	*Poem Lines*	*Double/Triple Words*	*Frequency*
1.	2	3	10	*Bhalolage* (to appear good to one)	1
2.	3	1, 4	2, 9	*Shuni* (to listen), *Kayte* (to speak)	2
3.	6	4, 7	9, 19	*Chhinnokoro* (to split)	2
4.	10	1, 2, 3, 4	3, 9, 12, 17	*Sobar* (for all)	4
5.	11	6	17	*Mukti* (to be free from earthly bondage)	2
6.	16	2	2	*Dhonyoholo* (to be gratified)	1
7.	19	3	9	*Hobe* (to be done)	1
8.	27	1, 2, 12, 13	1, 2, 25, 26	*Alo Jwalo* (to light up)	4
9.	38	1, 2	1, 7	*Chai* (desire)	2
10.	42	1	2, 4	*Bhese* (float), *Kon deshe* (which country)	2
11.	45	1	1	*Ashe (come)*	1
12.	91	1, 3, 6, 9	2, 7, 17, 27	*Moron* (death)	4
13.	103	1,2	1, 2, 7, 8, 13, 14, 19, 20	*Ekti namaskare* (in one namaskar)	8

Table 3.59: Repetition of Single Word in a Sentence in *Gitanjali*

Sl. No.	Poem No.	Line(s) in Poems	Repeated Words	Frequency
1	2	3	*Chhalchhal* (tearfulness)	1
2	13	13	*Khhone Khhone* (frequently)	1
3	14	7, 15	*Dine Dine* (day by day), *Jani Jani* (to know)	2
4	16	9	*Gane Gane* (in songs)	1
5	19	9	*Hobe Hobe* (to be done)	1
6	23	6	*Bare Bar* (time and again)	1
7	24	5	*Dhire Dhire* (slowly)	1
8	27	14, 17, 18	*Jhori* (to fall), *Mori* (to die)	3
9	28	10	*Rashi Rashi* (heaps of)	1
10	30	3	*Sathe Sathe* (with)	1
11	45	3	*Juge Juge* (era after era), *Pole Pole* (in moments)	2
12	46	11, 12	*Theke Theke* (at times), *Khnepe Khnepe* (trembling)	2
13	66	15, 22	*Chupe Chupe* (silently), *Deshe Deshe* (at home and abroad)	2
14	70	5, 8	Dike *Dike* (everywhere), *Dheyea Dheyea* (to chase)	2
15	84	2, 5, 9	*Bhubane Bhubane* (at all places), *Taray Taray* (from star to star), *Ghore Ghore* (at every home)	3
16	100	3	*Ghate Ghate* (from ghat to ghat)	1
17	101	5	*Ghore Ghore*, *Dware Dware* (from door to door)	2
			Giti-malya	
1	1	4, 7	*Nabo Nabo* (newly), *Phire Phire* (again and again)	2
2	5	14	*Chokhe Chokhe* (constant watch)	1
3	12	5, 22	*Benke Benke* (curve), *Aacho Aacho* (are)	2
4	20	5	*Majhe Majhe* (from time to time)	1
5	21	9	*Cholcholie* (noise of running water)	1
6	44	15, 16, 17	*Khhone Khhone*, *Mone Mone* (in mind), *Rohi Rohi* (at intervals)	3
7	53	2, 4, 14	*Taray Taray*, *Borne Borne* (word by word)	3
8	55	21	*Pae Pae* (at every step)	1
9	68	9	*Nobo Nobo*, *Borone* (respectful reception)	2
10	72	13, 15	*Gopone Gopone* (secretly), *Niti Niti* (always)	2
11	89	2, 4	*Khhone Khhone*, *Gane Gane*	2
12	98	7	*Thore Thore* (in stratum)	1

(Contd.)

Table 3.59: *(Contd.)*

			Naivedya	
1	25	1, 3	*Majhe Majhe, Til Til* (slowly)	2
2	35	7	*Deshe Deshe, Dishe Dishe* (everywhere)	2
3	40	8, 10	*Pole Pole* (at every moment), *Songharo Songharo* (destroy)	2
4	43	12	*Theke Theke*	1
5	67	67	*Nai Nai* (non-existence)	1
6	69	1, 5, 6, 7, 11	*Shiray Shiray* (in veins), *Chupe Chupe*, *Lakkho Lakkho* (in lakhs), *Trine Trine* (in grasses), *Boroshe Boroshe* (year after year), *Ange Ange* (in limbs)	6
7	81	1, 5	*Majhe Majhe*, *Antore Antore* (in heart)	2
8	82	11	*Dite Dite* (to give)	1
			Kheya	
1	41	25	*Cheye Cheye* (to see)	1
2	48	4, 19	*Bhare Bhare* (large quantity), *Jhure Jhure* (continuous travelling)	2
3	50	2, 3, 19, 20	*Pothe Pothe* (in roads), *Dware Dware*, *Mutha Mutha* (handful), *Bhare Bhare*	4
4	51	15, 25, 28	*Ghore Ghore*, *Khhone Khhone*, *Jhonjhoni* (expressing of striking a thin metal)	3
5	78	8	*Dole Dole* (in flocks)	1
6	80	14, 17	*Nobo Nobo*, *Borne Borne*	2
			Sisu	
1	61	32, 40	*Ghire Ghire* (to surround)	2
2	62	8	*Patay Patay* (in leafs)	1
			Achalayatan	
1	57	9, 10	*Majhe Majhe*, *Patay Patay*	2
			Kalpana	
1	88	2, 4	*Theke Theke*, *Phire Phire*	2
			Chaitali	
1	92	6	*Ghare Ghare*	1
			Utsarga	
1	102	9, 25, 26, 35	*Ki Jani, Ki Jani* (Unknown), *Khhone Khhone*	4

Rabindranath used homonyms in a sentence even in a line with different literary connotations in his poems and that is true in case of *Gitanjali* also as indicated in Tables 3.60 and 3. 61 respectively.

Table 3.60: Use of Homonyms in a Sentence in *Gitanjali*

Sl. No.	*Poem No.*	*Line(s) in Poems*	*Statistics (No. of Words Occurrence)*
1	11	13	1
2	13	16	1
3	16	10	1
4	17	16	1
5	28	1	1
6	29	3	1
7	34	5	1
8	38	6	1
9	45	3	1
10	46	5	1
11	58	6	1
20	103	18	1
		Naivedya	
12	63	3, 11, 7	5 (one word thrice in line.2)
13	66	23	1
14	74	12	1
15	77	12	1
16	84	12	1
17	90	8, 12	2
18	91	6	1
19	101	12	1
1	4	2	1
2	25	14	1
3	35	3	1
4	36	5	1
5	43	9	1
6	69	2, 9, 10	3
7	82	2	1
8	95	9	1
		Kheya	
1	31	21	1
2	41	9, 19	2
3	48	11	1
4	78	27	1
		Giti-malya	
1	44	3, 7	2
2	71	11, 14, 19, 27, 31	5
3	72	7	1
4	89	6, 15	2

(Contd.)

Table 3.60: *(Contd.)*

		Sisu	
1	61	4, 10	2
		Chaitali	
1	92	6	1

Table 3.61: Use of Homonyms in a line in *Gitanjali*

Sl. No.	*Poem No.*	*Line(s) in Poems*	*Statistics (No. of Occurrences)*
1	37	4	1
2	39	4	1
3	45	6	1
4	83	5	1
		Naivedya	
1	73	2	1
2	95	1	1
		Kheya	
1	31	7	1

Actually many poems of Rabindranath are songs, and poems of *Gitanjali* are no exception. Table 3.62 justifies this statement as 42 out of 103 poems are songs of which notations are scattered in different volumes of *Swarabitan* (book of notations) published by Visva-Bharati.

Table 3.62: *Gitanjali* Songs

Sl. No.	*Poem No.*	*Notation First Published by Visva-Bharati*	*Volume in Swarabitan*
1	1	Gitalekha vol.1/1324-27 (B.S.)	39
2	3	Gitanjali/1927	38
3	5	Gitalipi vol.6/1910-18	39
4	10	Gitanjali/1927	38
5	13	Gitalipi vol. 2/1910-18	38
6	14	Brahmasangit vol.5/1311-18 (B.S.)	24
7	15	Gitalipi vol.2/1910-18	38
8	16	Gitalipi vol.5/1910-18	37
9	18	Gitalipi vol.3/1910-18	37
10	21	Gitalekha vol. 1/1324-27 (B.S.)	39
11	22	Gitalipi vol. 3/1910-18	11
12	23	Gitalipi vol. 3/1910-18	11
13	26	Gitalipi vol. 5/1910-18	38
14	27	Gitalipi vol. 6/1910-18	11

(Contd.)

Table 3.62: *(Contd.)*

Sl. No.	*Poem No.*	*Notation First Published by Visva-Bharati*	*Volume in Swarabitan*
15	28	Gitalipi vol. 5/1910-18	37
16	39	Gitalipi vol. 5/1910-18	38
17	44	Gitalekha vol. 3/1324-27 (B.S.)	41
18	45	Gitalipi vol. 3/1910-18	38
19	46	Gitalipi vol. 1/1910-18	37
20	49	Gitalipi vol. 5/1910-18	37
21	53	Gitanjali/1927	42
22	55	Gitalekha/1324-27 (B.S.)	39
23	56	Gitalipi vol. 4/1910-18	37
24	57	Gitanjali/1927	52
25	59	Gitalipi vol. 3/1910-18	38
26	63	Brahmasangit vol. 6/1311-18 (B.S.)	26
27	65	Gitalipi vol. 4/1910-18	38
28	70	Gitalipi vol. 2/1910-18	38
29	72	Gitalekha vol. 2/1324-27 (B.S.)	40
30	74	Gitalipi vol. 3/1910-18	38
31	76	Brahmasangit vol. 4/1311-18 (B.S.)	24
32	77	Gitalipi vol. 5/1910-18	37
33	79	Gitalipi vol. 1/1910-18	38
34	83	Gitanjali/1917	50
35	84	Gitalekha vol. 2/1324-27 (B.S.)	37
36	89	Gitalekha vol. 1/1324-27 (B.S.)	39
37	93	Gitalipi vol. 6/11910-18	40
38	94	Gitanjali/1917	41
39	97	Gitalipi vol. 3/1910-18	37
40	98	Gitalekha vol. 1/1324-27 (B.S.)	39
41	100	Gitalipi vol. 1/1910-18	38
42	103	Gitanjali/1917	38

Zipf's law of frequency of different words is justified in *Gitanjali*. Occurrence of words and their corresponding rank is computed in Table 3.63. The table is computed on the basis of statistics of how many times a particular word used in *Gitanjali* (for example a word used once, twice or two hundred five times), how many words used for how many (f) times (for example a word used once only in 1740 occasions, words used twice in 467 occasions or a single word used in 205 occasions etc.), preparing of rank (r) of words according to descending order of f and corresponding $\log_{10}$ value of f and r. It is observed from the statistics of words prepared for this study that in Gitanjali 3091 different words used in different frequencies. The descending order of first five words in respect of highest number of times used (rank) are: *Amar* (mine), *Tomar* (your), *Na* (no), *Je* (that), *Tumi* (you).

Table 3.63: Rank-frequency of Different Words of *Gitanjali*

Statistics(f) (How many times a word used)	*How Many Words Used f times*	*Rank (r) according to descending order of f*	*Log 10 f*	*Log 10 f*
1	1740	1352-3091	0	3.1310-3.4901
2	467	885-1351	0.3010	2.9469-3.1306
3	238	647-884	0.4771	2.8109-2.9464
4	139	508-646	0.6021	2.7059-2.8102
5	100	408-507	0.6990	2.6107-2.7050
6	65	343-407	0.7781	2.5353-2.6096
7	51	292-342	0.8451	2.4654-2.5340
8	39	253-291	0.9031	2.4031-2.4639
9	29	224-252	0.9542	2.3502-2.4014
10	26	198-223	1.0000	2.2967-2.3483
11	26	172-197	1.0414	2.2355-2.2945
12	15	157-171	1.0792	2.1959-2.2330
13	9	148-156	1.1139	2.1703-2.1931
14	13	135-147	1.1461	2.1303-2.1673
15	17	118-134	1.1761	2.0719-2.1271
16	8	110-117	1.2041	2.0414-2.0682
17	14	96-109	1.2304	1.9823-2.0374
18	7	89-95	1.2553	1.9494-1.9778
19	9	80-88	1.2787	1.9031-1.9445
20	4	76-79	1.3010	1.8808-1.8976
21	1	75	1.3222	1.8751
22	5	70-74	1.3424	1.8451-1.8692
23	4	66-69	1.3616	1.8195-1.8388
24	4	62-65	1.3802	1.7924-1.8129
25	3	59-61	1.3979	1.7708-1.7853
26	1	58	1.4150	1.7634
27	4	54-57	1.4314	1.7324-1.7559
29	2	52-53	1.4624	1.7160-1.7243
30	3	49-51	1.4771	1.6902-1.7076
31	1	48	1.4914	1.6812
32	1	47	1.5051	1.6701
33	2	45-46	1.5185	1.6532-1.6627
34	2	43-44	1.5315	1.6335-1.6434
35	2	41-42	1.5441	1.6128-1.6232
36	4	37-40	1.5563	1.5682-1.6021
37	5	32-36	1.5682	1.5051-1.5563
38	1	31	1.5798	1.4914
39	1	30	1.5911	1.4771
40	2	28-29	1.6021	1.4472-1.4624

(Contd.)

Table 3.63: *(Contd.)*

Statistics(f) (How many times a word used)	*How Many Words Used f times*	*Rank (r) according to descending order of f*	*Log 10 f*	*Log 10 f*
41	1	27	1.6128	1.4314
43	1	26	1.6335	1.4150
44	1	25	1.6435	1.3979
46	1	24	1.6628	1.3802
48	1	23	1.6812	1.3617
49	2	21-22	1.6902	1.3222-1.3424
50	3	18-20	1.6990	1.2553-1.3010
53	1	17	1.7243	1.2304
56	2	15-16	1.7482	1.1761-1.2041
57	1	14	1.7559	1.1461
62	1	13	1.7924	1.1139
64	1	12	1.8062	1.0792
72	1	11	1.8573	1.0414
78	1	10	1.8921	1.0000
79	1	9	1.8976	0.9542
84	1	8	1.9243	0.9031
86	1	7	1.9345	0.8451
89	1	6	1.9494	0.7781
91	1	5	1.9590	0.6990
129	1	4	2.1106	0.6021
158	1	3	2.1987	0.4771
199	1	2	2.2299	0.3010
205	1	1	2.3118	0

The above rank-frequency of different words of *Gitanjali* can graphically be plotted as under which justifies Zipf's law.

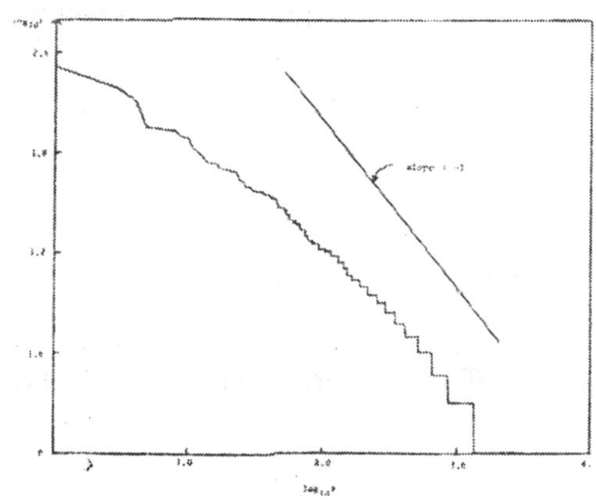

3.7 Conclusion

From the above analysis of *Gitanjali* it may be concluded that:

(i) The first poem of *Gitanjali* was written in 1895 and the last poem was written in 1913. The maximum number of poems (33) was written in 1911. Thus, it appears that Rabindranath never wrote the poems of *Gitanjali* consciously for Nobel Prize purpose.
(ii) From the available dates it is found that Rabindranath wrote 17.476 per cent poems at Bolpur-Santiniketan—where Tagore established his experimental school.
(iii) Most of the poems (21.798%) are of 16 lines and 52.27 per cent poems are of 14 to 20 lines.
(iv) Rabindranath used double or triple words on 33 occasions, repetition of single words 90 times and homonyms on 60 occasions.
(v) About 41 per cent poems of *Gitanjali* are songs scattered in different volumes of *Swarabitan*.
(vi) In all 3091 different words used in *Gitanjali* in different frequencies led to 11,521 words algother [87]. Thus, the number of unique words is more than one-third of the total number of words (11521/3091 = 3.73), whereas Zipf considers number of unique words about one-tenth of the full text. It can be observed from Table 5.62 that:
   (a) Rank frequency increases gradually from rank 1 to rank 1740. Most conspicuous difference is between rank 467 and rank 1740. Such a contrast is quite predictable because when the rank increases the frequency remains constant at 1. Zipf also finds similar results for Ulysses.
   (b) From the graph it is clear that the rank-frequency is approximately constant in the middle ranks. These tallies with Zipf's findings that show that the approximation is much better for the middle rank.
   (c) From the Table it is also clear that as the rank increases, the frequency decreases and the change of words sharing the same frequency increases.

Thus, from the table and the associated graph it justifies that the frequencies of different words used in *Gitanjali* follow the Zipf's law of word frequencies. The Zipf's law states that the frequency of occurrence of the r—the root frequent word (r= 1, 2, 3...) tends to be inversely proportional to r. It appears from the graph that the rank-frequency relation on the log-log scale follows Zipf's law though it is flatter to some extent.

It can be observed from actual words that first two words (rank 1 and rank 2) are pronouns, *Amar* (f 205) and *Tomar* (f 199) [88]. The poet offers his prayer to God, so the word *Amar* (my) and *Tomar* (your) appears frequently than other words in the whole text. As Rabindranath wrote in a letter to Indira Devi Chaudhurani ".... *I was not consciously writing poetry when writing the songs of Gitanjali. They were an expression of my feelings; they were my humble prayers, my sincere sadhana and also a reflection of my joys and sorrows*"[89]. Reflections of such '*feeling*' can be found in many songs of *Gitanjali*. One such reflection is here as under:

> "*Where the mind is without fear and the head is held high;*
> *Where knowledge is free;*
> *Where the world has not been broken up into fragments by narrow domestic walls;*
> *Where words come out from the depth of truth;*
> *Where tireless striving stretches the arms towards perfection;*
> *Where the clear stream of reason has not lost its way into the dreary desert sand of dead habit;*
> *Where the mind is led forward by thee into ever-widening thought and action;*
> *Into that heaven of freedom, my father, let my country awake*" [90].

NOTES AND REFERENCES

1. TAGORE (Rabindranath). *Santiniketan brahmacaryasram*. 1358 (B.S.). Visva-Bharati; Santiniketan; p. 26.
2. TAGORE (Rabindranath). *Santiniketan adiparba*. 1349 (B.S.). Visva-Bharati; Santiniketan; p. 19.
3. TAGORE (Rabindranath). *My school Santiniketan*: 1901-51.1951. Visva-Bharati Granthan Vibhaga; Calcutta; pp. 6-7.
4. TAGORE (Rabindranath). *Vichtra prabandha*. 1388 (B.S.). Visva-Bharati Granthan Vibhaga; Calcutta; p. 35.
5. Rabindranath as the Chairman of Reception Committee of All India Libraries Association prepared this speech. Due to his illness this was

read out by Mr. Hirendranath Dutta. Later it was published in *The Indian Library Journal,* Vol. 2, No. 2-4. 1929.

6. *Ibid.*
7. *Ibid.*
8. TAGORE (Rabindranath). *Kshanika.* 1359 (B.S.). Visva-Bharati Granthan Vibhaga; Calcutta; p. 23.
9. TAGORE (Rabindranath). Library and its use. *The Indian Library Journal.* 2, 3; 1929; 21-28.
10. *Ibid.*
11. *Ibid.*
12. TAGORE (Rabindranath). Sikshar bikiran: address. In *Siksha.* 1405 (B.S.). Visva-Bharati Granthan Vibhaga; Calcutta; p. 214.
13. TAGORE (Rabindranath). *Sahitya.* 1398 (B.S.). Visva-Bharati Granthan Vibhaga; Calcutta; p. 14.
14. TAGORE (Rabindranath). *Japane-Parasha.* 1343 (B.S.). Visva-Bharati Granthan Vibhaga; Calcutta; p. 146.
15. TAGORE (Rabindranath). *Siksha.* 1342 (B.S.). Visva-Bharati; Santiniketan; p. 87.
16. BISI (Pramathanath). *Rabindranath O Santiniketan.* 1402 (B.S.). Visva-Bharati Granthan Vibhaga; Calcutta; p. 129.
17. TAGORE (Rabindranath). *Punascha.* 1372 (B.S.). Visva-Bharati Granthan Vibhaga; Calcutta; pp. 13-64.
18. TAGORE (Rabindranath). *Naukadubi.* 1951. Visva-Bharati Granthan Vibhaga; Calcutta; p. 222.
19. TAGORE (Rabindranath). *Janmadine.* 1957. Visva-Bharati Granthan Vibhaga; Calcutta; p. 20.
20. TAGORE (Rabindranath). 1351. *Vithika.* 1351 (B.S.). Visva-Bharati Granthan Vibhaga; Calcutta; p. 21.
21. TAGORE (Rabindranath) *Chhinapatravali.* 1367 (B.S.). Visva-Bharati Granthan Vibhaga; Calcutta; pp. 251-252.
22. TAGORE (Rabindranath). *Jivansmriti.* 1405 (B.S.). Visva-Bharati Granthan Vibhaga; Calcutta; p. 13.
23. TAGORE (Rabindranath). *Vithika.* 1351 (B.S.). Visva-Bharati Granthan Vibhaga; Calcutta; pp. 21-23.
24. TAGORE (Rabindranath). *Chithipatra.* Vol. 5. 1352. Visva-Bharati Granthan Vibhaga; Calcutta; p. 139.
25. TAGORE (Rabindranath). *Rabindra rachanavali.* Vol. 4. 1385 (B.S.). Visva-Bharati Granthan Vibhaga; Calcutta; p. 559.
26. TAGORE (Rabindranath). *Jivansmriti.* 1405 (B.S.). Visva-Bharati Granthan Vibhaga; Calcutta; pp. 70-71.
27. TAGORE (Rabindranath). *Siksha.* 1342 (B.S.). Visva-Bharati; Santiniketan; pp. 70-71.
28. *Ibid.*, pp. 20-25.
29. TAGORE (Rabindranath). *Rabindra rachnavali.* Vol. 8. 1385 (B.S.). Visva-Bharati Granthan Vibhaga; Calcutta; p. 471.

30. TAGORE (Rabindranath). *Katha O Kahini*. 1401 (B.S.). Visva-Bharati Granthan Vibhaga; Calcutta; 169 p.
31. TAGORE (Rabindranath). *Kshanika*. 1359 (B.S.). Visva-Bharati Granthan Vibhaga; Calcutta; p. 25.
32. TAGORE (Rabindranath). *Sisu*. 1958. Visva-Bharati Granthan Vibhaga; Calcutta; p. 86.
33. TAGORE (Rabindranath). *Chokher Bali*. 1395 (B.S.). Visva-Bharati Granthan Vibhaga; Calcutta; 242 p.
34. TAGORE (Rabindranath). *Sesher kavita*. 1351 (B.S). Visva-Bharati Granthan Vibhaga; Calcutta; pp. 44, 75, 40.
35. TAGORE (Rabindranath). *Chhinapatravali*. 1367 (B.S.). Visva-Bharati Granthan Vibhaga; Calcutta; pp. 186-87.
36. TAGORE (Rabindranath). *Kshanika*. 1306 (B.S.). Visva-Bharati Granthan Vibhaga; Calcutta; p. 5.
37. TAGORE (Rabindranath). *Santiniketan Brahmacharyasram*. 1338 (B.S.). Visva-Bharati; Santiniketan; pp. 40-41.
38. TAGORE (Rabindranath). *Katha sahitya*. 1367 (B.S.). Visva-Bharati Granthan Vibhaga; Calcutta; p. 267.
39. DEVARAJAN (G). *Research in library and information science*. 2002. Ess Ess Publication; New Delhi; pp. 6-7.
40. TAGORE (Rabindranath). *Rabindra rachnavali*. 1962. Visva-Bharati Granthan Vibhaga.
41. FAIRTHORNE (RA). Empirical hyperbolic distribution (Bradford Ziff-Model bort) for bibliometric description and production. *Journal of Documentation*. 25, 1969; p. 326.
42. CHUNKAPURA (Jose). *The God of Rabindranath Tagore*. 2002. Visva-Bharati Granthan Vibhaga; Calcutta; p. 87.
43. TAGORE (Rabindranath). *Letters from Russia*. 1367 (B.S.). Visva-Bharati Granthan Vibhaga; Calcutta; pp. 9-11.
44. Tagore's comment on Granthagar to Kumar Munindra Debray. 1344 (B.S.). Later Kumar handed over the letter to Tagore. Kept in Rabindra Bhavana.
45. TAGORE (Rabindranath). *Siksha*. 1342 (B.S.) Visva-Bharati; Santiniketan; p. 270.
46. TAGORE (Rabindranath). *Sikshar svangikaran*. In Siksha. Vol. 1. 1351 (B.S.). Visva-Bharati; Santiniketan; p. 315.
47. *Viava-Bharati Bulletin no. 11*. 1928. Visva-Bharati; Santiniketan; p. 1.
48. *Visva-Bharati Annual Report 1927*.
49. CHAKRABORTY (Satyadas). *Sriniketaner gorar katha*. 1985. Sahitya Samaj; Sriniketan; pp. 51-52.
50. LAL (Prem Chand). *Reconstruction and education in rural India*. 1952. George Allen & Unwin; London; pp. 82-83.
51. TAGORE (Rabindranath). *Siksha*. 1973. Visva-Bharati Granthan Vibhaga; Calcutta; p. 226.
52. *Annual Report. 2005-06*. 2006. Rural extension centre. Sriniketan.

53. O'CONNELL (Kathleen M). *Rabindranath Tagore: the poet as educator*. 2002. Visva-Bharati; Santiniketan; p. 15.
54. TAGORE (Rabindranath). *Rabindra rachanavali*. Vol. 1961. Visva-Bharati Granthan Vibhaga; Calcutta; p. 582.
55. TAGORE (Rabindranath). Schoolmaster. *Modern Review*. 36, 3; p. 313.
56. TAGORE (Rabindranath). *Siksha*. 1972. Visva-Bharati Granthan Vibhaga; Santiniketan; p. 20.
57. TAGORE (Rabindranath). *Personality*. 1959. Macmillan; London; p. 116.
58. BANDYOPADHYAY (Somendranath). *Rabindra-chitrakala: Rabindrasahitytyer patabhumika*. 1982. Dey's Publishing; Calcutta; p. 18.
59. It is difficult to access the actual number of Rabindranath's paintings and drawings as many may be in the personal collection in India and abroad. There are 1573 paintings and drawings in Rabindra-Bhavana, Visva-Bharati, about 100 at National Gallery of Modern Art, New Delhi, 45 at Rabindra Bharati Museum, Calcutta, 19 at Dartinghall Trust, 32 are held by the Academy of Fine Arts. A thorough bibliometric study requires immense time-consuming research. Here a study on the collection of 1573 paintings and drawings held by Visva-Bharati has been made.
60. TAGORE (Rabindranath). *On the edges of times*. 1958. Orient Longman; Calcutta.
61. Letter of Rabindranath to William Rothenstein. March 1930. Kept in Rabindra Bhavana.
62. TAGORE (Rabindranath). My pictures. In NEOGY (Pritwish). Ed. *Rabindranath Tagore on art and aesthetics*. 1961. Orient Longman; New Delhi; pp. 97-98.
63. LAGO (Mary M). *Letters of William Rothenstein and Rabindranath Tagore 1911-1941*. 1978. Harvard University Press; Harvard.
64. MITTER (Parha). *The triumph of modernism: Indian artists and the avant-garde: 1922-1947*. 2007. Oxford University Press; New Delhi; p. 69.
65. TAGORE (Rabindranath). My pictures. In NEOGY (Pritwish). Ed. *Rabindranath Tagore on art and aesthetics*. 1961. Orient Longman; New Delhi; p. 104.
66. *Printed over Visva-Bharati News: Birthday No. Cover*: Vol. 2, No. 11. May 1934.
67. MUILLWARD (RM). Rabindranath Tagore in Paris. *Modern Review*. 11; 1930; 545.
68. BANDYOPADHYAY (Somendranath). *Rabindra-chitrakala: Rabindrasahityer patabhumika*. 1982. Dey's Publishing; Calcutta; p. 140.
69. TAGORE (Abanindranath). Exhibitions of paintings and drawings of Rabindranath Tagore. In MAJUMDAR (Kamal). Ed. *Exhibition catalogue*. 1947.
70. RAFIQUE (Ahmad). *Rabindranather chitrasilpa*. 1996. National Academy of Fine and Performing Arts; Dhaka; p. 140.
71. MUKHOPADHAYA (Prabhatkumar). *Rabindrajibani Rabindrasahitya-prabashak*. Vol. 3. 1961. Visva-Bharati Granthan Vibhaga; Calcutta; p. 247.

72. BOSE (Nandalal). The paintings of Rabindranath. *Visva-Bharati Quarterly.* 14, 1; 1936; 31.
73. BAGCHI (Radhacharan). Rabindranath Tagore as a painter. In SENGUPTA (Santosh Chandra). Ed. *Homage from Visva-Bharati.* 1962. Visva-Bharati Granthan Vibhaga; Calcutta; p. 200.
74. SINGH (Nihar). Tagore's conversion with Yeats in Dublin. *Calcutta Municipal Gazette.* 13th Sept. 1941.
75. CHAUDHURI (Amit). Two giant brothers. *London Review of Books.* 28, 8; 2006; 27-30.
76. MUKHOPADHYAY (Prabhatkumar). *Rabindrajibani Rabindrasahitya-prabashak.* Vol. 2. 1994. Visva-Bharati Granthan Vibhaga; Calcutta; pp. 227-228.
77. TAGORE (Rabindranath). *Gitanjali: song offerings.* 1912. The India Society; London; 80p.
78. TAGORE (Rabindranath). Letter to Kshitimohan Sen, London, 20 June. Kept in Rabindra Bhavana.
79. ROBINSON (Andrew). *The art of Rabindranath Tagore.* 1989. Rupa & Co.; Calcutta. p. 33.
80. KUNDU (Kalian). *Rabindranath and the British Press (1912-1941).* 1990.The Tagore Research Centre; London; p. 31.
81. TAGORE (Rabindranath). *Gitanjali: songs offerings.* 1913. Macmillan Publishing Company; London; 81p.
82. TAGORE (Rabindranath). *Gitanjali: songs offerings.* 1999. Rabindra-Bhavana; Santiniketan; 274p.
83. TAGORE (Rabindranath). *Gitabitan.* 1380 (B.S.). Visva-Bharati Granthan Vibhaga; Calcutta; 1034p.
84. TAGORE (Rabindranath). *Swarabitan.* 60 Vols. 1982. Visva-Bharati Granthan Vibhaga; Calcutta.
85. *Gitimalya* published in the year 1914 after publication of English *Gitanjali,* but poems were written before and/included in *Gitanjali* from manuscript.
86. TAGORE (Rabindranath). *Gitanjali: songs offerings.* 1999. Rabindra-Bhavana; Santiniketan; p. 237.
87. MALLICK (BP), NARA (T) and BHATTACHARAYA (N). *Gitanjali: linguistic statistical analysis.* 1994. Indian Statistical Institute; Calcutta; pp. 3-97.
88. *Ibid.,* p. 123.
89. TAGORE (Rabindranath). *Chithipatra.* Vol. 5. 1400 (B.S.). Visva-Bharati Granthan Vibhaga. Calcutta; p. 33.
90. TAGORE (Rabindranath). *Gitanjali: songs offerings.* 1999. Rabindra-Bhavana; Santiniketan; p. 87.

4

A Comparative Study of Publications of Tagore's Literature Five Years before and After the Expiry of Copyright (1997-2006)

4.1 Introduction

The first book of Rabindranath *Kavi-Kahini* was published in the year 1878 by his friend Prabodh Chandra Ghosh. Regarding this publication Rabindranath wrote "*When I was in Ahmedabad with my brother, my friend astonished me by sending this book*"[1]. The second one *Banaphul* was published in the year 1880 by the poet's elder brother Somendranath. Sailesh Chandra Majumdar of Majumdar Library was the first professional publisher who first published *Kavyagrantha* (collected works) of Rabindranath in the year 1903-04. Before that Rabindranath had to publish his works using his own fund with the exception of *Kadi o Komal* (published in 1886 by People's Library), *Chithipatra* (published in 1887 by Saratkumar Lahiri and Co.), and *Panchabhut* (published in 1897 by Sur Company). Books published from Adi Brahmasamaj Jantra were exclusively funded from his own fund given by his father Debendranath Tagore. Sometimes Rabindranath had to face serious scarcity of funds for publication as well as to meet the expenses of Santiniketan Ashrama. Tagoreana was even sold in half price from bookshops like Sri Chaitanya Pustakalaya, 9 Cornwallis Street, Kolkata in the year 1304 (B.S.) through press advertisement. Even Rabindranath expressed his willingness to give up copyright of his collected works and publications up to Kshanika (1900) for rupees six thousand only to any person in a letter addressed to Priyanath Sen in 1307 (B.S.)[2].

But the situation changed with the establishment of Visva-Bharati Granthan Vibhaga (VBGV), the Publishing Department of the University, as an integral part of Visva-Bharati. It was established by Rabindranath in the year 1923 and published dance drama *Basanta* in the same year. But regular publication started from the year 1925 with the publication of *Puravi.* Before that the publication right of Tagoreana was given to Chintamani Ghosh, owner of Indian Press/ Indian Publishing House of Allahabad. In a letter dated 18th September, 1922 Rabindranath wrote "*I have given the right of all my Bengali books to Visva-Bharati in a deed and relieved now*" [3]. According to Tagore's biographer Prabhatkumar "Chintamoni Kar took the responsibility of publishing the poet's publication with the negotiation of Ramananda Chattopadhaya in 1908. The stock value of 100 books published up to 1923 was Rs. 78,000. Chintamanibabu gave his entire stock to Visva-Bharati at the cost of Rs. 26,000 only..." [4].

4.2 Visva-Bharati Granthan Vibhaga: Activities at the Beginning

VBGV started its functioning in the house named 'Mahatashram' at Cornwallis Street near Vidyasagar College in Calcutta with the initial capital of Rs. 26,000, taken as loan from central fund of Visva-Bharati which the institute repaid during next nineteen years [5]. The objectives of the department are based on a set of rules laid down by Rabindranath himself:

1. The complete works of Tagore should be available at an affordable cost ('*Sulabh Rabindranath*').
2. These should be accurately published in respect of spelling, style, presentation and format ('*Bisuddha Rabindranath*').
3. The complete writings of Tagore ('*Samagra Rabindranath*') should be published [6].

To fulfil the aforesaid objectives the principal activities of the publishing department included:

A. Publishing of Books (Bengali, English, Hindi, and Sanskrit) Other than Textbooks

1. by Rabindranath Tagore

2. on Rabindranath Tagore
3. on Rabindranath's associates, disciplines and students
4. on Visva-Bharati and Santiniketan
5. on various other topics (both fiction and non-fiction)

B. Publishing of Textbooks

1. taught in Visva-Bharati
2. taught by others (including books of the West Bengal Council of Higher Secondary Education)

C. Selling of Books

1. through its own bookshops at Kolkata and Santiniketan
2. through agents
3. at different book fairs including Calcutta Book Fair and Santiniketan Pous Mela.

At the initial years after the establishment of VBGV Rabindranath was anxious about its success. But in course of time it was observed that the readers as well as sales of Tagoreana increased day by day as found from following sales figure:

Table 4.1: Turnover of VBGV: 1921-22 to 1926-27

Financial Year	*Sale (Rs.)*
1921-22	19800
1922-23	19743
1923-24	22000
1924-25	16594
1925-26	25039
1926-27	28738

Source: Visva-Bharati Granthan Vibhaga: Panchasatvarsha Parikrama.

Prasantachandra Mahalanobis served the institute as its first director. The successive directors were Kishorimohan Santra, Charuchandra Bhattacharya, Pulinbehari Sen. The members of the first publishing committee besides Rabindranath were Surendranath Tagore, Ramananda Chattopadhyay, Tapanmohan Chattopadhyay, Nepalchandra Ray, Rathindranath Tagore and Prasantachandra

Mahalanobis. Right from the beginning Prasantachandra started to provide details information about a book of Rabindranath published by VBGV under the heading "*Path-parichaya*" and included it either at the beginning or at the end of a book. Later on "*Path-parichaya*" termed as '*Granthaparichaya*" and included at the end of the book. Granthaparichaya included detailed information about the first publications, later editions, criticism, changes in manuscripts, and Rabindranath's comment on his own writings. Later on, it was also included in Rabindra-Rachanavali by Prasantachandra. The same process was followed and further developed by the successive directors. Thus VBGV is the pioneer publisher of Bengali book world with special research-based information. The institute published not only collected works on special themes, but also publications of new editions with collection from different editions of the same book. As a result the institute was able to establish itself as a centre for Tagoreana culture and research [7]. For maintaining spelling and pronouncing standard uniformly for all publications of Tagoreana Prasantachandra took special care obviously in consultation with Rabindranath. Sunitikumar Chattopadhyay and Kalidas Nag also helped him in this respect [8]. Thus VBGV from its very beginning tried to be one of the best publishing houses as well as centre for Rabindra culture with its printing and editorial quality, uniform spelling throughout all the publications as well as house style to fulfil Tagore's vision of Samagra Rabindranath and Bisuddha Rabindranath. The intellectual reader community accepted it which can be established from the sales figures recorded in Table 4.2.

Table 4.2: Turnover of VBGV: 1960-61 to 1964-65

Financial Year	*Sale (Rs.)*
1960-61	13,85,288
1961-62	18,17,637
1962-63	14,64,007
1963-64	14,26,699
1964-65	15,40,755

Source: Visva-Bharati Granthan Vibhaga: Panchasatvarsha Parikrama.

Sales figures significantly increased in the financial year 1961-62 as 1961 was celebrated as Rabindranath's centenary year throughout the country. Though VBGV started its career with publications of

Tagoreana in the year 1923 but from the year 1942 it started to publish books on Rabindranath, Rabindra associates, Visva-Bharati, and Santiniketan as well. Meanwhile VBGV started publishing Rabindra Rachanavali (Collected works of Rabindranath) from the year 1939 under the directorship of Charuchandra Bhattacharaya [9]. Visva-Bharati became the Central University and declared as a Centre of National Importance by the Parliament of India in the year 1952; from then the activities of VBGV became more formal.

4.3 Activities of Visva-Bharati Granthan Vibhaga (1997-2006)

VBGV is rendering its services continuously for nearly seven decades. Rabindranath's intention was not only to see his works published properly and to keep these in print, but also to provide constant financial support to the parent organization out of the income generated by the department. The department remained a self-sufficient unit of Visva-Bharati until the last decade. With the global slump in book industry as a whole, the rise of private publishers, the flouting of publication ethics and copyright rules, the apathy of the sector, the VBGV is now in crisis. The situation started deteriorating with the increase in cost of production and establishment.

The activities of VBGV (1997-2006) in respect of its holdings, distribution network, sales promotion activities, and discount structure, turnover as well as new publications can be observed from the following tables:

Table 4.3: Tagoreana Published by VBGV

Sl. No.	*Literary Form*	*No. of Titles*
1.	**Fictions** (Gora, Ghare-Baire, Chaturanga, Chokher Bali, Dui Bon, Naukadubi, Bau-Thakuranir Hat, Malancha, Char Adhyay, Rajarshi, Shsher Kavita, Yogayog, Rabindra Upanayas Samagra (Collection of Rabindra fictions)	13
2.	**Poems and songs** (Nadi, Chitra, Kanika, Katha o Kahini, Kalpana, Kshanika, Smaran, Kheya, Gitanjali, Chaitali, Gitali, Giti-malya, Utsarga, Balaka, Palataka, Sisu Bholanath, Puravi, Pravahini, Mahua, Vanabani, Gitabitan, Sanchayita, Parisesh, Punascha, Sesh Saptak, Vithika, Patraput, Syamali, Khapchhada, Chhadar Chhabi, Prantik, Senjuti, Prahasini, Akash-pradip, Navajatak, Sanai, Rogasajyay, Arogya, Janmadine, Chhada, Sesh Lekha, Sphulinga, Sandhya Sangit, Chhabi o Gan, Sonar Tari, Naivedya, Baul, Sisu, Lekhan,	62

Bhanusimgha Thakurer Padavali—with notation, Bhanusimgha Thakurer Padavali, Baikali, Chitravichitra, Bhagnahriday, Kadi o Komal, Manasi, Surjabarta,, Chotoder Chhada, Birpurus, Rakshi, Sankalpa o Swadesh, Sanchyan)

3. **Drama** (Goday Galad, Baikunther Khata, Hasya-Kautuk, Mukut, Raja, Dakghar, Achalayatan, Arupratan, Muktadhara, Grihapravesh, Chirakumar Sabha, Sodh-bodh, Natir Puja, Raktakarabi, Kaler Yatra, Chandalika, Taser Desh, Bansari, Malancha, Phalguni, Sesh Raksha, Muktir Upay, Vyanga-Kautuk, Saradotsav, Prayaschitta, Phalguni, Vasanta, Yogayog, Tapati, Rabindra Natya Samgraha (Collection of Drama)) 29
4. **Stories** (Galpaguchha, Galpasalpa, Tin-Sangi, Lipika, Se) 5
5. **Drawings and paintings** (Chitralipi-1 and 2) 2
6. **Kavyanatya** (Drama in Verse) (Chitrangada, Kahini, Sapmochan, Prakritir Pratisodh, Rituranga, Viday Abhishap, Visarjan, Raja o Rani, Malini, Lakshmir Pariksha) 10
7. **Essays** (Kalantar, Svadesh, Sabhyatar Sankat) 3
8. **Biography** (Aurobindo Ghosh, Atmaparichaya, Christo, Ram Mohan Ray, Vidyasagar-Charit, Jivansmriti, Mahatma Gandhi, Buddhadeva, Maharshi Debendranath, Chhelebala, Chhelebela (Illustrated), Charitapuja, Buddhadeva o Buddha Samskriti) 13
9. **Religion** (Dharma, Manusher Dharma, Santiniketan, Sanchay) 4
10. **Science** (Visva-parichay with change of manuscript, Visvaparichaya) 2
11. **Miscellaneous** (Itihas, Kabir Bhanita, Mukul, Rabindra Parichaya, Vichitra Prabandha, Vichitrita, Samavaya Niti, Svadesi Samaj, Sangit-Chinta, Chhada, Palliprakriti, Bankimchandra, Kausarak, Panchabhut, Michael Madhusudan Dutta, Prasanga Rabindranath, Rupantar, Samkalan, Hey Chiranutun—Mostly collection from Tagore's writings) 19
12. **Linguistics** (Prachin Sahitya, Lokasahitya, Sahitya, Adhunik Sahitya, Sabdatattva, Banghabasha Parichaya, Sahityer Pathe, Sahityer Svarup) 8
13. **Travel** (Europe-Pravasir Patra, Europe-Yatrir Dairi, Japan-Yatrir Patra, Russiar Chithi, Japan-Yatri, Pather Sanchay, Parasya-Yatri, Paschim-Yatrir Dairi-Paschhatta Brahman) 8
14. **Education** (Visva-Bharati, Santiniketan Brahmacharyasram, Siksha, Asramer Rup o Vikas) 5
15. **Letters** (Written to different persons) 23
16. **Swarabitan** (Notation of Rabindra Sangit) 74
17. **Swarabitan-New Series** (Notation of Rabindra Sangit) 6
18. **Rabindra Rachanavali** (Collected works). 31 vols. 1
19. **Rabindra Rachanavali** (Collected works) 18 vols. Low Price Edition 1
20. **Rabindra Rachanavali** (Non-conventional collection). 2 vols 1
21. **Loksiksha Granthamala** [10]. 3
22. **English writings of Rabindranath** (My Boyhood Days, Boundless Sky, The Centre of Indian Culture, The Co-operative Principles, Crisis of Civilization, Introduction to Tagore, Letters from Russia, Mahatma Gandhi, The Religion of an Artist, The Religion of Man, A Vision of Indian History, Gitanjali, Gitanjali (Bilingual edition), Journey to Persia and Iraq, Santiniketan 1901-1951, 25 Portraits of Rabindranath, Visva- 24

	Bharati and its Institutions, Four Chapters, Two Sisters, The Runaway and other Stories, The Parrot's Training and other Stories, Chitralipi, Poems, Syamali)	
23.	**Translation of Tagore's work in Sanskrit, Hindi** (Gitanjali—Sanskrit translation, Mera Bachpan (Hindi translation of Chhelebela, Nati-ke-puja (Hindi translation of drama Natir puja, Chaturanga, Do Bahne—Hindi translation of Dui Bon, Phuleadi—Hindi translation of Malini, Swarabitan (Notation of Rabindra Sangit)	7
24.	**Textbook for school** [11].	21

Source: VBGV Catalogue.

Table 4.4: Works on Rabindranath Published by VBGV

Sl. No.	*Literary Form*	*No. of Titles*
1.	Essays, bibliography, biography, etc.—Bengali	59
2.	Biography, drawings, history, etc.—English	31
3.	Visva-Bharati Quarterly (journal)[12]	1
4.	Visva-Bharati Research Publication	15
5.	Rabindra Bhavana Publications	68
	Total	**174**

Source: VBGV Catalogue.

Table 4.5: Other Publications of VBGV

Sl. No.	*Literary Form*	*No. of Titles*
1.	Textbook (English, Bengali)	19
2.	Miscellaneous writings on art, culture, biography, history, etc. (English, Bengali, Hindi)	68
3.	Loksiksha Granthamala	7
4.	Visvavidya Granthamala	135
5.	Galpasalpa Granthamala	5
6.	Sanskrit Sahitya Granthamala	1
7.	Visva-Bharati Research Publication	114
8.	Visva-Bharati Journal of Philosophy	1
9.	Visva-Bharati Annals	1
10.	Santiniketan Pustak-Prakash Samiti	4
11.	Visva-Bharati Patrika—Quarterly [13]	1
	Total	**356**

Source: VBGV Catalogue.

Thus, there are 864 titles at the disposal of VBGV. It also distributes Visva-Bharati research publications and journals. The publishing department published 19 text books for West Bengal Board of Higher Secondary Education besides 21 school text books written by Rabindranath.

Distribution Network (1997-2006)

VBGV distributes its publications through a network of distributors for distributing its publications in India, Bangladesh and other foreign countries through its head office (6, Acharya Jagadish Chandra Bose Road, Kolkata-17), two sales counters at Kolkata (2, Bankim Chatterjee Street, Kolkata-73 and 210, Bidhan Sarani, Kolkata-6) and one in Santiniketan (inaugurated in August 2003). For sales promotion activity VBGV regularly participates in different book fairs and exhibitions in Kolkata, as well as in national, state, district book fairs and exhibitions as indicated below:

Table 4.6: Distribution Network of VBGV (1997-98 to 2006-07)

Year	*Calcutta*	*Other Places*	*Bangladesh and Other Foreign Countries*	*Total*
1997-98	4	8	7 (All located in Calcutta)	19
1998-99	4	8	7	19
1999-00	3	8	7	18
2000-01	3	7	7	17
2001-02	3	7	7	17
2002-03	3	6	8	17
2003-04	4	7	7	18
2004-05	4	8	7	19
2005-06	6	9	7	22
2006-07	6	8	6	20

Source: Visva-Bharati Annual Report: 1997-98 to 2006-07.

It is significant to note that all the distributors are from India, including those specially appointed for distribution of books in Bangladesh and other foreign countries. Among Indian states there was an agent only in Tripura up to 2001-02. Even there is no agent in many districts of West Bengal as there are only 6-9 agents in the state.

Publication (1997-2006)

VBGV regularly publishes new books on Rabindranath, reprint Tagoreana and other textbooks as shown in Table 4.7.

Table 4.7: Publication of New Books, Reprints, etc. of VBGV (1997-2006)

Year	*New Books*	*Reprinted Text Books (Tagore)*	*Reprinted Tagoreana*	*Other Reprints*	*Reprinted Textbooks (Others)*	*Total*
1997-98	9					9
1998-99	9	11	53	9	7	89
1999-00	10	12	38	10	13	83
2000-01	16	16	23	14	15	84
2001-02	1	17	47	8	9	82
2002-03	12	9	50	7	9	87
2003-04	15	10	72	6	9	112
2004-05	4	16	57	6	9	92
2005-06	13		39	3		55
2006-07	6		47	5	9	67

Source: Visva-Bharati Annual Report: 1997-98 to 2006-07.

Table 4.7 indicates that VBGV regularly publishes new books, reprint Tagoreana and textbooks. New books are mainly on Tagore written by Rabindra associates like Prabhatkumar Mukhopadhyaya, Prasantachandra Mahalanobis, Pulinbehari Sen, Pratima Devi, etc. and renowned Bengali scholars like Prasantakumar Pal, Uma Dasgupta, Amitrasudan Bhattacharyaya, Baridbaran Ghosh and so on.

Promotional Activity (1997-2006)

To promote its publications VBGV regularly participates in national, state and district book fairs and exhibitions as indicated in Table 4.8.

From the Table it is clear that VBGV stopped its participation in National Book Fair, New Delhi from 2000-01 and participation in state book fairs is limited to two fairs only from 2001-02. Participation in district book fair is mainly Calcutta-centric as the publishing department participates only in one or two district book fairs of West Bengal.

Discount Structure

Up to the financial year 1998-99, VBGV used to offer 12.5 to 25 per cent discount to different categories of customers and special discount offered for a limited period on the occasion of Tagore's

Table 4.8: Participation of VBGV in Book Fairs and Exhibitions (1997-2006)

Year	*State/National Book Fair*	*District Book Fair, Exhibitions, etc.*	*Total*
1997-98	4 (Calcutta, New Delhi, Agartala, Assam)	5 (Calcutta 4, Hooghly 1)	9
1998-99	4 (Calcutta, New Delhi, Jamshedpur, Agartala)	4 [Calcutta1, Santiniketan 1, District 2 (Burdwan, Hooghly)]	8
1999-00	5 (Calcutta, New Delhi, Jamshedpur, Assam, Agartala)	5 [Calcutta 2, Santiniketan 1, District 2 (Burdwan, Hooghly)]	10
2000-01	3 (Calcutta, Mumbai, Agartala)	5 [Calcutta 2, Santiniketan 1, District 2 (Burdwan, Hooghly)]	8
2001-02	2 (Calcutta, Jamshedpur)	5 [Calcutta 2, Santiniketan 1, District 2 (Howrah, Hooghly)]	7
2002-03	2 (Calcutta, Jamshedpur)	3 (Calcutta 2, Santiniketan 1)	5
2003-04	2 (Calcutta, Jamshedpur)	5 [Calcutta 3, Santiniketan 1, District 1 (Brudwan)]	7
2004-05	2 (Calcutta, Jamshedpur)	4 (Calcutta 3, Sntiniketan1)	6
2005-06	2 (Calcutta, Jamshedpur)	6 [Calcutta 4, Santiniketan 1, District 1 (Kalyani)]	8
2006-07	1 (Jamshedpur)	5 [Calcutta 3, Santiniketan 1, District 1 (Nadia)]	6

Source: Visva-Bharati Annual Report: 1997-98 to 2006-07.

Birth Anniversary to all customers. But from the financial year 1999-2000 onwards VBGV started to expand the period of special discount. For example in the financial year 1999-2000 special discounts offered throughout the year on ten titles of Tagoreana (*Dui Bon, Sey, Galpasalpa, Sandhya Sangit, Shyamali, Prahasini, Sesh Lekha, Bansari, Europe Prabasir Patra, Swadeshi Samaj*). Similarly in the financial year 2000-01 special discount was offered on seven titles (*Ghare-Baire, Galpasalpa, Prabahini, Lekhen, Prakitar Pratisodh, Palli Prakriti, Parasya Yatri*) and in the financial year 2001-02 on eight titles (*Malancha, Galpasalpa, Akash Pradeep, Parisesh, Rabindra Natya samgraha Vol. 1 and 2, Maharshi Debendranath, Amader Santiniketan*).

In the financial year 2002-03 the institute restructured its discount structure from existing 12.5 to 25 per cent to 20 to 33.3 per cent for different categories of customers as indicated in the following table:

Table 4.9: Discount Structure of VBGV for Different Categories of Customers (2002-03)

Customer	*% of Discount*
Book sellers outside West Bengal	33.33
Book sellers of West Bengal	30
Students and employees of Visva-Bharati	30
Public Libraries and Educational Institutions	25
General customers	20

Source: Visva-Bharati Annual Report: 2002-03.

Realizing the difficulties of marketing of its publications after the expiry of copyright, at the same time with the object of popularizing its publications, Granthan Vibhaga from the financial year 2003-04 onwards categorized its publications into two categories and increased its discount structure of 2002-03 and allowed the following discount for different categories of customers.

Table 4.10: Discount Structure of VBGV (2003-04 onwards)

Category of Customers	*% Discount on Granthan Vibhaga Own Publication*	*% of Discount on Rabindra Rachanabali Popular Ed.), Rabindra Bhavana Pub., Research Pub., etc.*
All Agents	35	30
All Booksellers	30	25
Students and Employees of Visva-Bharati	30	25
Public Libraries and Educational Institutions.	20	20
General Customers	15	15

Source: Visva-Bharati Annual Report: 2003-04.

Thus, it is clear that VBGV started expanding its special discount offer period two years prior to the expiry of copyright and increased its discount structure twice after the expiry of copyright to increase its business.

Sale of Publications

After the expiry of copyright there was an impression that all the leading as well as other relatively small private publishers will start publishing Tagoreana and turnover of Visva-Bharati publications will reduce significantly. The following turnover Table may unveil the truth:

Table 4.11: Turnover of VBGV (1997-2006)

Financial Year	*Sale (Rs.)*
1997-98	2,18,35,671.00
1998-99	2,10,92,814.00
1999-00	2,28,69,990.00
2000-01	2,50,81,547.00
2001-02	2,20,04,541.00
2002-03	2,30,92,791.00
2003-04	2,01,75,016.00
2004-05	1,69,02,235.00
2005-06	6,39,88,728.00
2006-07	6,98,82,018.00

Source: Visva-Bharati Annual Report and Annual Audited Account.

From the above figure of turnover of five years before and after the expiry of copyright it is evident that the expiry of copyright did not affect the turnover of the publishing unit, though marginal sales decrease is observed in the financial year 2004-05. But the sales increased three times in the financial year 2005-06 and 2006-07. This is mainly due to publications and sales of textbooks of West Bengal secondary and higher secondary levels.

Along with the publication of books VBGV started releasing compact disc (CD) with the first publication of '*Visva-Bina*' in the year 2002-03. It has also started an ambitious e-commerce project in collaboration with M/s. Brainware from 9th March, 2005, where all Visva-Bharati publications, CD, paintings, etc. will be available for sale through Internet and e-commerce [14]. VBGV is at present working towards computerization of its official activity through in-service training of its personnel at Brainware training centre in Calcutta. The work of computerized digitization process started with Sanchayita [15]. But the progress of the work is very slow.

The VBGV had been accredited the status of an Institute or a Bhavana (i.e. faculty) by Clause 19 of the Statute of Visva-Bharati. However, the VBGV is functioning as an autonomous self-financing organization since its inception in 1923 without any budgetary support from the University. All appointments, transfer and promotion orders for the employees are issued by the Registrar, Visva-Bharati following the Common Seniority Rules and financial control is exercised by the University's Finance Officer, ever since Visva-Bharati has become a Central university. As the situation stands, the funding responsibility of VBGV should also rest with University Grants Commission like its parent organization, but this has not happened yet [16].

The staff payment is made out of royalties and interest on deposit. The sanctioned staff strength is 85, but to cope with the situation of increasing expenditure the vacant positions are now not being filled up, as a result at present only 50 personnel are in the pay roll of VBGV. That has been possible as the Vibhaga managed to get a contract for supplying textbooks of West Bengal Higher Secondary Board [17]. An apprehension is natural that the quality control as well as innovative publications might be hampered and publication of '*Bisuddha Rabindranath*' as well as '*Samagra Rabindranath*' would be a difficult task.

4.4 Publication of Tagoreana by Private Publishers after the Expiry of Copyright

After the expiry of copyright in December 2001 Rabindranath's treasure is open and private publishers are free to publish Tagoreana. The following Tables give some idea about total number of publishers publishing Tagoreana.

Table 4.12: Publishers of Bengali Books (2002-2006)

Sl. No.	*Year*	*No. of Publishers Publishing Bengali Books*	*No. of Publishers Publishing Tagoreana*	*% of Publishers Publishing Tagoreana*
1.	2002	688	12	1.74
2.	2003	688	12	1.74
3.	2004	755	32	4.24
4.	2005	755	38	5.03
5.	2006	658	38	5.76

Source: Books in Print from West Bengal and Fair Directory 2002-2006.

From Table 4.12, it is evident that only a meagre percentage of publishers are publishing Tagoreana even five years after the expiry of copyright. Moreover, names of many publishers like Ranar, Nandita, Saroj, etc. are in the Books in Print but books are not available in the market and many publishers publish only one or two books like *Sahaj Path*. Thus, for this study twenty-five publishers were considered. The list of publishers and their publications are given in Table 4.13.

Table 4.13: Tagoreana Published by Private Publishers

Sl. No.	Publisher	Printer(s)	No. of Books	Title of the Books
1.	Kamini Prakashalaya, 5, Nabin Chandra Pal Lane, Ko kata-9.	1. Basu Mudran, 19/A, Sikdar Bagan Lane, Kolkata-4 2. A.B.C. Printers, 41, Simla Road, Kolkata-6. 3. Hindustan Art and Engraving, 24, Dr. Kartick Bose Street, Kolkata-9 4. Parijat Printers, 7, Garudas Datta Garden Lane, Kolkata-67 5. New Age Offset, 23, Pataldanga Street, Kolkata-9 6. Indralekha Press, 16, Hemendra Sen Street, Kolkata-6 7. Progressive Art Concern, 159/1-A.B.B. Ganguly Street, Kolkata-12 8. Essar Graphics, 1C,	45	Gitanjali, Sanchayita, Gitabitan, Galpaguchchha, Ghare-Baire, Naukadubi, Chaturanga, Char Adhyay, Bau-Thakuranir Hat, Rajarshi, Dui Bon, Chokher Bali, Malancha, Yogayog, Gora, Sesher Kavita, Dakghar, Raktakarabi, Sisu, Sisu Bholanath, Chandalika, Chitrangada, Raja o Rani, Tin-Sangi, Chhinnapatra, Chhada Samargha, Katha o Kahini, Visarjan, Sonar Tari, Jivansmriti, Natir Puja, Punascha, Sampatti Samarpan, Swarna Mriga, Khoka Babur Pratyabartan, Cabuliwala, Postmaster, Kshudhita Pashan, Nasta-Nir, Streer Patra, Patra o Patri, Gupta Dhan, Malyadan, Dristidan, Manihara

(*Contd.*)

Table 4.15 (Contd.)

Sl. No.	Publisher	Printer(s)	No. of Books	Title of the Books
		Gour Laha Street, Kolkata-6 7, Compu Colour, 41, Simla Road, Kolkata-6 9. Dijendra Offset, 36 Kailash Bose Street, Kolkata-81 10. Nabalok Press, 32/2, Sahitya Parisad Street, Kolkata-6 11. Colour and Colour, 4, Nabin Chandra Pal Lane, Kolkata-9 12. Jagadhatri Printers, 60, Patuatala Lane, Kolkata-9		
2.	Juthika Book Stall. 12, Bankim Chatterjee Street, Kolkata-73	1. Das Offset Processor, 25, Gulu Ostagar Lane, Kolkata-6 2. Purnima Printers, T/2A/1, Gurudas Dutta Garden Lane, Kolkata-67 3. New Bangasree Press, 12/2, Madan Mitra Lane, Kolkata-6 4. Annapurna Agency, 61, Surja Sen Street, Kolkata-9	18	Gitanjali, Sanchayita, Gitabitan, Galpaguchchha, Naukadubi, Char Adhyay, Bau-Thakuranir Hat, Rajarshi, Chokher Bali, Yogayog, Sesher Kavita, Visarjan, Sonar Tari, Rakta–karabi, Chhinnapatra, Jivansmriti, Chitra, Lipika

(*Contd.*)

Table 4.15 (Contd.)

Sl. No.	Publisher	Printer(s)	No. of Books	Title of the Books
		5. Pritha Printing Works, 1/1A, Priyanath Banerjee Street, Kolkata-9		
3.	United Publishers, 77A. Patandanga St., Kolkata-9	1. Nabalok Press, 32/2, Sahitya Parisad Street, Kolkata-6. 2. Loknath Printers, 26, Bidhan Sarani, Kolkata-6 3. Perfect Print and Process, 1/1B, Dr. Amal Raychowdhury Lane, Kolkata-9	15	Gitanjali, Ghare-Baire, Naukadubi, Chaturanga, Char Adhyay, Bau-Thakuranir Hat, Rajarshi, Dui Bon, Malancha, Yogayog, Gora, Chhinnapatra, Sisu, Sisu Bholanath, Chhelebela o Cabuliwala
4.	Patraj Publication, 2, S C. Dey Street Kolkata-73	1. Nabalok Press, 32/2, Sahitya Parisad Street, Kolkata-6. 2. Rajendra Offset, 11, Panchanan Ghosh Street, Kolkata-6 3. Fair Print, 6, Panchanan Ghosh Street, Kolkata-9 4. Nivedita Press, 19D, Goabagan Street, Kolkata-6	15	Gitanjali, Sanchayita, Gitabitan, Galpaguchchha, Ghare-Baire, Naukadubi, Chaturanga, Char Adhyay, Bau-Thakuranir Hat, Rajarshi, Dui Bon, Chokher Bali, Karuna, Malancha, Yogayog
5.	Punascha, 9A, Nabin Kundu Lane, Kolkata-9	Dotline Print and Process, 114N, Dr. S.C. Banerjee Road, Kolkata-10	11	Gitanjali, Sanchayita, Gitabitan, Galpaguchchha,, Gora, Ghare-Baire, Naukadubi, Chaturanga, Char Adhyay, Bau-Thakuranir Hat, Rajarshi

(Contd.)

Table 4.15 (Contd.)

Sl. No.	*Publisher*	*Printer(s)*	*No. of Books*	*Title of the Books*
6.	Ashok Book Agency, 36B, College Row, Kolkata-9	1. New Jaikali Press, 8A, Dinabandhu Lane. Kolkata-6 2. Spectram Offset, 5B, Kundu Lane, Kolkata-37 3. Puberun Press, 1/1A, Goabagan Lane, Kolkata-6	10	Gitanjali, Sanchayita, Gitabitan, Galpaguchchha, Naukadubi, Chokher Bali, Yogayog, Sonar Tari, Rabindranather Jivansmriti, Punascha
7.	Granthasambhar, 3, College Row, Kolkata-9	1. The G.B. Printers, 19 E. Goabagan Street, Kolkata-6 2. Indralekha Press, 16, Hemendra Sen Street, Kolkata-6 3. Nabalok Press, 32/2, Sahitya Parisad Street, Kolkata-6	9	Gitanjali, Sanchayita, Ghare-Baire, Naukadubi, Chokher Bali, Malancha, Yogayog, Gora, Chhinnapatra
8.	Sahityam, 18, B.S.C. Dey Street, Kolkata-73	1. Printing Centre Chhidam Mudi Lane, Kolkata-6. 2. Progressive Art Concern, 159/1A, BB Ganguly Street, Kolkata-12 3. Loknath Printing and Binding Works,	7	Gitanjali, Sanchayita, Gitabitan, Galpaguchchha, Sesher Kavita, Sisu, Sisu Bholanath

(*Contd.*)

Table 4.15 (Contd.)

Sl. No.	Publisher	Printer(s)	No. of Books	Title of the Books
		24B, College Row, Kolkata-47		
9.	Gitanjali 3/161, Seth Bagan Road, Kolkata-30	1. Padmanava Impression, 17, Vimghosh Lane, Kolkata-6 2. Loknath Printers, 26, Bidhan Sarani, Kolkata-6	6	Sesher Kavita, Sisu, Sisu Bholanath, Chhinnapatra, Chhelebela, Kshudhita Pashan
10.	Tuli-Kalam, 1A, College Row, Kolkata-9	1. Friends Graphics, 11B, Bidan Row, Kolkata-6 2. Kamal De, T/2A/1, Gurudas Dutta Garden Lane, Kolkata-67 3. Essar Graphics, 1C, Gour Laha Street, Kolkata-6 4. Eastern Press, 22/6, Budu Ostagar Lane, Kolkata-9	6	Gitanjali, Sanchayita, Gitabitan, Galpaguchchha, Chhelebela, Lipika o Sey
11.	Patra Bharati, 3/1, College Row, Kolkata-9	Hemprabha Printing House, 1/1, Brindaban Mallick Lane. Kolkata-9	6	Ghare-Baire, Chaturanga, Char Adhyay, Malancha, Sesher Kavita, Khoka Babur Pratyabartan
12.	Nirmal Book Agency, 89, M.G. Road, Kolkata-7	Loknath Printing and Binding Works, 24B, College Row, Kolkata-47	5	Chhelebela, Khapchhada, Khoka Babur Pratyabartan, Chhuti, Cabuliwala

(*Contd.*)

Table 4.15 (Contd.)

Sl. No.	Publisher	Printer(s)	No. of Books	Title of the Books
13.	Asia Publishing Company, A-132, 133, College Street Market, Kolkata-7	1. Nabapress Private Limited, 66 Gray Street, Kolkata-6 2. Print-o-Graph, 9-C, M.G. Road, Kolkata-9	5	Gitanjali (Bi-lingual), Sanchayita, Gitabitan, Galpaguchchha, Chhotader Lekha.
14.	Narayan Pustakalaya, 8, Shyamacharan De Street Kolkata-73	Shila Printing Works., 6, Rev, Kali Banerjee Road, Kolkata-6	4	Gitanjali, Sanchayita, Gitabitan, Galpaguchchha
15.	Mitra and Ghosh Publishers, 10, Shyamacharan Dey Street, Kolkata-73	1. Chayanika Press, 1, Ramanath Majumdar Street, Kolkata-9 2. Progressive Art Concern, 159/1-A, B.B. Ganguly Street, Kolkata-12	4	Jivansmriti, Sahajpath-1 and 2, Kishor Rabindra Rachanavali.
16.	Radha Pustkalaya, 8, Shyama Charan De Street, Kolkata-73	1. Modern Press, 11, Raja Subodh Mallick Square, Kolkata-13 2. New Kalimata Printers, 19A/H/2, Goabagan Street, Kolkata-6	3	Sanchayita Gitabitan, Galpaguchchha
17.	Reflect Publication, 30, M.G. Road, Kolkata-9	Arun Offset, Sonarpur, 24 Parganas	3	Sanchayita, Gitabitan, Galpaguchchha
18.	Das Sahitya Kutir, 10, Akhil Mistri Lane, Kolkata-9	1. Padmanava Impression, 17, Bhimghosh Lane, Kolkata-6	3	Chaturanga, Char Adhyay, Dui Bon

(Contd.)

Table 4.15 (Contd.)

Sl. No.	Publisher	Printer(s)	No. of Books	Title of the Books
		2. Haridas Printers, 10, Jadu Srimani Lane, Kolkata-6		
19.	Bookfront Publication Forum, AJ 162, Sector-2 Bidhannagar, Kolkata-91	Press Shop, 77/2/1, Lenin Sarani, Kolkata-13	3	Postmaster, Kshudhita Pashan, Atithi
20.	Prakash Bhavana, 15, Bankim Chatterjee Street Kolkata-73	Tarakeswar Press, 6, Sibu Biswas Lane, Kolkata-6	2	Sisu Bholanath, Chhelebela
21.	Sahitya Bharati Publications, 211/1, Bidhan Sarani, Kolkata-6	C.21/30A-B, Pischapmochan, Varanasi-10	2	Sahaj Path 1 and 2
22.	Babli Prakashani, 8/1A, Shyamacharan Dey Street, Kolkata-73	Calcutta Art Studio, 185/1, B.B. Ganguly Street, Kolkata-12	1	Sahai Path
23.	Baksahitya, 33, College Row, Kolkata-9	Tarakeswar Press, 6, Sibu Biswas Lane, Kolkata-6	1	Rajarshi
24.	Rajarshi Prakashan, 42c, J.K. Mitra Road, Kolkata-37	Essar Graphics, 1C, Gour Laha Street, Kolkata-73	1	Shsher Kavita
25.	Suranjana Prakashani, Banamalipur, Barasat, 24 Parganas	D and P Graphics, Ganganagar, 24 Parganas	I	Shsher Kavita

(Contd.)

A comparative study of the above publications with Visva-Bharati Publications reveals that only 39 titles are published by private publishers after the expiry of copyright in comparison of 334 titles of VBGV. Even if English publications, translations into other languages and textbooks of Visva-Bharati are excluded, the ratio would be 282:39. The number of publications of private publishers excludes selective publications from short stories which are part of *Galpaguchchha* (Collection of short stories) published by VBGV. Actually most of the publishers published books with the titles of one or two short stories like *Khoka Babur Partyabartan*, *Cabuliwala, Postmater*, etc. selecting from *Galpaguchchha*. Another important feature may be observed that most of the publishers published *Gitanjali, Sanchayita, Gitabitan* and *Galpaguchchha*. The remaining books are mostly novels, one or two dramas and autobiography of Rabindranath. But books on songs, dramas, essays, religious writings, travel, education, rural development and Rabindra Rachanavali are not yet published by private publishers. Publishers getting their books printed from many printers indicate that most of them have no in-house printing press. Leading publishers of Bengali books like Ananda Publishers, Dey's Publishing, Sahityaloke have not yet started publishing Tagoreana and Mitra and Ghosh published only four books. Relatively new publishers with less number of titles in their credit as observed from their current catalogue like Juthika Book Stall (05 titles), United Publishers (147 titles), Ashok Book Agency (138 titles), Granthasambhar (53 titles), Gitanjali (79 titles), Asia Publishing Company (107 titles), Radha Pustakalaya (144 titles) etc. started publishing Tagoreana who generally publish children's books, classics and books of authors whose copyright expired like Rabindranath Tagore, Saratchandra Chattopadhyay, Bankim Chandra Chattopadhyay, Sukumar Ray, and Dakshinaranjan Ray.

4.5 Comparison of Price of Tagoreana Published by Visva-Bharati and Private Publishers

For marketing of books, besides sales channel, discount structure, advertisement etc. price plays a vital role. It is more important after the expiry of copyright as no monopoly of Visva-Bharati exists now. Table 4.14 will help to have an idea about comparative price of titles, as discount structure of all the publishers are almost the same, i.e. 33.3 per cent to booksellers.

Table 4.14: Comparative Statement of Price: VBGV and Private Publishers

Part I

Title	*VBGV*	*Kamini*	*Juthika*	*United*	*Patraj*	*Punascha*	*Ashok*	*Grantha-sambhar*
Gitanjali	50.00	40.00	30.00	40.00	40.00	35.00	25.00	45.00
Sanchayita	160.00	100.00	100.00		110.00	90.00	130.00	120.00
Gitabitan	325.00	100.00	120.00		120.00	90.00	150.00	
Galpaguchchha	225.00	110.00	120.00		120.00	110.00	110.00	
Ghare-Baire	70.00	40.00		30.00	50.00	35.00		50.00
Naukadubi	70.00	50.00	50.00	45.00	60.00	45.00	65.00	60.00
Chaturanga	35.00	25.00		25.00	25.00	38.00		
Char Adhyay	35.00	25.00	40.00	25.00	30.00	25.00		
Bau-Thakuranir Hat	60.00	30.00	30.00	30.00	35.00	25.00		
Rajarshi	40.00	30.00	40.00	25.00	35.00	25.00		
Dui Bon	12.00	25.00		25.00	30.00			
Chokher Bali	65.00	50.00	50.00		40.00		55.00	50.00
Malancha	13.00	25.00		25.00	20.00			50.00
Yogayog	40.00	50.00	40.00	40.00	60.00		45.00	50.00
Gora	130.00	80.00		70.00		60.00		80.00
Sesher Kavita	45.00	30.00	40.00					
Dakghar	20.00	30.00						
Raktakarabi	25.00	25.00	35.00					
Sisu	45.00	25.00		35.00				
Sisu Bholanath	25.00	25.00		30.00				
Chandalika	8.00	30.00						
Chitrangada	35.00	30.00		30.00				
Raja o Rani	55.00	30.00						
Tin-Sangi	40.00	30.00						
Chhinnapatra	100.00	40.00	45.00					45.00
Katha o Kahini	40.00	25.00						
Visarjan	25.00	25.00	30.00					
Sonar Tari	35.00	40.00	40.00				45.00	
Jivansmriti	40.00	50.00	40.00				45.00	
Natir Puja	20.00	30.00						
Punascha	60.00	30.00					45.00	
Chitra	40.00		40.00					
Lipika	60.00		22.00					

(Contd.)

Part II

Title	*VBGV*	*Sahityan*	*Gitanjali*	*Tuli-Kalam*	*Patra Bharati*	*Nirmal Book*	*Asia Pub.*	*Narayan*
Gitanjali	50.00	16.00		30.00			60.00	45.00
Sanchayita	160.00	80.00		80.00			125.00	120.00
Gitabitan	325.00	100.00		100.00			150.00	130.00
Galpaguchchha	225.00	100.00		80.00			150.00	130.00
Ghare-Baire	70.00				40.00			
Chaturanga	35.00				15.00			
Char Adhyay	35.00				15.00			
Malancha	13.00				15.00			
Sesher Kavita	45.00	20.00	30.00		25.00			
Sisu	45.00	20.00	30.00					
Sisu Bholanath	25.00	15.00	25.00					
Chhinnapatra	100.00		40.00					
Chhelebela	20.00		25.00	20.00		25.00		
Khapchhada	225.00					60.00		

Part III

Title	*VBGV*	*Mitra and Ghosh*	*Radha*	*Reflect Pub.*	*Das Sahitya Kutir*	*Prakash Bhavana*	*Sahitya Bharati*	*Baksahitya*	*Rajarshi*
Gitanjali	50.00								
Sanchayita	160.00		130.00	50.00					
Gitabitan	325.00		140.00	70.00					
Galpaguchchha	225.00		130.00	70.00					
Chaturanga	35.00				25.00				
Char Adhyay	35.00				30.00				
Rajarshi	40.00							50.00	
Dui Bon	12.00				30.00				
Sesher Kavita	45.00								30.00
Sisu Bholanath	25.00					30.00			
Jivansmriti	40.00	150.00				25.00			
Chhelebela	20.00								
Sahajpath-1	16.00	16.00					20.00		
Sahajpath-2	17.00	16.00					30.00		

It is evident from the above table that the price of most of the titles of VBGV is higher than any other private publishers though all the titles of Visva-Bharati in the comparative table are paperback except *Sanchayita, Gitabitan, Galpaguchchha* and *Sey*. Books published by private publishers are hardbound (except four titles of Sahityan: *Gitanjali, Sesher Kavita, Sisu* and *Sisu Bholanath*, two titles of Prakash Bhavana: *Jivansmriti* and *Chhelebela*, one title each of Bak-Sahitya: Rajarshi, Suranjana Prakashani: *Sesher Kavita* and *Sahaj Path* of Babli, Mitra & Ghosh and Patra Bharati), but the binding quality is poor in general except books published by Mitra & Ghosh. It appears that the price of *Dui Bon* published by Kamini Prakashalaya is much higher (Rs. 25.00) than Visva-Bharati (Rs. 12.00) but *Dui Bon* published by Kamini included four other short stories, namely *Sampatti Samarpan, Khoka Babur Pratyabartan, Thakurda* and *Taraprasannar Kriti*. Similarly along with *Malancha* two other short stories *Guptadhan* and *Kankal* are included. *Dakghar* is a combination of three dramas *Dakghar, Malini* and *Mukut*. *Chandalika* is a combination of two dramas—*Chandalika* and *Tapati*. *Natir Puja* and *Arupratan* are combined together under one cover. The price of *Gitanjali*—bilingual edition of Asia Publishing seems to be higher but the price of the same edition of Visva-Bharati is much higher, i.e. Rs. 125.00. *Jivansmriti* published by Mitra & Ghosh is an edited volume by Baridbaran Ghosh with good number of notes and references and contains more pages (N=352) than that of VBGV (N=163). *Sahaj Path* published by Patra Bharati and Babli contains exercise with more number of pages.

In this comparative price statement titles not published by VBGV as a separate book was not considered. For that reason *Karuna* published by Patraj, books separately published by the name of short stories, titles made on selective writings like Chhotodar Lekha of Asia or Kishor Rabindranath of Mitra & Ghosh are not considered.

4.6 Comparison of Page and Size of Tagoreana Published by Visva-Bharati and Private Publishers

Price is related to number of pages, size of the book, paper and printing quality, illustrations, etc. So, a comparative statement of pages along with size of the book may throw some light on the above aspect of comparative price statement.

Table 4.15: Comparative Statement of Page and Size (in cm.) VBGV and Private Publishers

Part I

Title	*VBGV*	*Kamini*	*Juthika*	*United*	*Patraj*	*Punascha*	*Ashok*	*Grantha-sambhar*
Gitanjali	194 18×12	152 21.7×13.7	104 22×13.5	152 21.7×13.5	128 22×14	176 21.8×14	128 21.7×13.6	152 21.7×14
Sanchayita	918 21.8×14.5	736 21.7×13.7	606 22×14		607 21.5×14	575 21.8 ×14	664 21.9×13.7	720 21.7×13.8
Gitabitan	1034 21.8×14.5	784 21.7×13.7	764 22×14		706 22.3×14	660 21.8×14	784 22.3×14.2	
Galpaguchchha	882 21.5×14.5	848 21.7×13.7	768 22×14		848 22×14	672 21.8×14.5	879 22.1×14.2	
Ghare-Baire	220 21.3×13.8	136 21.7×13.7		136 21.7×13.5	160 22×14	96 21.8×14		136 21.5×14
Naukadubi	279 21.5×14	176 21.7×13.7	176 21.5×13.7	176 21.7×13.5	208 22×14	134 21.11×14	208 21.7×14	176 21.5×14
Chaturanga	117 18.3×12.3	64 21.7×13.7		64 21.7×13.5	72 22×14	144 21.10×14		
Char Adhyay	116 18.5×12.5	80 21.7 × 13.7	40 21.7×13.5	64 21.7×13.5	71 21.7×13.8	62 21.10×14		
Bau-Thakuranir Hat	208 18×12	104 21.7×13.7	96 22×13.6	104 21.7×13.5	120 22×14	78 21.10×14		
Rajarshi	175 18×12	96 21.7×13.7	88 22×13.5	96 21.7×13.5	112 22.2×13.9	68 22×14		

(*Contd.*)

Table 4.15 (Contd.)

Title	*VBGV*	*Kamini*	*Juthika*	*United*	*Patraj*	*Punascha*	*Ashok*	*Grantha-sambhar*
Dui Bon	103 17.6×12	80 21.7×13.7		64 21.7×13.5	61 22×14			
Chokher Bali	242 21.6×13.7	160 21.7×13.7	152 21.5×13.5		167 22×14		168 21.7×14	160 21.5×14
Malancha	96 17.8×12.1	72 21.7×13.7		48 21.7×13.5	56 22×14			216 21.5×14
Yogayog	237 21.4×13.9	144 21.7×13.7	136 22×13.7	144 21.7×13.5	19122×14		160 22×13.7	144 21.5×14
Gora	503 21.6×14	288 21.7×13.7		288 21.7×13.5		228 22×14		288 21.5×14
Sesher Kavita	190 17.9×12	96 21.7×13.7	72 22×13.7					
Dakghar	79 17.8x12	96 21.7×13.7						
Raktakarabi	123 21.5x13.5	80 21.7×13.7	72 21.8×14					
Sisu	204 17.5x12	72 21.7×13.7		112 21.7×13.5				
Sisu Bholanath	90 18x12.2	64 21.7×13.7		64 21.7×13.5				
Chandalika	47 18x12	96 21.7×13.7						
Chitrangada	61 20.8x13.1	96 21.7×13.7						

(*Contd.*)

Table 4.15 (Contd.)

Title	*VBGV*	*Kamini*	*Juthika*	*United*	*Patraj*	*Punascha*	*Ashok*	*Grantha-sambhar*
Raja o Rani	159 18x12	96 21.7×13.7						
Tin-Sangi	126 21.3x14	88 21.7×13.7						
Chhinnapatra	311 21.5x13.6	128 21.7×13.7	120 22×13.9	126 21.7×13.5				128 21.5×14
Katha o Kahini	171 18x12.2	80 21.7×13.7						
Visarjan	128 18.12.2	80 21.7×13.7	70 21.5×13.5					
Sonar Tari	177 18x12	128 21.7×13.7	120 22×13.7				144 22×13.7	
Jivansmriti	163 21.2x13.5	160 21.7×13.7	114 21.4×13.9				128 21.8×13.8	
Natir Puja	88 18x12	96 21.7×13.7						
Punascha	217 21.5x13.8	104 21.7×13.7					128 21.8×13.8	
Chitra	175 17.5x12		127 22×13.3					
Lipika	180 18x12		72 21.5×13.5					

(Contd.)

Part II

Table 4.15 (Contd.)

Title	VBGV	Sahityan	Gitanjali	Tuli-Kalam	Patra Bharati	Nirmal Book	Asia Publishing	Narayan
Gitanjali	194 18×12	151 17.5×12.2		192 21.5×13.5			239 19×10.5	176 21.7×14
Sanchayita	918 21.8×14.5	632 22×14.3		780 22×14			640 21.7×14	722 22×13.8
Gitabitan	1034 21.8×14.5	783 22×14.5		959 22×14			824 22×14	764 21.8×14
Galpaguchchha	882 21.5×14.5	896 22×14.5		800 22×14			904 22×14	848 22×13.8
Ghare-Baire	220 21.3×13.8				250 17.7×11.4			
Chaturanga	117 18.3×12.3				96 17.9×11.2			
Char Adhyay	116 18.5×12.5				96 17.8×11.4			
Malancha	96 17.8×12.1				95 17.8×11.4			
Sesher Kavita	190 17.9×12	128 18×12.3	96 21.5×13.7		144 18×11.5			
Sisu	204 17.5x12	175 18×12	96 21.5×13.5					

(Contd.)

Table 4.15 (Contd.)

Title	VBGV	Sahityan	Gitanjali	Tuli-Kalam	Patra Bharati	Nirmal Book	Asia Publishing	Narayan
Sisu Bholanath	90 18x12.2	80 18×12	64 21.5×13.5					
Chhinnapatra	311 21.5x13.6		120 21.5×13.5					
Chhelebela	83 18×12.4		64 21.5×13.5	72 22×13.8		64 24.5×18.5		
Khapchha-da	160.00 25×19.5					159 24.5×19		

Part III

Title	VBGV	Mitra and Ghosh	Radha	Reflect Pub.	Das Sahitya Kutir	Prakash Bhavana	Sahitya Bharati	Baksahitya	Rajarshi
Gitanjali	194 18×12								
Sanchayita	918 21.8×14.5		720 22.5×13.5	416 22.4×14					
Gitabitan	1034 21.8×14.5		764 21.5×13.5	560 22.5×14					
Galpaguchchha	882 21.5×14.5		848 21.5×13.5	616 22.5×14.3					
Chaturanga	117 18.3×12.3				64 21.5×13.5				

(Contd.)

Table 4.15 (Contd.)

Title	VBGV	Mitra and Ghosh	Radha	Reflect Pub.	Das Sahitya Kutir	Prakash Bhavana	Sahitya Bharati	Baksahitya	Rajarshi
Char Adhyay	116 18.5×12.5				104 21.5×13.5				
Rajarshi	175 18×12							144 21.2×13.1	
Dui Bon	103 17.6×12				96 21.5×13.5				
Sesher Kavita	190 17.9×12								96 21.8×13.6
Sisu Bholanath	90 18x12.2					30 21.2×13.5			
Jivansmriti	163 21.2x13.5	352 21.6×14.5							
Chhelebela	83 18×12.4					56 21.3×13.5			
Sahajpath-1	53 20.2×16.5	56 23.7×15.7					64 24×18.5		
Sahajpath-2	59 20.3×16.3	60 23.4×15.4					72 24×18.5		

Other two titles are: *Sahaj Path* Part-I published by Babli contains 46 pages, having size 23.8 × 18.2 cm and *Sesher Kavita* published by Suranjana contains 112 pages, and having the size 17.9 × 12 cm. From the above table it is clear that the number of pages of the books published by VBGV is much higher in many cases nearly twice in comparison to the number of pages of books published by private publishers through the size remains more or less same. In some cases like *Malancha* of Granthasambhar it may be noticed that the number of pages is higher but it is a combination of four novels, namely *Malancha, Dui Bon, Char Adhyay* and *Chaturanga.* The actual page of *Malancha* is 48 only. Thus, it is evident that to keep price low, the private publishers compromised on paper, binding and printing quality, font size, space between lines and also top and bottom margins which in many cases violate aesthetic beauty and also publishing quality.

4.7 Growth of Publication of Tagoreana by Private Publishers

Copyright of Tagoreana expired in December 2001. Publishers started publishing Tagoreana from January 2002. A brief statement of first publication of Tagoreana by various private publishers will indicate the growth of publication as well as flow of business interest of private publishers in publishing Tagoreana after the expiry of copyright.

From Table 4.16 it is clear that 81 per cent (151 out of 186) books published in the year 2002 immediately after the expiry of copyright. Nearly 13 per cent (22 out of 186) books (new titles not published in 2002) were published in the year 2003. So, remaining 6 per cent books published in the last three years (2004-06). Moreover, most of the books published in 2002 were in between January to May 2002. The year of publication has not been mentioned in case of *Sesher Kavita* published by *Gitanjali* and two titles each of Prakash Bhavana and Sahitya Bharati entitled *Sisu Bholanath* and *Jivansmriti* and *Sahajpath* Part-I and II respectively. Thus, majority of publishers published books in a hurry immediately after the expiry of copyright which increased the possibility of mistakes.

Table 4.16: Year of First Publication of Tagoreana by Private Publishers

Publisher	*2002*	*2003*	*2004*	*2005*	*2006*	*Total*
Kamini	39	6				45
Juthika	18					18
United	15					15
Patraj	15					15
Punascha	11					11
Ashok	8	2				10
Granthasambhar	9					9
Sahityam	4	2	1			7
Gitanjali	4			1		5
Tuli-kalam	5			1		6
Patra Bharati	4	2				6
Nirmal	1	4				5
Asia	5					5
Narayan	4					4
Mitra and Ghosh		3			1	4
Radha					3	3
Reflect	3					3
Das Sahitya Kutir	2	1				3
Book Front	3					3
Prakash Bhavana						2
Sahitya Bharati						2
Babli	1					1
Bak Sahitya		1				1
Rajarshi			1			1
Suranjana		1				1

4.8 Tagoreana and International Standard Book Number (ISBN)

International Standard Book Number (ISBN) allotted by Raja Rammohun Roy Library Foundation, Calcutta is an important tool for bibliographic control. Tagoreana published by Visva-Bharati incorporated it. So a study of Tagoreana published after the expiry of copyright by private publishers with ISBN may reveal the real situation in this respect.

From Table 4.17 it is clear that five publishers (Patraj, Punascha, Mitra & Ghosh, Reflect and Book Front) published Tagoreana with ISBN. In other words, five publishers out of twenty-five (i.e. 20%) published Tagoreana with ISBN. If titles having ISBN is considered, the figure would be 36 out of 186 titles, i.e. 19 per cent only. It indicates less bibliographical control over publication of Tagoreana after expiry of copyright.

Table 4.17: Tagoreana Published by Private Publishers with ISBN

Publisher	*With ISBN*	*Without ISBN*	*Total*	*Percentage of Titles with ISBN*
Kamini		45	45	00
Juthika		18	18	00
United		15	15	00
Patraj	15		15	100
Punascha	11		11	100
Ashok		10	10	00
Granthasambhar		9	9	00
Sahityam		7	7	00
Gitanjali		6	6	00
Tuli-kalam		6	6	00
Patra Bharati		6	6	00
Nirmal		5	5	00
Asia		5	5	00
Narayan		4	4	00
Mitra and Ghosh	4		4	100
Radha		3	3	00
Reflect	3		3	100
Das Sahitya Kutir		3	3	00
Book Front	3		3	100
Prakash Bhavana		2	2	00
Sahitya Bharati		2	2	00
Babli		1	1	00
Bak Sahitya		1	1	00
Rajarshi		1	1	00
Suranjana		1	1	00

Regarding copyright declarations only three publishers (Granthasambhar, Mitra & Ghosh, and Reflect) had clearly mentioned that they reserved the copyright. Five publishers (Kamini, Punascha, Sahityayan, Juthika and United) mentioned the title as the publisher's first edition but without any sign of copyright. The remaining 17 publishers are silent regarding copyright issue.

4.9 Textual Comparison of Tagoreana Published by Private Publishers and Visva-Bharati

Besides the above bibliographical comparison in respect of titles published by private publishers, price, pagination and size of books, first publication, ISBN and copyright, a publisher-wise comparative study of titles with Visva-Bharati publications in respect of mistakes in punctuation marks, spelling, omission of word(s) or line(s), style of presentation etc. would focus on the truth that after the expiry of copyright whether '*Bisuddha Rabindranath*' is being published or not.

In the first literary comparison (Table 4.18), punctuation marks used in the books published by private publishers and punctuation marks used in Visva-Bharati edition have been compared. Similarly, the second Table (4.18a) shows additional punctuation marks used in the text. In the third Table (4.18b) spelling mistakes, omission or addition of word(s) or line(s), paragraph/line clubbed/separated are considered. Here a line in case of poems considered as a paragraph.

During the study it was observed that important access point to enter the thought content was not used in many books published by Kamini, e.g. subject and first line index of poems in *Sonar Tari*, first line index in *Sanchayita* and *Sisu Bholanath*. From the above comparative table it is clear that *Gitanjali* is the best book published by Kamini Prakashalaya has fewer mistakes in the thought content. *Sanchayita, Gitabitan* and *Galpaguchha* are also good books published by Kamini with fewer mistakes. On the contrary *Ghare-Baire, Chaturanga* and *Gora* are having the highest mistakes—13, 11 and 9 per page respectively in respect of other punctuation marks used or punctuation marks omitted. In *Chandalika*, *Rajarshi* and *Gora* maximum number of additional punctuation marks—5, 1.5 and 1 respectively per page are used. In case of other mistakes it can be observed that *Tinsangi* is having 7 spelling mistakes in 9 pages and *Sesher Kavita* has 9 spelling mistakes in 10 pages. Even incidents like sentence omission can be found in 5 cases and word deleted in 6 occasions out of 45 books compared. Paragraphs (line in case poems) have been clubbed in *Chokher Bali* as many as 19 times in 16 pages. This has happened in many other books. It is done mainly to reduce the number of pages to keep price relatively low.

In *Gitabitan* published by Visva-Bharati in the index reference of the songs of *Swarabitan* (book of notation) is given, but publication by Juthika lacks it. And in *Raktakarabi* title is divided in the title page as *Rakta Karabi*. From Tables 4.19, 4.19a, 4.19b it may be concluded that in case of use of other punctuation marks or punctuation marks not given the chronological order of books having higher mistakes would be *Sesher Kavita* (9 per page), *Rajarshi* (8.33 mistakes per page), *Char Adhyay* (8.25 mistakes per page) and so on. On the other hand no mistake in this category can be found in *Sonar Tari* and *Lipika*. The highest number of

Table 4.18: Textual Comparison: Kamini Prakashalaya
Punctuation Marks: Other Punctuation Marks Used or Omitted

Titles	*Page No. Compared*	.	,	:	;	?	!	“ ” ‘ ’	’	—	-	*Total*
Gitanjali	15											0
Sanchayita	70	3	1				1				2	7
Gitabitan	70	4	3						1	1	1	10
Galpaguchchha	84	1	11				4		1		5	22
Ghare-Baire	14	48	44		14	3	19		3	33	23	187
Naukadubi	18	2	7		1	2	3				3	18
Chaturanga	6	10	4		6			39		4	3	66
Char Adhyay	8	7	5		1		2				6	21
Bau-Thakuranir Hat	10	3	6		1	1	1				3	15
Rajarshi	10	1	20		6	8	5			4	2	46
Dui Bon	8	1	8	1	1		2	2			3	18
Chokher Bali	16	7	17		9	1	6	1		1	16	59
Malancha	7	1	11			13	3				4	32
Yogayog	14	7	14		3	2	4	1		2	12	45
Gora	29	30	95		30	11	31	15	1	44	18	275
Sesher Kavita	10	4	14		6	11		7	1	5	10	58
Dakghar	9	2	6			3	6		2	9	2	30
Raktakarabi	7	1	1			1						3
Sisu	7	2	4		3	1	1	1		6	4	22
Sisu Bholanath	6									1		1
Chandalika	2					6	9			2	1	18
Chitrangada	9	4	18		3	15	10	1	4	10	6	71
Raja o Rani	9	9	18		7	1	28			8	7	78
Tin-Sangi	7	2	6		1				1	5	5	20

(*Contd.*)

Table **4.18** *(Contd.)*

Titles	*Page No. Compared*	.	,	:	;	?	!	“ ” ‘ ’	'	—	-	*Total*
Chhinnapatra	12	2					1			1	4	8
Chhada Samagra	5	3	1				2	5	6	8		25
Katha o Kahini	8	10	15		14	1	1	8	1	6	10	66
Visarjan	7	2	1			3	3	1			2	12
Sonar Tari	13	2									1	3
Jivansmriti	16							1			1	2
Natir Puja	9	11	25		2	6	12		1		13	61
Punascha	10	5	20		9	1	3	6	1	11	4	60
Sampatti Samarpan	8		1									1
Swarna Mriga	8	1			1		1					3
Khoka Babur Pratyabartan	8		1				1					2
Cabuliwala	8		1								1	2
Postmaster	8		1									1
Kshudhita Pashan	8										1	1
Nasta-Nir	8											0
Streer Patra	8										1	1
Patra o Patri	8	1			1		1					3
Gupta Dhan	11						1					1
Malyadan	8		1									1
Dristidan	8						1				1	2
Manihara	8									1		1

(Contd.)

Table 4.18a: Punctuation Marks: Additional Punctuations Used

Titles	*Page No. Compared*	.	,	;	:	?	!	“ “ ‘ ‘	’	—	-	*Total*
Gitanjali	15											0
Sanchayita	70											0
Gitabitan	70											0
Galpaguchchha	84		1									1
Ghare-Baire	14		2						1			3
Naukadubi	18		3								4	7
Chaturanga	6											0
Char Adhyay	8										6	6
Bau Thakuranir Hat	10											0
Rajarshi	10		12								3	15
Dui Bon	8										2	2
Chokher Bali	16		9								4	13
Malancha	7		1								3	4
Yogayog	14		5								5	10
Gora	29		15					1			11	27
Sesher Kavita	10		3								3	6
Dakghar	9		4						1		1	6
Raktakarabi	7		1								1	2
Sisu	7		1					2			1	4
Sisu Bholanath	6											0
Chandalika	2	2	5								3	10
Chitrangada	9		2								4	6
Raja o Rani	9		5								3	8
Tin-Sangi	7		3						7		3	13
Chhinnapatra	12											0

(Contd.)

Table 4.18a (Contd.)

Titles	Page No. Compared	.	,	;	:	?	!	" " ' '	'	___	-	Total
Chhada Samagra	5		2						1		1	4
Katha o Kahini	8		4			1						5
Visarjan	7		1						1			2
Sonar Tari	13		1									1
Jivansmriti	16		1									1
Natir Puja	9		6								1	7
Punascha	10		3							2	4	9
Sampatti Samarpan	8							1				1
Swarna Mriga	8											0
Khoka Babur Pratyabartan	8											0
Cabuliwala	8										1	1
Postmaster	8											0
Kshudhita Pashan	8											0
Nasta-Nir	8											0
Streer Patra	8		1								1	2
Patra o Patri	8											0
Gupta Dhan	11								1			1
Malyadan	8											0
Dristidan	8										1	1
Manihara	8											0

Table 4.18b: Other Mistakes

Title	*Page Compared*	*Spelling Mistake*	*Sentence Omitted*	*Word Omitted*	*Sentence Added*	*Word Added*	*Para Clubbed*	*Para Separated*
Gitanjali	15							
Sanchayita	70	1						
Gitabitan	70	3	1	1				
Galpaguchchha	84	3						
Ghare-Baire	14	7	1				2	
Naukadubi	18	5						2
Chaturanga	6	1						
Char Adhyay	8	4					1	
Bau Thakuranir Hat	10	1						
Rajarshi	10	4					4	2
Dui Bon	8	5					5	1
Chokher Bali	16	6		1			19	
Malancha	7	4					4	1
Yogayog	14	10		1				
Gora	29	12					5	
Sesher Kavita	10	9					4	
Dakghar	9	2					3	
Raktakarabi	7					1		
Sisu	7	2					5	
Sisu Bholanath	6							
Chandalika	2							
Chitrangada	9	3						
Raja o Rani	9	2		1				
Tinsangi	7	9				1		

(Contd.)

Table 4.18b (Contd.)

Title	*Page Compared*	*Spelling Mistake*	*Sentence Omitted*	*Word Omitted*	*Sentence Added*	*Word Added*	*Para Clubbed*	*Para Separated*
Chhinnapatra	12	2	1	1				1
Chhada Samagra	5	5	1	1			5	
Katha o Kahini	8	4	1				1	
Visarjan	7							
Sonar Tari	13	1					1	
Jivansmriti	16							
Natir Puja	9	3		1				
Punascha	10	5					9	1
Sampatti Samarpan	8	1						
Swarna Mriga	8	1						
Khoka Babur Pratyabartan	8	2						
Cabuliwala	8	1						
Postmaster	8							
Kshudhita Pashan	8	1						
Nasta-Nir	8							
Streer Patra	8							
Patra o Patri	8						1	
Gupta Dhan	11			1				
Malyadan	8	2						
Dristidan	8	1		1				
Manihara	8	1						

Table 4.19: Textual Comparison: Juthika Book Stall.
Punctuation Marks: Other Punctuation Marks Used or Omitted

Titles	*Page No. Compared*	.	,	:	;	?	!	“ ” ‘ ’	’	—	-	*Total*
Gitanjali	10		6				1	2	1	6	3	19
Sanchayita	59	1	1						2		2	6
Gitabitan	70		4						1		1	6
Galpaguchchha	77	1	8		1			1	2		1	14
Naukadubi	18	9	15		3	4	5	2			10	48
Char Adhyay	4	14	7		1						11	33
Bau Thakuranir Hat	10	8	12		2	8	19	2			2	53
Rajarshi	9	9	26		11	12	6	3		3	5	75
Chokher Bali	15	11	29		18		8	2		2	10	80
Yogayog	14	2	6			1	3	2		1	6	21
Sesher Kavita	7	3	16	1	6	7	2	2	1	15	10	63
Visarjan	7						1					1
Sonar Tari	12											0
Rakta Karabi	7						1					1
Chhinnapatra	12									1		1
Jivansmriti	11		4								2	6
Chitra	13	1					1			1		3
Lipika	7											0

Table 4.19a: Punctuation Marks: Additional Punctuation Marks Used

Titles	*Page No. Compared*	.	,	:	;	?	!	“ ” ‘ ’	’	—	-	*Total*
Gitanjali	10		3						2		4	9
Sanchayita	59											0
Gitabitan	70		2				1					3
Galpaguchchha	77											0
Naukadubi	18		6						2		8	16
Char Adhyay	4		4								14	18
Bau Thakuranir Hat	10	1	5						1		5	12
Rajarshi	9		10								11	21
Chokher Bali	15		29								21	50
Yogayog	14		6						1	1	3	11
Sesher Kavita	7		16						2	1	7	26
Visarjan	7											0
Sonar Tari	12											0
Rakta Karabi	7											0
Chhinnapatra	12											0
Jivansmriti	11		1								2	3
Chitra	13								1			1
Lipika	7											0

Table 4.19b: Other Mistakes

Title	*Page Compared*	*Spelling Mistake*	*Sentence Omitted*	*Word Omitted*	*Sentence Added*	*Word Added*	*Para Clubbed*	*Para Separated*
Gitanjali	10	1						
Sanchayita	59	1		1				
Gitabitan	70	1						
Galpaguchchha	77	5						
Naukadubi	18	10					1	
Char Adhyay	4	9						
Bau-Thakuranir Hat	10	7						
Rajarshi	9	7				1	2	5
Chokher Bali	15	9		1	2		11	
Yogayog	14	3						1
Sesher Kavita	7	8						
Visarjan	7							
Sonar Tari	12	1						
Rakta Karabi	7							
Chhinnapatra	12	1	1					
Jivansmriti	11			2				
Chitra	13					3		
Lipika	7	1						

additional punctuation marks has been used in *Char Adhyay* (4.5 per page). The descending order would be *Sesher Kavita* (3.71 addition per page), *Chokher Bali* (3.33 addition per page)...Even in *Gitanjali* 9 punctuation marks have been added in 10 pages compared. One can observe the highest percentage of spelling mistakes in *Char Adhyay* (2.25 per page), sentences have been deleted in *Chhinnapatra* and *Lipika*, sentences have been added in *Chokher Bali* and the highest number of paragraphs has been clubbed in *Chokher Bali.*

From Table 4.20 it may be concluded that the highest number of change or omission of punctuation marks has been made in *Ghare-Baire* (15.14 per page) and the lowest number in *Gitanjali* (.06 per page). Similarly maximum numbers of punctuation marks are added in *Char Adhyay* (2.14 per page) and no punctuation marks added in *Gitanjali.* Maximum spelling mistakes have been noticed in *Dui Bon* (1 per page), sentences omitted in *Chhinnapatra* (1 sentence in 5 pages), words omitted in *Malancha* (2 words in 5 pages), sentences added in *Bau Thakuranir Hat*, words added in *Dui Bon*, paragraphs clubbed in *Malancha* (3 times in 5 pages), paragraphs separated in *Rajarshi* (5 times in 10 pages). During the study some other omissions/mistakes were observed such as: printing overlapped in pages 150-152 in *Gitanjali*, quote omitted in the entire text of *Chaturanga*. Rabindranath dedicated *Bau Thakuranir Hat* to Soudamini Devi through a poem of 24 lines and *Dui Bon* to Rajsekher Basu but the publication of United Publishers excludes this dedication.

A quick look into the table (4.21) would reveal that the highest and lowest number of other punctuation marks used or not given are *Chaturanga* (7 per page) and *Dui Bon* (no mistake) respectively. Similarly, the highest and lowest number of additional punctuation marks used is again in *Ghare-Baire* (2 per page) and *Gitanjali* (no addition). The highest and lowest number of additional punctuation marks have been used in *Malancha* (1.33 per page) and *Naukadubi* (no addition in 21 pages compared) respectively. The highest number of spelling mistakes occurred in *Karuna* (.66 per page), and sentences omitted in *Malancha* (1 sentence in six pages compared). One important thing that can be observed is even in case of *Gitanjali* there are mistakes in all the three categories. Clubbing of lines on five occasions in 12 pages obviously affects meter, mora and rhythm of the poems of *Gitanjali.* Rabindranath dedicated *Dui Bon* to Rajsekhar Basu but Patraj Publications dedicated it to all lovers of Tagore instead of Basu.

Table 4.20: Textual Comparison: United Publishers.
Punctuation Marks: Other Punctuation Marks Used or Omitted

Titles	*Page No. Compared*	.	,	:	;	?	!	" " ' '	'	—	-	*Total*
Gitanjali	15									1		1
Ghare-Baire	14	51	56		14	5	23			39	24	212
Naukadubi	17	4	14		3	6	3	2			10	42
Chaturanga	6	15	11		5			36		9	1	77
Char Adhyay	7	18	8				2		1	1	6	36
Bau Thakuranir Hat	10	4	12		2	4	6			2	2	32
Rajarshi	10	4	18		8	3	7		1	6	5	52
Dui Bon	7	6	12		4		1	2		1	3	29
Malancha	5	6	13		3	15	3			3	1	44
Yogayog	14	8	20		3	3	4	2		15	1	56
Gora	27	33	100		23	4	16	16		36	35	263
Chhinnapatra	12	1					1		1	1	2	6
Sisu	11	4	6				3	1	1	3	6	24
Sisu Bholanath	6	1	1									2
Chhelebela o Cabuliwala	6								1		1	2

Table 4.20a: Punctuation Marks: Additional Punctuations Used

Titles	Page No. Compared	.	,	:	;	?	!	“ ” ‘ ’	’	—	-	Total
Gitanjali	15											0
Ghare-Baire	14	1	8				1		6	1	12	29
Naukadubi	17		6						2		8	16
Chaturanga	6											0
Char Adhyay	7		4								11	15
Bau Thakuranir Hat	10		2								4	6
Rajarshi	10		7							2	1	10
Dui Bon	7		4								4	8
Malancha	5		5						1	2	2	10
Yogayog	14		5						1		10	16
Gora	27		29		1				1		18	49
Chhinnapatra	12											1
Sisu	11		4						1		6	11
Sisu Bholanath	6		1									1
Chhelebela o Cabuliwala	6										1	1

Table 4.20b: Other Mistakes

Title	*Page Compared*	*Spelling Mistake*	*Sentence Omitted*	*Word Omitted*	*Sentence Added*	*Word Added*	*Para Clubbed*	*Para Separated*
Gitanjali	15	2						
Ghare-Baire	14	9	1				1	5
Naukadubi	17	7		2			1	1
Chaturanga	6	1						
Char Adhyay	7	4						
Bau Thakuranir Hat	10	6			1			
Rajarshi	10	1				1	3	5
Dui Bon	7	7		1		1	2	1
Malancha	5	3		2			3	
Yogayog	14	6		3				
Gora	27	13		1			5	1
Chhinnapatra	12	5	1					
Sisu	11	7		1				
Sisu Bholanath	6							1
Chhelebela o Cabuliwala	6	1						

Table 4.21: Textual Comparison: Patraj Publications.
Punctuation Marks: Other Punctuation Marks Used or Omitted

Titles	*Page No. Compared*	.	,	:	;	?	!	“ ” ‘ ’	’	—	-	*Total*
Gitanjali	12		1									1
Sanchayita	60	1	3					1		1		6
Gitabitan	72	2	1					1		1		5
Galpaguchchha	85	2	18		4		7	3			1	35
Ghare-Baire	17	16	16		8	3	8	1	1	11	14	78
Naukadubi	21		1								1	2
Chaturanga	7	8	1		2		1	33			4	49
Char Adhyay	8	1						1				2
Bau Thakuranir Hat	12	2	9		5	3	11	7		2	4	43
Rajarshi	11									1		1
Dui Bon	6											0
Chokher Bali	17	8	10		11		3			2	11	45
Karuna	6	1	2								3	6
Malancha	6	3	5		3	12	21	2	1	1	3	51
Yogayog	19	2	4			2					1	9

Table 4.21a: Punctuation Marks: Additional Punctuation Marks Used

Titles	*Page No. Compared*	.	,	:	;	?	!	“ ” ‘ ’	’	—	-	*Total*
Gitanjali	12		1									1
Sanchayita	60		1									1
Gitabitan	72								1		3	4
Galpaguchchha	85		4						3		1	8
Ghare-Baire	17		3								3	6
Naukadubi	21											0
Chaturanga	7											0
Char Adhyay	8											0
Bau Thakuranir Hat	12		4								5	9
Rajarshi	11											0
Dui Bon	6											0
Chokher Bali	17		3								2	5
Karuna	6										1	1
Malancha	6		4								4	8
Yogayog	19		2								6	8

Table 4.21b: Other Mistakes

Title	*Page Compared*	*Spelling Mistake*	*Sentence Omitted*	*Word Omitted*	*Line Added*	*Word Added*	*Para Clubbed*	*Para Separated*
Gitanjali	12						5	
Sanchayita	60	3						
Gitabitan	72	5		2		5		
Galpaguchchha	85	6				1	3	
Ghare-Baire	17	4		1			2	1
Naukadubi	21	2	2					
Chaturanga	7	3					1	
Char Adhyay	8	2	1					
Bau Thakuranir Hat	12	3					2	
Rajarshi	11	5	1					
Dui Bon	6	1						
Chokher Bali	17		1		1		6	
Karuna	6	4		1				
Malancha	6	17	1				3	
Yogayog	19	4						

Table 4.22: Textual Comparison: Punascha.
Punctuation Marks: Other Punctuation Marks Used or Omitted

Titles	*Page No. Compared*	.	,	:	;	?	!	“ ” ‘ ’	’	—	-	*Total*
Gitanjali	17											0
Sanchayita	57	2								1	1	4
Gitabitan	66		1							1	2	4
Galpaguchchha	65	31	117	2	32	3	11	11	1	17	53	278
Gora	23	18	104		31	5	18	17		54	29	276
Ghare-Baire	9	53	50		19	4	19			30	22	197
Naukadubi	14	1	8		1	4	4	1		4	9	32
Chaturanga	14	7	36		13	1	2	11		1	13	84
Char Adhyay	6	14	16		2	13	17	1		7	11	81
Bau-Thakuranir Hat	7	5	8		1	7	4			2	1	28
Rajarshi	7	4	21		9	14	8	1	1	10	12	80

Table 4.22a: Punctuation Marks: Additional Punctuation Marks Used

Titles	*Page No. Compared*	.	,	:	;	?	!	" " ' '	'	—	-	*Total*
Gitanjali	17											0
Sanchayita	57		1									1
Gitabitan	66		1						1		3	5
Galpaguchchha	65		37						3	1	38	79
Gora	23		31					1		2	19	53
Ghare-Baire	9		10						1		15	26
Naukadubi	14		8								8	16
Chaturanga	14		9					1	1	1	6	18
Char Adhyay	6		9							1	8	18
Bau-Thakuranir Hat	7		2								2	4
Rajarshi	7		8								5	13

Table 4.22b: Other Mistakes

Title	*Page Compared*	*Spelling Mistake*	*Sentence Omitted*	*Word Omitted*	*Sentence Added*	*Word Added*	*Para Clubbed*	*Para Separated*
Gitanjali	17							
Sanchayita	57	3						
Gitabitan	66			2		3		
Galpaguchchha	65	52				14	7	1
Gora	23	14					1	
Ghare-Baire	9	3		1			1	
Naukadubi	14	8		1		2	2	
Chaturanga	14	2		1			1	
Char Adhyay	6	3	20					
Bau-Thakuranir Hat	7	6						
Rajarshi	7	6				1	2	6

From the comparative Tables (4.22, 4.22a, 4.22b) of books published by Punascha and Visva-Bharati it is clear that special care for publication of *Gitanjali* has been taken as it has no mistake in all the three categories. In case of others, punctuation marks used or not used and additional marks used, *Ghare-Baire* and *Chaturanga* commit the highest number of mistakes—22 per page and 3 per page respectively. The highest number of spelling mistakes occurred in *Char Adhyay* (.86 per page), words omitted in *Ghare-Baire* (1 in 9 page), and words added in *Galpaguchchha* (14 words in 65 pages). In *Char Adhyay* which is a combination of *Char Adhyay* and *Malancha* (Visva-Bharati has no such combined publication) 20 sentences (five paragraphs) have been omitted in *Malancha.* Actually it starts from sixth paragraph. *Saralipipanji* is an important reference of notation to the songs omitted in *Gitabitan* and Rabindranath's dedication of *Ghare-Baire* to Pramathanath Chowdhury not included.

Ashok Book Agency changed the title of *Jivansmriti* to *Rabindranather Jivansmriti* with the highest number of mistakes in the entire three categories such as change or omission of punctuation marks (17 per page), addition of punctuation marks (1.91 per page) and spelling mistakes (1.81 per page). On the other hand in *Gitanjali* (1 comma deleted, 1 comma added and one line clubbed in 12 pages compared) and in *Punascha* there are 4 mistakes in punctuation marks, 1 addition of punctuation mark and 1 spelling mistake. The publisher has no book without any mistakes. In Visva-Bharati edition of *Gitabitan,* saralipipanji, subject and photograph indexes as well as first-line-of-the-song index are provided, but the edition brought out by Ashok Book Agency lacks all these important references. The name of the printer in *Yogayog* and Rabindranath's dedication of Punascha to 'Nitu' are not included.

Out of 9 books published by Granthasambhar *Gitanjali* is their best production in respect of other punctuation marks used or not given, addition of punctuation marks and other mistakes (with 1 deletion of dash in page 131, and one spelling mistake in page 31 out of 15 pages compared). On the other in *Ghare-Baire, Gora* and *Malancha* maximum number of other punctuation marks used or deleted (14.93, 10.11 and 6.05 per page respectively). In *Chokher Bali, Gora* and *Ghare-Baire* maximum number of additional punctuation marks per page used (2.63, 1.79 and 1.71 per page) respectively. In *Ghare-Baire, Chokher Bali* and *Malancha* maximum number of spelling mistakes (.71, .62 and .56 per page) respectively

Table 4.23: Textual Comparison: Ashok Book Agency.
Punctuation Marks: Other Punctuation Marks Used or Omitted

Titles	*Page No. Compared*	.	,	:	;	?	!	" " ' '	'	—	-	*Total*
Gitanjali	12		1									1
Sanchayita	62	2	5		4	2	5	1		3	3	25
Gitabitan	72	1	4				2				2	9
Galpaguchchha	88	2	8		5		2				11	28
Naukadubi	21	6	7	1	1	2	8	1			11	37
Chokher Bali	17	2	4		3			1		1		11
Yogayog	16	3	13		3		6	4	1		23	53
Sonar Tari	12	4	21		4			1			28	58
Rabindranather Jivansmriti	13	4	99		11		4	15	1	5	82	221
Punascha	12		1				1				2	4

Table 4.23a: Punctuation Marks: Additional Punctuation Marks Used

Titles	*Page No. Compared*	.	,	:	;	?	!	“ “ ‘ ‘	’	—	-	*Total*
Gitanjali	12		1									1
Sanchayita	62		2						1			3
Gitabitan	72	1	3							1		5
Galpaguchchha	88	1	8						1		2	12
Naukadubi	21		7								4	11
Chokher Bali	17	1	8								2	11
Yogayog	16	1	6							1	9	17
Sonar Tari	12		6				1		3		11	21
Rabindranather Jivansmriti	13	1	7								15	23
Punascha	12		1									1

Table 4.23b: Other Mistakes

Titles	*Page Compared*	*Spelling Mistake*	*Sentence Omitted*	*Word Omitted*	*Line Added*	*Word Added*	*Para Clubbed*	*Para Separated*
Gitanjali	12			1			1	
Sanchayita	62	5						
Gitabitan	72	2	2					
Galpaguchchha	88	10						
Naukadubi	21	8				2		
Chokher Bali	17	1					1	1
Yogayog	16	9						
Sonar Tari	12	12						
Rabindranather Jivansmriti	13	23		1				
Punascha	12	1						

Table 4.24: Textual Comparison: Granthasambhar.
Punctuation Marks: Other Punctuation Marks Used or Omitted

Titles	*Page No. Compared*	.	,	:	;	?	!	“ ” ‘ ’	’	—	-	*Total*
Gitanjali	15									1		1
Sanchayita	70		3				2				2	7
Ghare-Baire	14	53	52	1	12	6	23		2	35	25	209
Naukadubi	17	4	14		3	6	3	2			10	42
Malancha	18	25	28	1	8	16	8	2	2	4	15	109
Yogayog	14	6	22		3	3	2			2	10	48
Gora	28	29	105		29	8	31	14		44	23	283
Chhinnapatra	12	2				1			1	1	4	9
Chokher Bali	16	9	24		14	3	7	2	1	4	17	81

Table 4.24a: Punctuation Marks: Additional Punctuation Marks Used

Titles	*Page No. Compared*	.	,	:	;	?	!	“ ” ‘ ’	’	—	-	*Total*
Gitanjali	15											0
Sanchayita	70											0
Ghare-Baire	14		10						2		12	24
Naukadubi	17		6						2		8	16
Malancha	18		10						1	2	13	26
Yogayog	14		5								8	13
Gora	28		31		1				1	1	16	50
Chhinnapatra	12										1	1
Chokher Bali	16		23								19	42

Table 4.24b: Other Mistakes

Title	*Page Compared*	*Spelling Mistake*	*Sentence Omitted*	*Word Omi-- tted*	*Sentence Added*	*Word Added*	*Para Clubbed*	*Para Separated*
Gitanjali	15	1						
Sanchayita	70	2		2				
Ghare-Baire	14	10	1				1	5
Naukadubi	17	7		2			1	1
Malancha	18	10		2			7	1
Yogayog	14	5		1				
Gora	28	15					3	2
Chhinnapatra	12	6						
Chokher Bali	16	10					12	

Table 4.25: Textual Comparison: Sahityam.
Punctuation Marks: Other Punctuation Marks Used or Omitted

Titles	*Page No. Compared*	.	,	:	;	?	!	“ ” ‘ ’	’	—	-	*Total*
Gitanjali	14											0
Sanchayita	62	1								3		4
Gitabitan	71		5		1		1		1			8
Galpaguchchha	89	12	28	1	4	1	4			5	30	85
Sesher Kavita	13		1		1							2
Sisu	17						1					1
Sisu Bholanath	8											0

Table 4.25a: Punctuation Marks: Additional Punctuation Marks Used

Titles	*Page No. Compared*	.	,	:	;	?	!	“ ” ‘ ’	’	—	-	*Total*
Gitanjali	14											0
Sanchayita	62											0
Gitabitan	71		2									2
Galpaguchchha	89	1	23		1				1		3	29
Sesher Kavita	13		2					1				3
Sisu	17											0
Sisu Bholanath	8											0

Table 4.25b: Other Mistakes

Title	*Page Compared*	*Spelling Mistake*	*Sentence Omitted*	*Word Omitted*	*Sentence Added*	*Word Added*	*Para Clubbed*	*Para Separated*
Gitanjali	14							1
Sanchayita	62	1					8	
Gitabitan	71	3						
Galpaguchchha	89	8		1		1		2
Sesher Kavita	13							
Sisu	17							
Sisu Bholanath	8							

can be observed. In *Ghare-Baire* 1 sentence has been omitted, 1 paragraph clubbed and 5 paragraphs separated. Thus *Ghare-Baire* happens to be the worst production in respect of mistakes of Granthasambhar.

Galpaguchchha published by Sahityam possesses the highest number of mistakes relating to the category 'other punctuation marks used, not used or additional marks used' (.96, .35 per page respectively). On the other hand, the best production is *Gitanjali* as far as punctuation marks are concerned; only one line of the first poem is divided into two lines. *Galpaguchchha* is having the highest number of spelling mistakes (8 in 89 pages compared) and *Sanchayita* the highest number of paragraphs (line in case of poem) clubbed. However, it does not hamper the flow or rhythm of the poems as all these clubbings are in places and dates of writing at the end of the poem.

Table 4.26: Textual Comparison: Gitanjali.
Punctuation Marks: Other Punctuation Marks Used or Omitted

Titles	*Page No. Compared*	.	,	:	;	?	!	" " ' '	'	—	-	*Total*
Sesher Kavita	10	6	21		11	2	2	4		10	16	72
Sisu	9	2									1	3
Sisu Bholanath	6										1	1
Chhinnapatra	12	1						1			3	5
Chhelebela	6	3	1					1		1	2	8
Kshudhita Pashan	9						1					1

Table 4.26a: Punctuation Marks: Additional Punctuation Marks Used

Titles	*Page No. Compared*	.	,	:	;	?	!	" " ' '	'	—	-	*Total*
Sesher Kavita	10		5		1			2	1		7	16
Sisu	9		1						1		1	3
Sisu Bholanath	6											0
Chhinnapatra	12										1	1
Chhelebela	6		3						1		1	5
Kshudhita Pashan	9											0

It is observed from the above tables (4.26, 4.26a, 4.26b) that *Sesher Kavita* published by Gitanjali contains the highest number of mistakes per page in the entire three categories (7.2 per page in other punctuation marks used or not given, 1.6 additional punctuation

Table 4.26b: Other Mistakes

Title	Page Compared	Spelling Mistake	Sentence Omitted	Word Omitted	Line Added	Word Added	Para Clubbed	Para Separated
Sesher Kavita	10	11				1	1	
Sisu	9	3						
Sisu Bholanath	6			1				
Chhinnapatra	12	8						1
Chhelebela	6	13				1		
Kshudhita Pashan	9	2						

punctuation marks per page, 1.1 spelling mistake per page). *Sisu Bholanath* and *Kshudhita Pashan* bear fewer mistakes—mark omitted (page 5), one word omitted, one punctuation mark changed (! used as.) and two spelling mistakes occurred in page 35.

Table 4.27: Textual Comparison: Tuli-Kalam.
Punctuation Marks: Other Punctuation Marks Used or Omitted

Titles	Page No. Compared	.	,	:	;	?	!	" " ' '	'	—	-	Total
Gitanjali	18										1	1
Sanchayita	77	7									1	8
Gitabitan	89	7								1		8
Galpaguchchha	77	31	186		23	7	27	30	11	30	122	467
Chhelebela	6	5	15		3		2	2	3	7	24	61
Lipika o Sey	19	4	19		4	21	12	1	12	8	28	109

Table 4.27a: Punctuation Marks: Additional Punctuation Marks Used

Titles	Page No. Compared	.	,	:	;	?	!	" " ' '	'	—	-	Total
Gitanjali	18		1									1
Sanchayita	77											0
Gitabitan	89								1			1
Galpaguchchha	77	1	79		1				6		36	123
Chhelebela	6		3						1		2	6
Lipika o Sey	19		14						1		6	21

Table 4.27b: Other Mistakes

Title	*Page Compared*	*Spelling Mistake*	*Sentence Omitted*	*Word Omitted*	*Sentence Added*	*Word Added*	*Para Clubbed*	*Para Separated*
Gitanjali	18							
Sanchayita	77				1		2	
Gitabitan	89	1						
Galpaguchchha	77	56					21	2
Chhelebela	6	31					4	2
Lipika o Sey	19	20	1			1	1	

Tuli-Kalam published two separate books *Lipika* and *Sey* under one cover with the title *Lipika o Sey*. The mistakes in respect of other punctuation marks used or omitted can be noticed in *Chhelebala* (10.17 per page), *Galpaguchchha* (6.07 per page) and in *Lipika o Sey* (5.74 per page) and additional punctuation marks used in *Galpaguchchha* (1.60 per page), *Lipika o Sey* (1.10 per page) and *Chhelebala* (1 per page). The highest number of spelling mistakes can also be observed again in these books *Chhelebala* (5.17 per page), *Lipika o Sey* (1.05 per page) and *Galpaguchchha* (.73 per page). Two punctuation-mark mistakes, deletion of one hyphen in page number 155 and addition of one comma in page 165 can also be observed. The second line of poem number XXIII of *Gitanjali* (it is bi-lingual edition) in page 155 starts with small letter ('the' used instead of 'The'). In *Gitanjali*, the important reference of Kavyagrantha wherefrom the poems are taken is not given.

Table 4.28: Textual Comparison: Patra-Bharati.
Punctuation Marks: Other Punctuation Marks Used or Omitted

Titles	*Page No. Compared*	.	,	:	;	?	!	" " ' '	'	—	-	*Total*
Ghare-Baire	25	2			1		1				1	5
Chaturanga	9	2	2		2			1		1		8
Char Adhyay	9										1	1
Malancha	9											0
Sesher Kavita	14	1	1								1	3

Table 4.28a: Punctuation Marks: Additional Punctuation Marks Used

Titles	*Page No. Compared*	.	,	:	;	?	!	" " ' '	,	__	-	*Total*
Ghare-Baire	25											0
Chaturanga	9										1	1
Char Adhyay	9											0
Malancha	9											0
Sesher Kavita	14											0

Table 4.28b: Other Mistakes

Title	*Page Compared*	*Spelling Mistake*	*Sentence Omitted*	*Word Omitted*	*Line Added*	*Word Added*	*Para Clubbed*	*Para Separated*
Ghare-Baire	25							
Chaturanga	9	3						
Char Adhyay	9							
Malancha	9							
Sesher Kavita	14							

Out of the six titles published by Patra Bharati *Chaturanga* contains the highest number of mistakes in respect of other punctuation marks used—0.89 per page, one additional punctuation mark was used and three spelling mistakes were noticed in 9 pages compared. Use of additional punctuation marks and other mistakes in respect of 'spelling, omission/addition of sentence/word' is less in comparison to many other publishers under study. It is significant to note that Patra Bharati has not published popular titles like *Gitanjali, Galpaguchchha, Gitabitan* and *Sanchayita.*

Table 4.29: Textual Comparison: Nirmal Book Agency
Punctuation Marks: Other Punctuation Marks Used or Omitted

Titles	*Page No. Compared*	.	,	:	;	?	!	" " ' '	,	__	-	*Total*
Chhelebela	7											0
Khapchhada	16											0
Khoka Babur Pratyabartan	8	4										4
Chhuti	8					1					1	2
Cabuliwala	8											0

Table 4.29a: Punctuation Marks: Additional Punctuation Marks Used

Titles	Page No. Compared	.	,	:	;	?	!	“ ” ‘ ’	,	__	-	Total
Chhelebela	7		3								3	6
Khapchhada	16											0
Khoka Babur Pratyabartan	8										1	1
Chhuti	8											0
Cabuliwala	8											0

Table 4.29b: Other Mistakes

Title	Page Compared	Spelling Mistake	Sentence Omitted	Word Omitted	Line Added	Word Added	Para Clubbed	Para Separated
Chhelebela	7		2	2				
Khapchhada	16							
Khoka Babur Pratyabartan	8							
Chhuti	8							
Cabuliwala	8							

All the five titles published by Nirmal Book Agency are for children of which three are short stories printed separately as individual title from *Galpaguchchha*. Illustrations included in three short stories—*Khoka Babur Pratyabartan, Chhuti* and *Cabuliwala* and also in *Chhelebela*. In *Khoka Babur Pratyabartan* the highest number of other punctuation marks used or omitted is found to be 0.5 per page, in *Chhelebela* maximum number of additional punctuation marks is noticed (.86 per page) and also two sentences and two words are omitted. But there are titles like *Khapchhada, Cabuliwala* with no mistakes in any category. A large portion of Granthaparichaya is copied in *Khapchhada* from Visva-Bharati without reference to it.

Table 4.30: Textual Comparison: Asia Publishing Company.
Punctuation Marks: Other Punctuation Marks Used or Omitted

Titles	Page No. Compared	.	,	:	;	?	!	“ ” ‘ ’	,	__	-	Total
Gitanjali	21	3	14			1	4	2	9		7	40
Sanchayita	57	2	1				2		24		1	30
Gitabitan	69	2							33			35
Galpaguchchha	73		2						13		1	16
Chhotader Lekha	38	25	50		4	10	18	3	38	25	32	205

Table 4.30a: Punctuation Marks: Additional Punctuation Marks Used

Titles	*Page No. Compared*	.	,	:	;	?	!	“ ” ‘ ’	,	—	-	*Total*
Gitanjali	21		8				2				9	19
Sanchayita	57											0
Gitabitan	69											0
Galpaguchchha	73										1	1
Chhotader Lekha	38		28							3	16	47

Table 4.30b: Other Mistakes

Title	*Page Compared*	*Spelling Mistake*	*Sentence Omitted*	*Word Omitted*	*Line Added*	*Word Added*	*Para Clubbed*	*Para Separated*
Gitanjali	21	8					39	
Sanchayita	57	24						
Gitabitan	69	48						
Galpaguchchha	73	125						
Chhotader Lekha	38	71	12	7			2	33

Chhotader Lekha is a collection of poems, songs, short stories, etc. from various writings of Tagoreana. But this book for children possesses the highest number of mistakes in all the three categories such as other punctuation marks used or omitted (5.39 per page), additional punctuation marks (1.90 per page) and spelling mistakes (1.89 per page). Even in case of *Gitanjali* proper care has not been taken as a result it conations 40 mistakes in other punctuation marks used or omitted group, 19 additional punctuation marks have been used and 8 spelling mistakes noticed in 21 pages compared. Not only those in 39 occasions lines are clubbed which certainly hampers the spirit, rhythm, even changes the meaning of poems in Gitanjali. In the content part of *Sanchayita* place, date of writing of poems is not provided like Visva-Bharati edition.

Table 4.31: Textual Comparison: Narayan Pustakalaya.
Punctuation Marks: Other Punctuation Marks Used or Omitted

Titles	*Page No. Compared*	.	,	:	;	?	!	" " ' '	,	—	-	*Total*
Gitanjali	15											0
Sanchayita	70	3	1				1				2	7
Gitabitan	70	4	3						1	1	1	10
Galpaguchchha	84	1	11				4		1		5	22

Table 4.31a: Punctuation Marks: Additional Punctuation Marks Used

Titles	*Page No. Compared*	.	,	;	:	?	!	" " ' '	;	—	-	*Total*
Gitanjali	15											0
Sanchayita	70											0
Gitabitan	70											0
Galpaguchchha	84		1									1

Table 4.31b: Other Mistakes

Title	*Page Compared*	*Spelling Mistake*	*Sentence Omitted*	*Word Omitted*	*Line Added*	*Word Added*	*Para Clubbed*	*Para Separated*
Gitanjali	15							
Sanchayita	70	1						
Gitabitan	70	3	1	1				
Galpaguccha	84	3						

Gitanjali is the best book published by Narayan Pustakalaya with no mistakes. *Galpaguchchha* contains maximum punctuation-mark mistakes (26 per page) and *Gitabitan* contains the highest number of spelling mistakes (3 in 70 pages compared) and sentence and word omitted (1 in each category). As a whole in comparison to other publishers Narayan Pustakalaya gave emphasis in proof reading. It is interesting to note that Narayan Pustakalaya commits the same mistakes as done by Kamini Prakashalaya in *Sanchayita, Gitabitan* and *Galpaguchchha*.

Table 4.32: Textual Comparison: Mitra and Ghosh
Punctuation Marks: Other Punctuation Marks Used or Omitted

Titles	*Page No. Compared*	.	,	:	;	?	!	" " ' '	,	—	-	*Total*
Jivansmriti	24		8		9			1		2	1	21
Sahaj Path-1	6											0
Sahaj Path-2	6											0
Kishor Rabindra Rachanavali	72	6	30		6	3	5		3	8	23	84

Table 4.32a: Punctuation Marks: Additional Punctuation Marks Used

Titles	*Page No. Compared*	.	,	:	;	?	!	" " ' '	,	__	-	*Total*
Jivansmriti	24									1	2	3
Sahaj Path-1	6											0
Sahaj Path-2	6											0
Kishor Rabindra Rachanavali	72		6							1	7	14

Table 4.32b: Other Mistakes

Title	*Page Compared*	*Spelling Mistake*	*Sentence Omitted*	*Word Omitted*	*Line Added*	*Word Added*	*Para Clubbed*	*Para Separated*
Jivansmriti	24	4						
Sahaj Path-1	6	1						
Sahaj Path-2	6	2						
Kishor Rabindra Rachanavali	72	5	1	1		1	2	1

Mitra and Ghosh, one of the leading publishers of Bengali Books in India, published only four books of Rabindranath so far. Out of four titles two (*Sahaj Path* 1 and 2) are school textbooks for Class I and Class II and *Kishor Rabindra Rachanavali* is a collection of poems, songs, short stories, drama, etc. for children. But *Kishor Rabindra Rachanavali* possesses higher number of mistakes (1.17 per page), in other punctuation marks used or omitted category, 19 per page in additional punctuation marks used and other mistakes category as well. Three spelling mistakes in *Sahaj Path* can be noticed, but in the half title page of this book there is a declaration that the publisher follows the spelling system of West Bengal Bangla Academy. In this study they are considered as mistakes. As *Jivansmriti* is an edited book by Baridbaran Ghosh it provides notes and references at the end of each chapter and an index of content at the end.

Table 4.33: Textual Comparison: Radha Pustakalaya.
Punctuation Marks: Other Punctuation Marks Used or Omitted

Titles	*Page No. Compared*	.	,	:	;	?	!	“ ” ‘ ’	’	—	-	*Total*
Sanchayita	70		2				1				1	4
Gitabitan	70		4							1		5
Galpaguchchha	84	1	11				4		1		5	22

Table 4.33a: Punctuation Marks: Additional Punctuation Marks Used

Titles	*Page No. Compared*	.	,	:	;	?	!	“ ” ‘ ’	’	—	-	*Total*
Sanchayita	70										1	1
Gitabitan	70		1				1					2
Galpaguchchha	84		1									1

Table 4.33b: Other Mistakes

Title	*Page Compared*	*Spelling Mistake*	*Sentence Omitted*	*Word Omitted*	*Line Added*	*Word Added*	*Para Clubbed*	*Para Separated*
Sanchayita	70	4	--	--	--	--	--	--
Gitabitan	70	2	--	--	--	--	--	--
Galpaguchchha	84	3	--	--	--	--	--	--

Out of the three books considered for comparison published by Radha Pustakalaya in *Galpaguchchha* the highest number of other punctuation marks has been used or omitted, similarly maximum additional punctuation marks are used in *Gitabitan* and maximum spelling mistakes are noticed in *Sanchayita* (4 in 70 pages compared). At the end of *Galpaguchchha* (pages 84) five lines of a letter of Rabindranath written to Bijaychandra Majumder dated 24th July, 1932 are not related to the text.

Table 4.34: Textual Comparison: Reflect Publication.
Punctuation Marks: Other Punctuation Marks Used or Omitted

Titles	*Page No. Compared*	.	,	:	;	?	!	“ ” ‘ ’	’	__	-	*Total*
Sanchayita	40	63	110		34	9	32	3	18	82	63	414
Gitabitan	52	14	15						5	4	1	39
Galpaguchchha	61	43	164		34	6	23	9	20	13	166	478

Table 4.34a: Punctuation Marks: Additional Punctuation Marks Used

Titles	*Page No. Compared*	.	,	:	;	?	!	“ ” ‘ ’	’	__	-	*Total*
Sanchayita	40	3	47					1	6	3	43	103
Gitabitan	52		3						1		11	15
Galpaguchchha	61	2	84				1			1	6	94

Table 4.34b: Other Mistakes

Title	*Page Compared*	*Spelling Mistake*	*Sentence Omitted*	*Word Omitted*	*Sentence Added*	*Word Added*	*Para Clubbed*	*Para Separated*
Sanchayita	40	32					1	
Gitabitan	52	3		1		1		
Galpaguchchha	61	73	1	1	1	1	11	5

The price offered by Reflect Publication is lowest in comparison to all other private publishers. Reflect Publication published *Sanchayita*, *Gitabitan* and *Galpaguchchha*. To keep the price low, the publisher reduced the number of pages in each title and used small font size and less space between lines and also in margin, which led to more mistakes in punctuation marks, spelling, etc. *Sanchayita* has been published with the highest number of mistakes in respect of use or omission of punctuation marks (10.35 per page) and also in addition of punctuation marks (2.58 per page) while the highest number of spelling mistakes (1.20 per page), sentence/word omission, addition and clubbing/separation of paragraph can be found in *Galpaguchchha*.

Table 4.35: Textual Comparison: Das Sahitya Kuthir.
Punctuation Marks: Other Punctuation Marks Used or Omitted

Titles	*Page No. Compared*	.	,	:	;	?	!	“ ” ‘ ’	’	—	-	*Total*
Chaturanga	6	16	14		7			34		8	2	81
Char Adhyay	11	17	12	1	5	1	3	3	2	1	12	57
Dui Bon	10	7	20	1	6	15	3	3	1	3	2	61

Table 4.35a: Punctuation Marks: Additional Punctuation Marks Used

Titles	*Page No. Compared*	.	,	:	;	?	!	“ ” ‘ ’	’	—	-	*Total*
Chaturanga	6		1								1	2
Char Adhyay	11		4			1			1		12	18
Dui Bon	10	1	10						1		7	19

Table 4.35b: Other Mistakes

Title	*Page Compared*	*Spelling Mistake*	*Sentence Omitted*	*Word Omitted*	*Line Added*	*Word Added*	*Para Clubbed*	*Para Separated*
Chaturanga	6	2						
Char Adhyay	11	3					3	1
Dui Bon	10	6		2			6	1

The maximum mistakes noticed in use of or omission of punctuation marks are as follows: *Chaturanga* (13.5 per page), *Dui Bon* (6.10 per page) and *Char Adhyay* (5.18 per page). In case of additional punctuation marks used *Dui Bon* (1.91 per page) ranks first followed by *Char Adhyay* (1.64 per page) and *Chaturanga* (.33 per page). The publisher made maximum mistakes in *Dui Bon*—spelling (.6 per page), word omission (.33 per page) and paragraph clubbed (.6 per page). It is interesting to note that page number starts from 833 in *Chaturanga*, 1370 in *Char Adhyay* and 1276 in *Dui Bon.*

Table 4.36: Textual Comparison: Bookfront Publication Forum.
Punctuation Marks: Other Punctuation Marks Used or Omitted

Titles	*Page No. Compared*	.	,	:	;	?	!	“ ” ‘ ’	’	—	-	*Total*
Postmaster o Chhuti	4		2		1						3	6
Kshudhita Pashan	4	1	2							1	4	8
Atithi	4	1	2					1		1	3	8

Table 4.36a: Punctuation Marks: Additional Punctuation Marks Used

Titles	*Page No. Compared*	.	,	:	;	?	!	“ ” ‘ ’	’	—	-	*Total*
Postmaster o Chhuti	4		1								1	2
Kshudhita Pashan	4		3									3
Atithi	4											0

Table 4.36b: Other Mistakes

Title	*Page Compared*	*Spelling Mistake*	*Sentence Omitted*	*Word Omitted*	*Line Added*	*Word Added*	*Para Clubbed*	*Para Separated*
Postmaster o Chhuti	4	14						
Kshudhita Pashan	4	3		1				
Atithi	4	2					1	

Bookfront Publication Forum published only four short stories as three individual titles from *Galpaguchchha* with larger font. Still it has made a good number of mistakes in the entire category. The title on the cover page of a book is given as *Postmaster o Chhuti* which is a combination of two short stories *Postmaster* and *Chhuti* but in title page ‘o’ is deleted.

Table 4.37: Textual Comparison: Prakash Bhavana.
Punctuation Marks: Other Punctuation Marks Used or Omitted

Titles	*Page No. Compared*	.	,	:	;	?	!	“ ” ‘ ’	’	—	-	*Total*
Sisu Bholanath	6											0
Chhelebela	5		2						1			3

Table: 4.37a: Punctuation Marks: Additional Punctuation Marks Used

Titles	*Page No. Compared*	.	,	:	;	?	!	“ ” ‘ ’	’	—	-	*Total*
Sisu Bholanath	6											0
Chhelebela	5										2	2

Table 4.37b: Other Mistakes

Title	*Page Compared*	*Spelling Mistake*	*Sentence Omitted*	*Word Omitted*	*Line Added*	*Word Added*	*Para Clubbed*	*Para Separated*
Sisu Bholanath	6							
Chhelebela	5	2						

Out of two titles published by Prakash Bhavana *Sisu Bholanath* has no mistake in the entire category and *Chhelebela* has fewer mistakes in comparison to many other publishers' books.

Table 4.38: Textual Comparison: Baksahitya.
Punctuation Marks: Other Punctuation Marks Used or Omitted

Titles	*Page No. Compared*	.	,	:	;	?	!	“ ” ‘ ’	’	—	-	*Total*
Rajarshi	14										2	2

Table 4.38a: Punctuation Marks: Additional Punctuation Marks Used

Titles	*Page No. Compared*	.	,	:	;	?	!	“ ” ‘ ’	’	—	-	*Total*
Rajarshi	14											0

Table 4.38b: Other Mistakes

Title	*Page Compared*	*Spelling Mistake*	*Sentence Omitted*	*Word Omitted*	*Line Added*	*Word Added*	*Para Clubbed*	*Para Separated*
Rajarshi	14		1					

Table 4.39: Textual Comparison: Rajarshi Prakashan.
Punctuation Marks: Other Punctuation Marks Used or Omitted

Titles	Page No. Compared	.	,	:	;	?	!	" " ' '	,	—	-	Total
Sesher Kavita	10	4	23	1	7	14		3	5	11	6	74

Table 4.39a: Punctuation Marks: Additional Punctuation Marks Used

Titles	Page No. Compared	.	,	:	;	?	!	" " ' '	,	—	-	Total
Sesher Kavita	10		15						1		11	17

Table 4.39b: Other Mistakes

Title	Page Compared	Spelling Mistake	Sentence Omitted	Word Omitted	Line Added	Word Added	Para Clubbed	Para Separated
Sesher Kavita	10	5		1			1	

Table 4.40: Textual Comparison: Suranjana Prakashani.
Punctuation Marks: Other Punctuation Marks Used or Omitted

Title	Page No. Compared	.	,	:	;	?	!	" " ' '	,	—	-	Total
Sesher Kavita	12	2	19		8	8	2	2	4	11	9	65

Table 4.40a: Punctuation Marks: Additional Punctuation Marks Used

Title	Page No. Compared	.	,	:	;	?	!	" " ' '	,	—	-	Total
Sesher Kavita	12	1	13					1			4	19

Table 4.40b: Other Mistakes

Title	Page Compared	Spelling Mistake	Sentence Omitted	Word Omitted	Line Added	Word Added	Para Clubbed	Para Separated
Sesher Kavita	12	6	1					

A comparative analysis of publishers publishing single book reveals that *Rajarshi* published by Baksahitya possesses less number of mistakes in punctuation marks but one sentence is omitted. *Sesher Kavita* published by Rajarshi Prakashan and Suranjana Prakashani contains a good number of mistakes in all categories. *Sahaj Path* was published by Visva-Bharati with black and white illustrations made by Nandalal Bose, one of the famous artists of India. But *Sahaj Path* published by Babli and Sahitya Bharati changed the illustrations; as a result, on many occasions the content and illustrations do not match, even the idea is violated sometimes. For example in the illustration of 5th and 6th letter of *swarabarna* drawn by Bose, two dogs are barking one raising his head and another just downing his head near the neck of the first one as if recognizing his call. But illustrations provided in *Sahaj Path* published by Babli for the same through two dogs chained in a pole are far away from the concept.

4.10 Conclusion

It was observed during the study that though most of the books published by private publishers are hardbound, the binding as well as paper and printing quality in general is poor except the publication of Mitra and Ghosh. Regarding design of cover page Visva-Bharati follows a house style of saffron cover (with such exceptions as *Raktakarabi*, *Chhinnapatra, Natir puja, Khapchhada, Chandalika* and *Sey*) which is the symbol of sacrifice with title and signature of Rabindranath Tagore in front cover in brown or red and Visva-Bharati logo, price and ISBN at the back cover. Out of 186 titles compared for this study, cover pages of 64 books contain photograph of Rabindranath, 21 contain paintings and drawings of Rabindranath, and theme of the story is drawn in 89 titles and 12 titles with theme and Rabindranath's photo both. The cover page with theme is mostly scene of cinematography of Rabindranath's popular novels.

In case of Tagoreana published by Visva-Bharati, either there is an introduction by Rabindranath Tagore himself (with the exception in *Gitanjali* where the introduction is by W.B. Yeats) or without any introduction. For example, out of 41 titles compared for this study, on 14 occasions Rabindranath wrote the introduction. In most of the cases books published by private publishers included the introduction of Rabindranath whenever available and at the same time introduction written by some others also included. It is interesting to note that Sudeb Mukhopadhyay (no official address given) wrote introductions for three publishers: Kamini Prakashalaya (in 14 books), United Publisher (in 2 books) and Granthasambhar (in 2 books). The same introduction was used thrice in *Gitanjali* published by three publishers, twice in *Chhinnapatra* published by Kamini Prakashalaya and Granthasambhar and twice in *Rajarshi* published by Kamini Prakashalaya and United Publisher. Other persons to introduce Tagoreana are Kamakshiprasad Bandyopadhyay (no address given)—one book entitled *Khapchhada* of Kamini Pustakalaya; Tarun Mukhopadhyay (Department of Bengali, University of Calcutta)—eleven books published by Juthika; renowned literary personality Prof. Pabitra Sarkar—two books of Punascha; Amitava Basu (home address given) and Basanta Bhattacharyay (no address given)—book of Ashok Book Agency, Dr. Parthajit Gangyopadhyay and Tirthapati Datta—one title each *Galpaguchchha* and *Chhelebela* respectively for Tuli-Kalam; writer Sunil Gangyopadhyay for five titles of Patra Bharati; Dr. Alok Kumar Sen (no address given) for all the four titles (*Gitanjali, Sanchayita, Gitabitan, Galpaguchchha)* of Narayani; Tirthapati Datta for *Sesher Kavita* published by Rajarshi; and Amitabha Chowdhury for *Sahaj Path* published by Sahitya Bharati. As most of the introducers did not give their official or residential addresses questions are likely be raised about the authenticity and also academic credibility to introduce Tagoreana.

In a good number of books published by Visva-Bharati, granthaparichaya has tremendous research value as it provides information regarding first publication, change in manuscript by Rabindranath, criticism, Rabindranath's own interpretation, etc. Out of 41 titles of Visva-Bharati compared, 23 have this kind of granthaparichaya. Most of the private publications of Tagoreana lack this kind of granthaparichaya though publishers like Patraj in *Sanchayita* and *Gitabitan* and Ashok Book Agency in *Sonar Tari* and *Punascha*, Patra Bharati in *Ghare-Baire*, included granthaparichaya of Visva-Bharati. It is worthy to note here that this granthaparichaya section was not written by Rabindranath, in later period it was added with the book by VBGV, first initiated by Charuchandra Bhattacharya. So copying of granthaparichaya is a clear violation of copyright. Only in ten books (two of Kamini—*Gitanjali* and *Gitabitan;* three of Tuli-Kalam—*Gitabitan, Galpaguchchha, Lipika*; four of Patrabharati—*Sesher Kavita, Malancha, Chaturanga, Char Adhyay*;

one of Nirmal Book Agency—*Khapchhada)* granthaparichaya has been added as publishers own contribution, but a large portion of it is copied from Visva-Bharati granthaparichaya. In two books published by Mitra and Ghosh—*Jivansmriti* edited by Baridbaran Ghosh; and *Kishor Rabindra Rachanavali* edited by Amitrasudan Bhattacharya provided sufficient notes and references.

From the above discussion it may be concluded that most of the private publishers published Tagoreana with low price which resulted in poor quality in respect of physical as well as intellectual part of the thought content with huge number of punctuation-mark mistakes, spelling mistakes, line/word omission/addition, and paragraph clubbed/separated. One significant thing observed during comparison is that the mistakes in three books named *Sanchayita, Gitabitan* and *Galpaguchchha* published by Narayan Pustakalaya are same as the mistakes of books published by Kamini Prakashanalaya though printers are different. A very small portion of Tagoreana has been published by private publishers even five years after the expiry of copyright. Thus, though Tagoreana is now available easily at less cost '*Bisuddha Rabindranath*' as well as '*Samagra Rabindranath*' are still a distant dream.

NOTES AND REFERENCES

1. Tagore (Rabindranath). *Jibansmriti.* 1405 (B.S.). Visva-Bharati Granthan Vibhaga; Calcutta; p. 161.
2. *Visva-Bharati Granthan Vibhaga: Panchasatvarsha parikrama: 1923-73. 1974.* Visva-Bharati Granthan Vibhaga; Calcutta; pp. 12-14.
3. Das (Anathnath). Visva-Bharati Granthan Vibhaga. In BASU (Arun Kumar). Ed. *Saraswat: a collection of profiles of some learned bodies of West Bengal.* 2008. Paschimbanga Bangla Academy; Kolkata; p. 317.
4. Mukhopadhyaya (Prabhatkumar). *Rabindrajibini o Rabindrasahitya-prabashak.* Vol. 3. 1961. Visva-Bharati Granthan Vibhaga; Calcutta; p. 145.
5. *Visva-Bharati Granthan Vibhaga: panchasatvarsha parikrama: 1923-1973.* 1974. Visva-Bharati Granthan Vibhaga; Calcutta; p. 9.
6. *Visva-Bharati: report of the high level committee.* 2006. Raj Bhavana Press; Kolkata; p. 164.
7. *Visva-Bharati Granthan Vibhaga o Charuchandra Bhattacharyya.* 1984. Visva-Bharati Granthan Vibhaga; Calcutta; 54p.
8. Das (Anathnath). Visva-Bharati Granthan Vibhaga. In BASU (Arun Kumar). Ed. *Saraswat: a collection of profiles of some learned bodies of West Bengal.* 2008. Paschimbanga Bangla Academy; Kolkata; p. 317.

9. *Ibid.*, p. 323.
10. Publication for mass education which Rabindranath initiated for the purpose of distance education also. Tagore himself wrote Itihas, Visva-Parichaya, and Sahityer Svarup for this series.
11. Written by Rabindranath such as *Sahaj Path, Chhelebala, Sisu,* etc. or selection from his writings.
12. It is a quarterly research journal published by Visva-Bharati. Rabindranath himself was its first editor.
13. Published in three languages—Hindi, Bengali and Oriya.
14. *Visva-Bharati Annual Report 2002-03*. 2003. Santiniketan. p. 232.
15. *Visva-Bharati Annual Report 2006-07*. 2007. Santiniketan. p. 274.
16. *Visva-Bharati Annual Report 2004-05*. 2005. Santiniketan. p. 262.
17. *Visva-Bharati: report of the high level committee*. 2006. Raj Bhavana Press; Kolkata; pp. 165-66.

5

Conclusion

5.1 Introduction

Rabindranath was not only a poet, dramatist, novelist, short story writer, musician, painter, critic, philosopher, educationist, patriot but also a man of action who tried to give his vision a concrete shape with the establishment of his experimental school at *Santiniketan* and Institute of Rural Development at *Srinikatan*. Thus, Annada Sankar Ray rightly observed "His life is, in fact" is "Rabindranath's greatest work" [1]. Rabindranath was the 'discoverer and spokesman' of traditional India, that is 'basically humanist and universal, simple yet profound' [2]. Thus a study of Tagoreana is only a part of studying the activity of this *'universal man'* [3].

Regarding corrections of manuscripts, first publications in journals, publication in book form Rabindranath was very careful [4]. Sajanikanta Das handed over after correcting printing mistakes of *Puravi* Kavyagrantha to Rabindranath. Rabindranath became furious and ordered to burn the copies. But the mistakes were not huge though higher in comparison to other published books [5]. This is one of the examples of Tagore's concern about accurate publication of his writings. For this reason after the establishment of Visva-Bharati Granthan Vibhaga, there was an effort for uniform standard spelling, obviously according to the advice of Rabindranath and a special kind of house style in presentation, cover design, colour, etc. in publishing Tagoreana.

5.2 Major Findings of the Study

- From the publication of *Kavi-Kahini* in 1878 till the

publication of *Arogya, Janmadine, Galpasalpa, Sabhyatar Sankat* and *Asramer Rup o Vikas* in the year of his departure from this earthly world in 1941 Rabindranath faced the untold grief of numerous deaths. But these deaths could not stop or even slow down his mighty pen.

- Personal letters which form substantial part of Tagoreana throw light on Rabindranath's personal relationship with different people, and on the period of the correspondence. Through a study of these letters Tagore as an individual could be better understood and appreciated. Private publishers have not been interested for publication of such letters.
- A statistical account of publication of books on song, songs in dramas and year-wise growth of Rabindrasangit helps us to know the position of sangit (music) in Tagoreana and proves that even three years before publication of *Kavi-Kahini* in the year 1878 Rabindranath composed songs (1875).
- Rabindranath's vision on library and its services as reflected in his numerous writings (1888-1938) in all kinds of literary forms covers both philosophical as well as functional aspects of library. Rabindranath was also the pioneer of providing mobile library service (*'Chalantika'*) to rural India right from 1925.
- In a span of 12 years (15.3.1929-3.11.1940) Rabindranath drew a good number of paintings which cover at least twenty-seven themes. Rabindranath used different combinations of media (at least 21) predominantly ink (41.53%) on plain paper (96.88%) though in other twelve canvases used. Rabindranath put his signature on paintings in Bengali, English and a combination of both (Bengali signature 94.26%) of different sizes in different location on different dates. Rabindranath even had drawn six pictures on a single day (11.11.1936) and on forty-six occasions gave name to his paintings.
- *Gitanjali* (Song Offerings) is a collection of 103 poems from ten books (*Chaitali, Kalpana, Naivedya, Swaran, Sisu, Utsarga, Kheya, Gitanjali, Achayalatan, Giti-malya*) written between 2nd April, 1895 to 26th June, 1913 of which 42 are songs. The writings have maximum length of 72 (in one poem)

lines and minimum length of 12 lines (in six poems). The words in the writings follow Zipf's law with maximum frequency of the words '*amar*' (my) and '*tomar*' (your). Songs/poems of *Gitanjali* are basically devotional, where the poet offers his prayer to Almighty.

- Only a small portion (13.83%) of Tagoreana, mainly *Gitanjali*, novels, collected works (*Sanchayita, Gitabitan* and *Galpaguchha*) and selections from short stories as individual titles are being published by private publishers. Thus, only commercially viable and fast saleable titles have attracted the private publishers.
- Price of Tagoreana published by private publishers is less compared to Visva-Bharati's price, but binding and paper quality are poor, impression is not good and font size, space between lines and margins are small.
- Only a small portion of private publishers (5.78%) are publishing Tagoreana in Bengali even after five years of the expiry of copyright and the leading publishers are yet to start publishing Tagoreana.
- Readers of Tagoreana still consider Visva-Bharati publications as standard as sales of Visva-Bharati publications did not decline even five years after the expiry of copyright.
- Maximum number (81%) of titles was published in 2002 immediately after the expiry of copyright. After that only 19 per cent of titles published in four years 2003-2006.
- Only 20 per cent titles of Tagoreana published by private publishers bear ISBN. It indicates the scenario of less bibliographical control in the form of ISBN.
- Private publishers in general made good number of mistakes in punctuation marks, spelling mistakes, even deleted/added words/lines in the text and also clubbed paragraphs and lines. It indicates poor proof reading and lack of sincerity and seriousness of the houses in publishing Tagoreana.
- Some publishers violated copyright act by copying *Granthaparichaya*, which is not written by Rabindranath. The copyright of this is still with Visva-Bharati.

5.3 Conclusion

Visva-Bharati publications of Tagoreana are considered as standard as Rabindranath himself corrected his manuscripts, first as well as subsequent editions. The evidence of this kind of corrections can be found from the publications of different 'pathantar chayan' (selection from various editions) like *Pathantar Chayan: Rabindranather Gadyakabita* (prose poems) [6], *Pathantar Chayan: Rabindranather Upanyas* (Novel) [7], and *Sonar Tari: Bishoy Pathantar* [8]. Thus last editions published during Tagore's lifetime are considered as standard for this study.

As only a small portion of Tagoreana is published by private publishers, Visva-Bharati has the responsibility to fulfil Tagore's motto to disseminate his complete writings ('*Samagra Rabindranath*') accurately (*'Bisuddha Rabindranath')* to the mass at affordable cost ('*Sulabh Rabindranath*'). Visva-Bharati publications in some titles like *Sesher Kavita, Sisu, Punascha,* etc. provide more space in between lines and also margins that increase the number of pages and obviously the cost of production. Thus to keep price competitive the publishing department may alter their formats. This is also necessary to maintain uniformity in all the publications as in some titles like *Sonar Tari* and *Galpaguchchha* the font size is small with less space in between lines. It is observed during study that only four titles (*Sanchayita, Gitabitan, Galpaguchchha,* and *Sey*) out of 41 titles are hard bound. Thus, VBGV may consider publishing hardbound editions of more titles on demand.

For sale of Visva-Bharati publications, there is still scope of expanding market in foreign countries especially in Bangladesh. But it was noticed that Visva-Bharati has no distributor of its publications in Bangladesh. Foreign distributors are located in Kolkata only. Visva-Bharati needs to explore the possibility of expanding its distribution channel, especially in the competitive market, after the expiry of copyright.

Galpaguchchha is a voluminous book (882 pages) which contains 95 short stories. Most of the publishers published single or selection of two or three short stories from *Galpaguchchha* as individual title mainly for children. Visva-Bharati published only one title *Tinsangi* with three short stories (*Rabibar, Seshkatha* and *Laboratory*), but there is enough scope and demand for more such kind of titles with large font size, which will be easy to handle, especially for children.

Granthaparichaya provided at the end of the book is a speciality of Visva-Bharati publications which has tremendous research value. But in some books like *Char Adhyay, Malancha, Chaturanga* granthaparichaya is not provided. Rabindra Charcha Kendra (Centre of Tagorean Research) at Rabindra Bhavana may be entrusted with the responsibility of preparing granthaparichaya for these titles and incorporate it.

As the treasure of manuscript of Rabindranath is in the custody of Visva-Bharati, the institute may consider publishing existing titles with new illustrations, notes and incorporating copy of some manuscripts in it.

Visva-Bharati published only seven translations of Tagore's work. There is ample scope of translating Tagoreana in other Indian languages as well as foreign languages. Visva-Bharati has the moral responsibility to disseminate Tagorean thought to non-Bengali speaking people throughout the country and the globe by translating Tagoreana.

Modern age is the age information communication technology. Now books and journals are being published in electronic form. Visva-Bharati may consider publishing Tagoreana in large scale in compact discs and e-book form including manuscript. The copyright of these publications will be with Visva-Bharati.

Mistakes in any kind of punctuation mark either addition, omission or change affect the meaning, meter, mora and rhythm of writings. This is especially true in case of literature. Clubbing of paragraphs or sentences in poems destroy the essence and rhythm even meaning of the sentences. Change of words, sentences, mistakes in spelling are obviously an indication of injustice to the authors. Thus publishers publishing Tagoreana in the copyright free world should be more careful and that would be the best way to pay homage to the greatest literary personality, India had ever produced.

5.4 Suggestions for Further Study

- Rabindranath produced a good number of writings in English also and there are many translated works in English published (mainly by Macmillan) during his lifetime. English editions of Tagoreana are now being published in copyright free world by many private publishers. So, a comparative study of Tagoreana published in English after the expiry of copyright may be conducted.

- Tagoreana is now being published in foreign countries (especially Bangladesh) in many languages (mainly Bengali and English). So, a comparative study of Tagoreana published in India and foreign countries with special reference to Bangladesh after the expiry of copyright may be conducted.
- A comparative study of all editions of Tagoreana, including first and last editions published during Tagore's lifetime may be conducted to know the change of texts published by Visva-Bharati.
- A comparative study of copyright free publications of Tagoreana and other authors (Indian or foreign) may be conducted.
- A study on the trends of publications of Tagoreana in Indian languages after the expiry of copyright may be conducted.
- Bibliometric studies on selected titles (like *Gitanjali*, *Sonar Tari*, etc.) of Tagoreana may be conducted and applications of various bibliometric laws tested.
- Bibliometric study on year-wise, month-wise and date-wise growth of Tagoreana considering place, time of writings, theme, etc. may be conducted.
- Comparative study on illustrations of Tagoreana published in Indian languages with the illustrations drawn by Rabindranath himself and Visva-Bharati may be conducted.
- Users study on the readers of Tagoreana after the expiry of copyright may be conducted.
- Rabindra sangit is the treasure of Tagoreana now being sung with different notations other than notations composed by Rabindranath and his associates and recommended by Visva-Bharati. A comparative study on notations of Rabindra sangit before and after the expiry of copyright may be conducted.

REFERENCES

1. RAY (Anandasankar). Rabindranath: an artist in life. In *Rabindranath Tagore centenary volume: 1861-1961*. 1961. Sahitya Akademi; New Delhi; p. 217.

2. RAY (Niharranjan). Rabindranath Tagore and Indian tradition. In *Rabindranath Tagore centenary volume: 1861-1961*. 1961. Sahitya Akademi; New Delhi; pp. 223-232.
3. THOMPSON (Edward). *Rabindranath Tagore: poet and dramatist*. 1979. Rddhi-India; Calcutta; 335p.
4. BAGCHI (Sanatkumar). *Rabindranather pandulipi: samiksha o bislashan*. 1989. Pustak Bipani; Calcutta; p. 316.
5. DAS (Anathnath). Visva-Bharati Granthan Vibhaga. In BASU (Arun Kumar). Ed. *Saraswat: a collection of profiles of some learned bodies of West Bengal*. 2008. West Bengal Bangla Academy; Kolkata; pp. 317-324.
6. BHATTACHARYAY (Amitrasudan) and DAS (Pareshnath). *Pathantar chayan: Rabindranather gadyakabita*. 2006. Visva-Bharati Granthan Vibhaga; Calcutta; 424p.
7. BHATTACHARYAY (Amitrasudan). *Pathantar chayan: Rabindra upanyas*. 1410. (B.S.). Visva-Bharati Granthan Vibhaga; Calcutta; 272p.
8. GHOSH (Debkumar). *Sonar Tari: bishay pathantar*. 1987. Sahitya O Desh; Hooghly; 174p.

Appendix A

Tagore Family Tree

- Dwarakanath 1794-1846, Dwigambari Devi ?-1839
  - Daughter, Short life
  - Devendranath 1817-1905, Sarada Devi
    - Daughter 1838, short life
    - Dwijendranath 1840-1926, Sarvasundari Devi
      - Dwipendranath (Elder) 1862-1922, Sushila Devi, Hemlata Devi
        - Dwipendranath
      - Sudhindranath (Fourth son) 1869-1929, Charubala Devi
    - Satyendranath 1842-1923, Iyanadanandini Devi
      - Surendranath 1872-1940, Sangya Devi
      - Indira Devi 1873-1960, Pramath Choudhury
      - Kabindranath 1875-1879
    - Hemendranath 1844-1884, Nipamayi Devi
      - Pratibha (Elder) 1875-1922, Ashutosh Choudhury
    - Birendranath 1845-1915, Prafullyamayi Devi
      - Balendranath 1870-1899, Sahana Devi (no children)
    - Soudamani 1847-1920, Naradaprasad Gangopadhyay
      - Satyaprasad (Elder) 1859-1933
      - Iravati (Elder) 1861-1918, Nityaranjan Mukhopadhyay
    - Jyotirindranath 1849-1925, Kadambari Devi (no children)
    - Sukumari ?1850-1864
    - Punyendranath
    - Saratkumari 1854-1920, Jadunath Mukhopadhyay
      - Sushila (Elder), Sitalakanta Chattopadhyay
    - Swarnakumari ?1856-1932, Janakinath Ghosal
      - Hiranmayee 1868-1925
      - Jyotsnanath 1871
      - Sarala 1872-1945
      - Urmila 1873-?
    - Barnakumari 1858-1948, Satischandra Mukhopadhyay
    - Somarendranath 1859-1922, Unmarried
    - Rabindranath** 1861-1941, Mrinalini Devi
    - Budhendranath 1863-1864
  - Narendranath, live for 3 years, ?1851-1857
  - Girindranath* 1820-1954, Yogmaya Devi
  - Bhupendranath 1826-1839
  - Nagendranath 1829-1858, Tripurasundari Devi (no children)

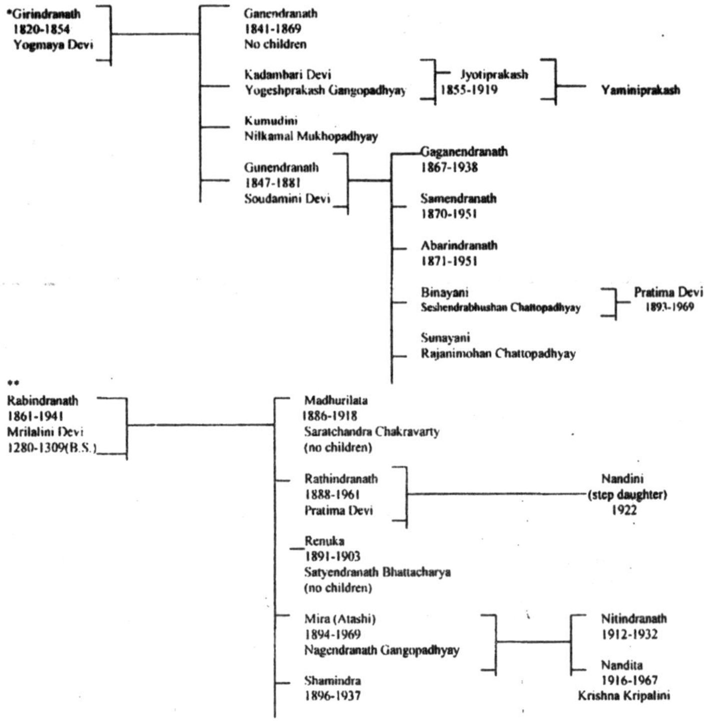
*Girindranath
1820-1854
Yogmaya Devi
Ganendranath
1841-1869
No children
Kadambari Devi
Yogeshprakash Gangopadhyay
Jyotiprakash
1855-1919
Yaminiprakash
Kumudini
Nilkamal Mukhopadhyay
Gunendranath
1847-1881
Soudamini Devi
Gaganendranath
1867-1938
Samendranath
1870-1951
Abarindranath
1871-1951
Binayani
Seshendrabhushan Chattopadhyay
Pratima Devi
1893-1969
Sunayani
Rajanimohan Chattopadhyay
**
Rabindranath
1861-1941
Mrilalini Devi
1280-1309(B.S.)
Madhurilata
1886-1918
Saratchandra Chakravarty
(no children)
Rathindranath
1888-1961
Pratima Devi
Nandini
(step daughter)
1922
Renuka
1891-1903
Satyendranath Bhattacharya
(no children)
Mira (Atashi)
1894-1969
Nagendranath Gangopadhyay
Nitindranath
1912-1932
Nandita
1916-1967
Krishna Kripalini
Shamindra
1896-1937

Appendix B

Catalogue of First Edition of Tagoreana in Rabindra Bhavana

Sl. No.	*Classification No.*	*Bibliographic Description*
1.	891.44194	*Kavi-Kahini*. 1285 (B.S.). Calcutta: Prabodhchandra Ghosh. 53p. (Verse)
2.	891.44194	*Bana-phul*. 1286 (B.S.). Calcutta: Gupta Press. 93p. (Verse)
3.	891.44194	*Bhagnahriday*. 1288. Calcutta: Kalikinkar Chakraborty. 196p. (Drama, in verse)
4.	891.44194	*Sandhya Sangit*. 1288. Calcutta. Kalidas Chakraborty. 141p. (Verse)
5.	891.4427	*Rudrachanda*. 1288. Calcutta: Kalikinkar Chakraborty. 54p. (Drama, in verse)
6.	910.4	*Europe-Pravasir Patra*. 1288. Calcutta: Saradaprasad Gangyopadhaya. 256p. (Letters, Corrected by Rabindranath Tagore)
7.	891.44194	*Chhabi O Gan*. 1290. Calcutta: Kalidas Chakraborty. 185p. (Verse)
8.	891.44194	*Prabhat Sangit*. 1290. Calcutta: Kalidas Chakraborty. 125p. (Verse)
9.	891.4445	*Vividha Prasanga*. 1290. Calcutta: Kalidas Chakraborty. 149p. (Essays)

10.	891.44153	*Bhanusimha Thakurer Padavali*. 1291. Calcutta: Rabindranath Tagore. 60p. (Poems and songs)
11.	891.44194	*Saisav Sangit*. 1291. Calcutta: Adi Brahma Samaj. 149p. (Verse)
12.	891.4427	*Prakritir Pratisodh*. 1291. Calcutta: Kalidas Chakraborty. 81p. (Drama, in verse)
13.	891.4445	*Alochana*. 1291. 133p. (Essays)
14.	923.6	*Rammohun Ray*. 1291. Calcutta: Adi Brahma Samaj. 34p. (Verse)
15.	780.954	*Rabichachhaya*. 1292. Calcutta: Jogendranarayan Mitra. 171p. (Songs)
16.	891.44194	*Kadi O Komal*. 1293. Calcutta: Peoples Library. 263p. (Verse)
17.	891.4434	*Rajarshi*. 1293. Calcutta: Adi Brahma Samaj Jantra. 242p. (Novel)
18.	891.446	*Chithipatra*. 1294. Calcutta: Sri Saratkumar Lahiri. 69p. (Essays)
19.	891.4427	*Mayar Khele*. 1295. Calcutta: Adi Brahma Samaj. 64p. (Musical drama)
20.	891.4427	*Raja O Rani*. 1296. Calcutta: Kalidas Chakraborty. 149p. (Drama, in verse)
21.	891.4427	*Visarjan*. 1297. 154p. (Drama, in verse)
22.	910.4	*Europe-Yatrir Dayari*: *Part: 1*. 1298. Calcutta: Kalidas Chakraborty. 78p. (Travel)
23.	910.4	*Europe-Yatrir Dayari: Part 2*. 1300. Calcutta: Kalidas Chakraborty. 98p. (Travel. Correction made by Rabindranath Tagore)
24.	891.44247	*Goday Galad*. 1299. Calcutta: Kalidas Chakraborty. 136p. (Comedy)

25. 891.4427 *Chitrangada*. 1299. Calcutta: Kalidas Chakraborty. 41p.
(Drama, in verse)

26. 780.954 *Ganar Bahi O Balmiki Prativa*. 1300. Calcutta: Adi Brahma Samaj. 407p.
(Musical drama)

27. 891.44194 *Sonar Tari*. 1300. Calcutta: Kalidas Chakraborty. 209p.
(Verse)

28. 891.4434 *Chhoto Galpa*. 1300. Calcutta: Kalidas Chakraborty. 189p
(Short stories)

29. 891.4427 *Chitrangada O Viday-Abhisap*. 1301. Calcutta: Kalidas Chakraborty. 103p.
(Drama, in verse)

30. 891.44194 *Chitra*. 1302. Calcutta: Kalidas Chakraborty. 151p.
(Verse)

31. 891.44194 *Nadi*. 1302. Calcutta: Adi Brahma Samaj. 34p.
(Verse)

32. 891.4434 *Galpa-Dasak*. 1302. Calcutta: Kalidas Chakraborty. 220p
(Short stories)

33. 891.44194 *Kavya-Granthavali*. Calcutta: Satyendranath Gangyopadhaya. 476p.
(Poems)

34. 891.44247 *Baikunther Khata*. 1303. Calcutta: Kalidas Chakraborty. 55p.
(Comedy)

35. 891.4445 *Panchabhut*. 1304. Calcutta: Sur Company. 95p.
(Essays)

36. 891.44194 *Katha*. 1306. 110p.
(Verse)

37. 891.4427 *Kahini*. 1306. Calcutta: Debendranath Bhattacharya. 164p.
(Verse-drama and verse)

38. 891.44194 *Kalpana*. 1307. 114p.
(Verse, Corrected by Rabindranath)

39. 891.44194 *Kshanika*. 1307. Calcutta: Indian Publishing House. 157p.

40. 891.4434 *Galpaguccha: Part* 1. 1307. Calcutta: Majumder Agency. 448p.
(Short stories)

41.	891.4434	*Galpaguchchha: Part 2*. 1308. Calcutta: Majumder Agency. 449p. (Short stories)
42.	294.14	*Upanishad Brahma*. 1308. 42p. (Essays)
43.	891.44194	*Naivedya*. 1308. Calcutta. 200p. (Verse)
44.	891.44194	*Smaran*. 1309. Calcutta: Indian Publishing House. 34p. (Verse)
45.	891.44194	*Kavya-Grantha*, 9 Vols. 1310. Calcutta: Majumder Library
46.	891.4434	*Karmaphal*. 1310. Calcutta: Hitendramohan Basu. 93p. (Story)
47.	891.44194	*Svadesh*. 1312. Calcutta: Majumder Library. 145p. (Essays)
48.	891.4445	*Bharatvarsha*. 1312. Calcutta: Majumder Library. 144p. (Essays)
49.	891.44194	*Kheya*. 1313. Bolpur: Brahmacharyasram. 74p. (Verse)
50.	891.4434	*Naukadubi*. 1313. Calcutta: Upendranath Mukhopadhyay. 404p. (Novel)
51.	891.9144	*Sabhapatir Avibhasan: Pabna Sammilani*. 1314. Calcutta: Adi Brahma Samaj Jantra. 50p. (Presidential Address: Pabna).
52.	801.95	*Sahitya*. 1314. Calcutta: Majumder Library. 163p. (Essays)
53	891.44274	*Vyangakautuk*. 1314. Calcutta: Majumder Library. 99p. (Comic plays)
54.	920.054	*Charitrapuja*. 1314. Santiniketan: Jagadananda Ray. 104p. (Essays)
55.	891.4445	*Gadya-Granthavali*. 16 Vols. 1314-. Calcutta: Majumder Library. (Collected works)
56.	204	*Santiniketan*. 17 Parts. 1315—Calcutta: Indian Publishing House. (Sermons)

57.	891.44194	*Katha O kahini*. 1315. Calcutta: Indian Publishing House. 80p. (Essays. Corrected by Rabindranath upto "Guru-Gobindo" of Katha)
58.	891.4427	*Sabdatattva*. 1513. Calcutta: Indian Publishing House. 167p. (Essays).
59.	891.4434	*Gora*. 1315. Calcutta: Prabashi Karjalaya. 166p. (Novel)
60.	375.42	*Engraji Sahaj Siksha*. 1316. Calcutta: Visva-Bharati Granthalaya. 48p. (How to learn English)
61.	375.49144	*Chhutir Pada*. 1316. Calcutta: Hitabadi Library. 124p. (Exercise)
62.	780.954	*Gan*. 1316. Allahabad: Indian Press. 412p. (Songs)
63.	891.44194	*Sisu*. 1316. Allahabad: Indian Press. 161p. (Poems)
64.	891.4427	*Prayaschitta*. 1316. Calcutta: Hitabadi Library. 116p. (Drama)
65.	891.4417	*Raja*. 1317. Calcutta: Indian Publishing House. 128p. (Drama)
66.	891.44194	*Chaitali*. 1318. Calcutta: Indian Publishing House. 66p. (Poems)
67.	891.4427	*Dakghar*. 1318. Calcutta: Indian Publishing House. 56p. (Drama)
68.	891.4427	*Malini*. 1318. Calcutta: Indian Publishing House. 49p. (Drama, in Verse)
69.	891.4434	*Galpa Chariti*. 1318. Calcutta: Ganendranath Chattopadhaya. 120p. (Stories)
70.	891.4434	*Aathti Galpa*. 1318. Calcutta: Indian Publishing House. 199p. (Stories)
71.	891.4427	*Achalayatan*. 1319. Calcutta: Ramgopal Chakraborty. 138p. (Drama)

72. 891.446 *Chhinnapatra*. 1319. Salaidaha: Nagendranath Gangyopadhyay. 233p.
(Letters)

73. 928 *Jivansmriti*. 1319. Salaidaha: Nagendranath. Gangyopadhayay.195p.
(Autobiography. Corrected by Rabindranath)

74. 780.954 *Gan*. 1321. Calcutta: Indian Publishing House. 168p.
(Songs)

75. 780.954 *Dharmasangit*. 1321. Allahabad: Indian Press Limited. 201p.
(Religious songs)

76. 891.44194 *Kavyagrantha*, 10 Vols. 1321-. Allahabad: Indian Press Limited.
(Collected works)

77. 891.44194 *Gitali*. 1321. Allahabad: Indian Press. 117p.
(Songs)

78. 891.4427 *Phalguni*. 1322. Allahabad: Indian Press. 84p
(Drama)

79. 891.4434 *Galpasaptak*. 1323. Allahabad: Indian Press. 204p.
(Short stories)

80. 891.4434 *Ghare-Baire*. 1323. Allahabad: Indian Press. 294p.
(Novel)

81. 891.4434 *Chaturanga*. 1323. Allahabad: Indian Press. 123p.
(Novel)

82. 891.4445 *Parichay*. 1323. Allahabad: Indian Press. 171p.
(Essays)

83. 891.4445 *Sanchay*. 1323. Allahabad: Indian Press. 126p.
(Essays)

84. 891.4427 *Guru*. 1324. Calcutta: Indian Publishing House. 51p.
(Drama)

85. 891.4427 *Arupratan*. 1326. Calcutta: Chintamoni Ghosh. 73p.
(Drama)

86. 910.4 *Japan-Yatri*. 1326. Calcutta: Indian Publishing House. 119p.
(Travel)

87. 891.4427 *Rinsodh*. 1328. Allahabad: Indian Press Limited. 96p
(Drama)

88. 891.44194 *Sisu Bholanath*. 1329. Allahabad: Indian Press Limited, 86p.
(Verse)

89. 891.4427 *Vasanta*. 1329. Santniketan: Jagadananda Ray. 32p.
(Muscal drama)

90. 891.4427 *Muktadhara*. 1329. Calcutta; Prabashi Karjalaya. 136p.
(Drama)

91. 891.4434 *Lipika*. 1329. Allahabad: Indian Press Limited. 182p.
(Prose poems)

92. 891.4427 *Raktakarabi*. 1331. Calcutta: Prabashi.
(Drama)

93. 780.954 *Pravahini*. 1332. Calcutta: Visva-Bharati. 180p.
(Songs. Signed by Rabindranath at the last page)

94. 891.4419 *Puravi*. 1332. Calcutta: Visva-Bharati. 254p.
(Verse)

95. 891.4427 *Grihapravesh*. 1332. Calcutta: Visva-Bharati. 102p.
(Songs. Corrected by Rabindranath)

96. 891.4427 *Chirakumar Sabha*. 1332. Calcutta: Visva-Bharati Granthalaya. 220
(Comedy)

97. 891.4427 *Ritu Utsav*. 1333. Calcutta: Visva-Bharati Granthalaya. 216p.
(Drama)

98. 891.4427 *Natir Puja*. 1333. Calcutta: Visva-Bharati Granthalaya. 82p.
(Drama)

99. 891.4427 *Raktakarabi*. 1333. Calcutta: Visva-Bharati Granthalaya. 203p.
(Drama)

100. 891.4427 *Sodh-bodh*. 1333. Calcutta: Visva-Bharati Granthalaya. 78p.
(Comedy)

101. 891.44194 *Lekhan*. 1334. Calcutta: Visva-Bharati. 65p.
(Epigrams—printed in facsimile of the poet's handwriting)

102. 891.4427 *Rituranga*. 1334. Calcutta: Visva-Bharati Granthalaya. 44p.
(Musical drama)

103. 891.4427 *Sesh Raksha*. 1335. Calcutta: Visva-Bharati Granthalaya. 133p.
(Drama, Corrected by Rabindranath)

104. 375.49144 *Pathprichay: Part III*. 1336. Calcutta: Visva-Bharati. 156p.
(Children book)

105. 375.49144 *Pathprichay: Part IV*. 1336. Calcutta: Visva-Bharati. 160p.
(Children book. Corrected by Rabindranath)

106. 891.44194 *Mahua*. 1336. Calcutta: Visva-Bharati Granthalaya. 175p.
(Verse)

107. 891.4427 *Tapati*. 1336. Calcutta: Visva-Bharati Granthalaya. 185p.
(Drama)

108. 891.4427 *Paritran*. 1336. Calcutta: Visva-Bharati Granthalaya. 41p.
(Drama)

109. 891.4434 *Yogayog*. 1336. Calcutta: Visva-Bharati. 471p.
(Novel)

110. 891.4434 *Sesher Kavita*. 1336. Calcutta: Visva-Bharati Granthalaya. 232p.
(Novel)

111. 891.446 *Bhanusimher Patravali*. 1336. Calcutta: Visva-Bharati Granthalaya. 158p.
(Letters. Corrected by Rabindranath)

112. 910.4 *Yatri*. 1336. Calcutta: Visva-Bharati Granthalaya. 315p.
(Travel)

113. 375.49144 *Sahaj Path: Part-I*. 1337. Santiniketan: Santiniketan Press. 53p.
(Children book. Corrected by Rabindranath)

114. 375.49144 *Sahaj Path: Part II*. 1337. Santiniketan: Santiniketan Press. 51p.
(Children book)

115. 891.4427 *Navin*. 1337. Calcutta: Visva-Bharati Granthalaya. 28p.
(Musical drama)

116. 780.954 *Gitabitan*. 1338. Calcutta: Visva-Bharati Granthalaya. 864p.
(Songs. Corrected by Rabindranath)

117. 891.44194 *Vanavani*. 1338. Calcutta: Visva-Bharati. 163p.
(Poem and songs)

118. 891.44194 *Sanchayita*. 1338. Calcutta: Visva-Bharati Granthalaya. 585p.
(Songs)

119. 910.4 *Russiar Chithi*. 1338. Calcutta: Visva-Bharati Granthalaya. 218p.
(Letters)

120.	089.9144	*Visvavidyalayar Rup*. 1339. Calcutta: Calcutta University. 30p. (Address)
121.	891.44194	*Parisesh*. 1339. Calcutta: Visva-Bharati. 162p. (Verse)
122.	891.44194	*Punascha*. 1339. Calcutta: Visva-Bharati Granthalaya. 123p. (Prose-poems)
123.	891.4427	*Kaler Yatra*. 1339. Calcutta: Visva-Bharati Granthalaya. 39p. (Drama)
124.	891.4434	*Dui Bon*. 1339. Calcutta: Visva-Bharati Granthalaya. 92p. (Novel)
125.	089.9144	*Bharatpathik Rammohun Roy*. 1340. Calcutta. 16p. (Essays and addresses)
126.	204	*Manusher Dharma*. 1340. Calcutta: Visva-Bharati Granthalaya. 119p. (Religion of man)
127.	891.44194	*Vichitrita*. 1340. Calcutta: Visva-Bharati Granthalaya. 60p. (Verse)
128.	891.4427	*Chandalika*. 1340. Calcutta: Visva-Bharati Granthalaya. 45p. (Drama)
129.	891.4427	*Taser Des*. 1340. Calcutta: Visva-Bharati Granthalaya. 69p. (Drama. Corrected by Rabindranath)
130.	891.4427	*Bansari*. Calcutta: Visva-Bharati Granthalaya. 130p. (Drama. Corrected by Rabindranath)
131.	891.4434	*Malancha*. 1340. Calcutta: Visva-Bharati Granthalaya. 63p. (Novel)
132.	891.4434	*Char Adhyay*. 1341. Calcutta: Visva-Bharati Granthalaya. 138p. (Novel)
133.	891.4427	*Sravan-Gatha*. 1341. Santiniketan: Santiniketan Press. 22p. (Musical drama)
134.	780.95409	*Sur O Sanggati*. 1342. Calcutta: Kundabhushan Bhaduri. 102p. (Letters)

135. 891.44194 — *Vithika*. 1342. Calcutta: Visva-Bharati Grantyhalaya. 232p.
(Verse)

136. 891.44194 — *Sesh Saptak*. 1342. Calcutta: Visva-Bharati. 170p.
(Prose-poem)

137. 891.4427 — *Nritya-natya Chitrangada*. 1342. Calcutta: Visva-Bharati Granthalaya. 33p.
(Dance-drama)

138. 089.9144 — *Chhatrasambashan*. 1343. Calcutta: Calcutta University Press. 17p.
(Address to students)

139. 370.1 — *Praktani*. 1343. Santiniketan: Santiniketan Ashram Sangha. 45p.
(Addresses)

140. 491.446 — *Chhanda*. 1343. Calcutta: Visva-Bharati Granthalaya. 239p.
(Essays)

141. 780.954 — *Nritya-natya Chandalika*. 1343. Calcutta: Visva-Bharati. 109p.
(Dance-drama)

142. 801 — *Sahityer Pathe*. 1343. Calcutta: Visva-Bharati Granthalaya. 174p.
(Essays)

143. 891.44194 — *Khapchhada*. 1343. Calcutta: Visva-Bharati Granthalaya. 144p.
(Nonsense rhymes)

144. 891.44194 — *Patraput*. 1343. Calcutta: Visva-Bharati Granthalaya. 64p.
(Prose-poems)

145. 891.44194 — *Syamali*. 1343. Calcutta: Visva-Bharati Granthalaya. 77p.
(Prose-poems)

146. 910.4 — *Japane-Parasye*. 1343. Calcutta: Visva-Bharati Granthalaya. 204p.
(Travel)

147. 910.4 — *Paschatta Brahman*. 1343. Calcutta: Visva-Bharati Granthalaya. 137p.
(Travel)

148. 523.1 — *Visva-Parichay*. 1344. Calcutta: Visva-Bharati Granthalaya. 95p.
(Essays. Corrected by Rabindranath)

149. 891.44194 — *Chhadar Chhabi*. 1344. Calcutta: Visva-Bharati Granthalaya. 93p.
(Verse)

150. 891.44194 — *Prantik*. 1344. Calcutta: Visva-Bharati Granthalaya. 33p.
(Verse)

151. 891.427 — *Chandalika*. 1344. Calcutta: Visva-Bharati Granthalaya. 45p.
(Dance-drama. Corrected by Rabindranath)

152. 891.4434 — *Sey*. 1344. Calcutta: Visva-Bharati. 148p.
(Stories)

153. 891.4445 — *Kalantar*. 1344. Calcutta: Visva-Bharati. 249p.
(Essays)

154. 491.44 — *Banglabhasha Parichay*. 345. Calcutta: Calcutta University. 180p.
(Essays. Corrected by Rabindranath)

155. 891.44108 — *Banglakavya Parichay*. 1345. Calcutta: Visva-Bharati Granthalaya. 349p.
(Essays. Mass education series 1)

156. 891.44194 — *Prahasini*. 1345. Calcutta: Visva-Bharati. 65p.
(Verse)

157. 891.44194 — *Senjuti*. 1345. Calcutta: Visva-Bharati Granthan Vibgha. 62p.
(Verse)

158. 891.446 — *Patradhara*. 3 vols. Calcutta: Visva-Bharati Granthalaya.
(Letters. Vol. 1. Chhinapatra, Vol. 2. Bhanusinghar Patrabali, Vol. 3. Pathe O Pather Prante)

159. 081 — *Rabindra Rachanavali*. Vol. 1. 1346. Calcutta: Visva-Bharati. 645p.
(Collected works)

160. 081 — *Rabindra Rachanavali*. Vol. 2. 1346. Calcutta: Visva-Bharati. 664p.
(Collected works)

161. 780.954 — *Syama*. 1346. Calcutta: Visva-Bharati. 92p.
(Dance-drama. Sarabitan-19)

162. 891.44194 — *Akash-pradip*. 1346. Calcutta: Visva-Bharati Granthalaya. 70p.
(Verse. Corrected by Rabindranath)

163. 910.4 — *Pather Sanchay*. 1345. Calcutta: Visva-Bharati Granthalaya. 86p.
(Essays and letters)

164. 081 *Rabindra Rachanavali*. Vol. 3. 1347. Calcutta: Visva-Bharati. 652p.
(Collected works)

165. 081 *Rabindra Rachanavali*. Vol. 4. 1347. Calcutta: Visva-Bharati. 567p.
(Collected works)

166. 081 *Rabindra Rachanavali*. Vol. 5. 1347. Calcutta: Visva-Bharati. 571p.
(Collected works)

167. 081 *Rabindra Rachanavali*. Vol. 6. 1347. Calcutta: Visva-Bharati. 674p.
(Collected works)

168. 759.954 *Chitralipi:* Part 1. 1347. Calcutta: Visva-Bharati Granthalaya. 37p.
(Collection of 18 paintings and 19 poems)

169. 891.44194 *Arogya*. 1347. Calcutta: Visva-Bharati Granthalaya. 39p.
(Verse)

170. 891.44194 *Navajatak*. 1347. Calcutta: Visva-Bharati Granthalaya. 96p.
(Verse)

171. 891.44194 *Rogasajyay*. 1347. Calcutta: Visva-Bharati Granthalaya. 47p.
(Verse)

172. 891.44194 *Sanai*. 1347. Calcutta: Visva-Bharati Granthalaya. 106p.
(Verse)

173. 891.4434 *Tin-Sangi*. 1347. Calcutta: Visva-Bharati Granthalaya. 151p.
(Short stories)

174. 928 *Chhelebela*. 1347. Calcutta: Visva-Bharati Granthalaya. 87p.
(Autobiography)

175. 081 *Rabindra Rachanavali*. Vol. 7. 1348. Calcutta: Visva-Bharati. 563p.
(Collected works)

176. 081 *Rabindra Rachanavali*. Vol. 8. 1348. Calcutta: Visva-Bharati. 547p.
(Collected works)

177. 081 *Rabindra Rachanavali*. Vol. 9. 1348. Calcutta: Visva-Bharati. 571p.
(Collected works)

179.	081	*Rabindra Rachanavali*. Vol. 10. 1348. Calcutta: Visva-Bharati. 675p. (Collected works)
180.	081	*Rabindra Rachanavali: Achalit Samgrah*. Vol. 2. 1348. Calcutta: Visva-Bharati. 772p.
181.	089.9144	*Sabhyatar Samkat*. 1348. Santiniketan: Santiniketan Press.11p. (Address)
182.	370.1	*Asamer Rup O Vikas*. 1348. Santiniketan: Santiniketan Press.14p (Essays)
183.	891.44194	*Janmadine*. 1348. Calcutta: Visva-Bharati Granthalaya. 45p. (Verse)
184.	891.4434	*Galpasalpa*. 1348. Calcutta: Visva-Bharati Granthalaya. 84p. (Stories and poems)

Bibliography

This bibliography excludes Tagoreana published by Visva-Bharati Granthan Vibhaga and private publishers as titles of Tagoreana included in Chapter VI and description of first edition of Tagoreana is also given in Appendix-B.

AHUJA (Ram). *Research methods*. 2001. Rawat Publications; Jaipur.

ARONSON (A). *Rabindranath Tagore through western eyes*. 1978. Rddhi-India; Calcutta.

BAGCHI (Radhacharan). Rabindranath Tagore as a painter. In SENGUPTA (Santosh Chandra). Ed. *Homage from Visva-Bharati*. 1962. Visva-Bharati Granthan Vibhaga; Calcutta. p. 200.

BAGCHI (Sanatkumar). *Rabindranather pandulipi: samiksha o bislehasan*. 1989. Pustak Bipani; Calcutta.

BAMANE (NJ). Legal implication to utilization of information technology products—intellectual property rights: Indian scenario and its future perspective. Paper presented in XX *IASLIC Conference*. 1995. Lucknow; pp. 145-150.

BANDYOPADHAYA (Brajendranath). *Rabindra grantha-parichay (1878-1943)*. 1349 (B.S.). Sahitya-Niketan; Calcutta.

BANDYOPADHYAY (Somendranath). *Rabindra-chitrakala: Rabindrasahityer patabhumika*. 1982. Dey's Publishing; Calcutta.

BANERJEE (H). *How thou singest my master: a study of Tagore's poetry*. 1961. Orient Longman; Bombay.

BASU CHOWDHURY (Alokranjan). Copyright free Rabindra creation: reaction of periodicals. *Rabindra Bhabna*. 26, 3; 2002; 19-29.

BHATTACHARYAY (Amitrasudan) and DAS (Pareshnath). *Pathantar chayan: Rabindranather gadyakabita*. 2006. Visva-Bharati Granthan Vibhaga; Calcutta.

BHATTACHARYAY (Amitrasudan). *Pathantar chayan: Rabindra upanyas*. 1410 (B.S.). Visva-Bharati Granthan Vibhaga; Calcutta.

BHATTACHARYA (B). *Towards universal man.* 1969. Asia Publishing House; Bombay.

BHATTACHARYYA (DK). *Research methodology*. 2004. Excel Books; New Delhi.

BISI (Pramathanath). *Rabindranath O Santiniketan.* 1402 (B.S). Visva-Bharati Granthan Vibhaga; Calcutta.

BOSE (Nandalal). The paintings of Rabindranath. *Visva-Bharati Quarterly.* 14, 1; 1936; 31.

BOSE (RN). *Rabindranath Tagore: a guru with difference.* 1976. Tagore Research Institute; Calcutta.

BRADFORD (SC). Sources of information on specific subjects. *Engineering.* 7, 13; 1934; 85-86.

CHAKRABORTY (Satyadas). *Sriniketaner gorar katha.* 1985. Sahitya Samaj; Sriniketan; 96p.

CHAKRAVARTI (BC). *Rabindranath Tagore, his mind and art.* 1971. Young India Publications; New Delhi.

CHAKRAVARTY (Bikash). ed. *Poets to poet.* 1998. Visva-Bharati Granthan Vibhaga; Calcutta.

CHATTERJEE (Ramananda). Rabindranath Tagore. *Modern Review.* 50, 6; 1931; 675.

CHATTOPADHYAY (Meera). *Rabindra rachanar ingreji-anubad-itibritta.* 2 vols. 1993. Sriguru Prakashan; Calcutta.

CHAUDHURI (Amit). Two giant brothers. *London Review of Books.* 28, 8; 2006; 27-30.

CHOWDHURANI (Indira Devi). *Rabindrasmriti.* 1962. Visva-Bharati Granthan Vibhaga; Calcutta.

CHUNKAPURA (Jose). *The God of Rabindranath Tagore: a study of the evolution of his understanding of God.* 2002. Visva-Bharati Granthan Vibhaga; Calcutta.

DAS (Anathnath). Publication of Rabindranath, copyright and copy left. *Desh.* 69, 12; 2002; 28-32.

DAS (Anathnath). Visva-Bharati Granthan Vibhaga. In BASU (Arun Kumar). Ed. *Saraswat: a collection of profiles of some learned bodies of West Bengal.* 2008. Paschimbanga Bangla Akademi; Kolkata; pp. 317-334.

DAS (Kshudiram). *Rabindranath Tagore: a 125th birth anniversary volume.* 1988. Government of West Bengal; Calcutta.

DASGUPTA (S). *Rabindranath Tagore, the man and his works.* 1964. N. Daniel Oliagi; Bombay.

DASGUPTA (Uma). Santiniketan and Sriniketan. *Visva-Bharati Quarterly.* 48, 1-4; 1982-83; 376-85.

DATTA (Bimal Kumar). *Rabindra sahitye granthagar.* 1989. Bengal Library Association; Calcutta.

DEVARAJAN (D). *Research in library and information science.* 2002. Ess Ess Publications; New Delhi.

DUTTA (Bhabatosh). Tagore: a short biography. In Chaudhury (Bhabatosh). Ed. *Introduction to Tagore.* 1983. Visva-Bharati Granthan Vibhaga; Calcutta; pp. 56-57.

DUTTA (Krishna) and ROBINSON (Andrew). 1995. *Rabindranah Tagore: the myriad-minded man.* 1995. Bloomsbury; London.

EDACHERIPARAMBIL (T). *God-concept in Gitanjali*; 1990. Claretian Publications; Bangalore.

FEATHER (John) and STRUGES (Paul). *International encyclopaedia of information and library science.* 2003. Routledge; London.

FAITHORNE (RA). Empirical hyperbolic distribution (Bradford Ziff-Model) for bibliometric description and production. *Journal of Documentation.* 25, 3; 1969; 317.

GHOSE (DN). *Rabindranath Tagore, his early life and works.* 1947. Modern Book Agency; Calcutta.

GHOSE (SK). *Rabindranath Tagore.* 1986. Sahitya Akademi; New Delhi.

GHOSH (Debkumar). *Sonar tari: bishay pathantar.* 1987. Sahitya O Desh; Hooghly.

GHOSH (Nityapriyo). Publication of Tagoreana, with pleasure. *Desh.* 69, 12; 2002; 25-27.

GHOSH (SN). *Rabindranath Tagore: his life and works.* 1947. Modern Book Agency; Calcutta.

HENN (Katherine). *Rabindranath Tagore: a biography.* 1985. Metuchen; New Jersey.

HULME (EW). *Statistical bibliography in relation to the growth of modern civilization.* 1923. Grafton; London.

HUMAYUN (K). *Rabindranath Tagore.* 1987. Pankaj Publications International; Delhi.

IYENGAR (KR Srinivasa). *Rabindranath Tagore: a critical introduction.* 1965. Sterling Publishers; New Delhi.

KAUR (Rajwant) and BHAGI (Rekha Goyal). Copyright in India: an overview. *International Library Movement (ILM)*, 27, 2; 2005; 61-77.

KEDIA (Onkar) and PANDEY (Manoj). *Common mans guide to right and facilities.* 2002. Publication Division; New Delhi.

KOTHARI (CR). *Research methodology.* 1992. Wiley Eastern Ltd., New Delhi.

KRIPALANI (Krishna). *Rabindranath Tagore: a biography.* 1980. Visva-Bharati Granthan Vibhaga; Calcutta.

KUNDU (Ashok Kumar). *Rabindra-dinopanji.* 1986. Banglabhasha Sahityo O Samskriti Gabashana Samsthan; Calcutta.

KUNDU (Kalian). *Rabindranath and the British Press (1912-1941).* 1990. The Tagore Research Centre; London.

LAGO (Mary M). *Letters of William Rothenstein and Rabindranath Tagore 1911-1941.* 1978. Harvard University Press; Harvard.

LAL (Prem Chand). *Reconstruction and education in rural India.* 1952. George Allen and Unwin; London.

LAWANI (SM). Bibliometrics: its theoretical foundations, methods and applications. *Libri.* 31, 4; 1981; 294-315.

LOTKA (AJ). The frequency distribution of scientific productivity. *Journal of Washington Academy of Science.* 16, 12; 1926; 317-323.

MAJUMDAR (Bimanbehari). *Heroines of Tagore: a study in the transformation of Indian society 1875-1941.* 1968. Firma K.L. Mukhopadhyay; Calcutta.

MAJUMDER (Swapan). *Rabindra granthasuchi.* Vol. 1. Part 1. 1395 (B.S.). National Library; Calcutta.

MALLIK (BP), NARA (T) and BHATTACHARAYA (N). *Gitanjali: linguistic statistical analysis.* 1994. Indian Statistical Institute; Calcutta; pp. 3-97.

MANDELBROT (Benoit). An informational theory of the statistical structure of language. In WILLS (Jackson) Ed. *Proceedings of the symposium on "application of communication theory".* 1953. Butterworth; London; pp. 486-502.

MITRA (Somnath). The letters of Rabindranath Tagore. In *Rabindranath Tagore: a centenary volume 1861-1961.* 1986. Sahitya Akademi; New Delhi; pp. 163-171.

MITTER (Parha). *The triumph of modernism: Indian artists and the avant-garde: 1922-1947.* 2007. Oxford University Press; New Delhi.

MANHEIM (Harry). *Sociological research: philosophy and methods.* 1977. The Dorsey Press; Illinois.

MOHSIN (SM). *Research methods in behavioural sciences.* 1989. Orient Longman; Calcutta.

MUKHERJEE (HB). *Education for fullness: a study of the educational thought and experiment of Rabindranath Tagore.* 1962. Asia Publishing House; Bombay.

MUKHERJEE (H). *Himself a true poem: a study of Rabindranath Tagore.* 1986. Peoples' Publishing Home; Delhi.

MUKHOPADHYAY (Arunkumar). *Rabindra-samiksha.* 2005. Dey's Publishing; Kolkata.

MUKHOPADHYAY (Prabhatkumar). *Gitabitan: kalanukramik suchi.* 1399 (B.S.). Tagore Research Institute; Calcutta.

MUKHOPADHAYA (Prabhatkumar). *Life of Tagore.* 1975. Indian Book Company; New Delhi.

MUKHOPADHYAY (Prabhatkumar). *Rabindragrantha parichiti.* 1385 (B.S). Visva-Bharati Research Publication; Santiniketan.

MUKHOPADHYAY (Prabhatkumar). *Rabindrajibani O Rabindrasahitya-prabashak*. 4 Vols. 1994. Visva-Bharati Granthan Vibhaga; Calcutta.

MUKHOPADHYAY (Prabhatkumar) *Ravindrajivankatha*. 1988. Ananda Publishers; Calcutta.

MUILLWARD (RM). Rabindranath Tagore in Paris. *Modern Review*. 11; 1930; 545.

NEOGY (Prithwish). *Rabindranath Tagore on art and aesthetics*. 1961. Orient Longman; Calcutta.

O'CONNELL (Kathleen M). *Rabindranath Tagore: the poet as educator*. 2002. Visva-Bharati; Santiniketan.

OSTLE (Bemard) and MENSING (Richard W). *Statistics in research*. 1975. The Iowa State University; Ames Iowa.

PAUL (Prasanta Kumar). *Rabijibani*. 9 vols. 1990-. Ananda Publisher; Calcutta.

PEARSON (Karl). *The grammar of science*. 1957. Meridian Books; New York; pp. 10-12.

PEARSON (William W). *Shantiniketan*. 1916. Macmillan; London.

PRITCHARD (A). Statistical bibliography or bibliometrics. *Journal of Documentation*. 24, 4; 1969; 348.

RAFIQUE (Ahmad). *Rabindranather chitrasilpa*. 1996. National Academy of Fine and Performing Arts; Dhaka.

RAI (N). *Rabindra sahityer bhumika*. 1962. New Age Publishers; Calcutta.

RAY (Annadasankar). Rabindranath: an artist in life. In *Rabindranath Tagore centenary volume: 1861-1961*. 1961. Sahitya Akademi; New Delhi.

RAY (Niharranjan). *An artist in life: a commentary on the life and works of Rabindranath Tagore*. 1967. University of Kerala; Trivandrum.

RAY (Niharranjan). Rabindranath Tagore and Indian tradition. In *Rabindranath Tagore centenary volume: 1861-1961*. 1961. Sahitya Akademi; New Delhi; pp. 223-232.

RAY (Partha Pratim), BISWAS (Bidhan Ch) and SEN (BK). Tagore's vision of knowledge and its communication. *Searls Journal of Information Management*. 44, 1; 2007; 3-14.

RAY (Partha Pratim). Vision of library in Tagoreana: a bibliometric approach. *Granthagar*. 54, 6; 2004; 153-58.

RAY (Partha Pratim), BISWAS (Bidhan Ch) and SEN (BK). Knowledge communication in Tagore's model for rural development: an overview. *Annals of Library and Information Studies*. 52, 3; 2005; 94-102.

ROBINSON (Andrew). *The art of Rabindranath Tagore*. 1989. Rupa & Co.; Calcutta.

ROY (Kshitish). *Rabindranath Tagore: a life story*. 1990. New Delhi: Ministry of Information and Broadcasting; New Delhi.

SAHA (Jadu). Problem and prospects of publication of translated works of Rabindranath after expiry of copyright. *Rabindra Bhabna.* 26, 4; 2002; 21-27.

SEN (Pulinbehari). *Rabindra granthapanji.* 1973. Visva-Bharati Granthan Vibhaga; Calcutta.

SENGUPTA (IN). Bibliometrics: a bird's eye-view. *IASLIC Bulletin.* 30, 4; 1985; 167-174.

SENGUPTA (SC). ed. *Rabindranath Tagore, homage from Visva-Bharati.* 1962. Visva-Bharati; Santiniketan.

SINGH (Nihar). Tagore's conversion with Yeats in Dublin. *Calcutta Municipal Gazette.* 13th Sept. 1941.

SINGLETON (Royce A) and STRAITS (Bruce C). *Approaches to social research.* 1999. Oxford University Press; New York.

SINHA (SC) and DHIMAN (AK). *Research methodology.* 2 vols. 2002. Ess Ess Publications; New Delhi.

TAGORE (Rabindranath). My pictures. In NEOGY (Pritwish). Ed. *Rabindranath Tagore on art and aesthetics.* 1961. Orient Longman; New Delhi; pp. 97-98.

TAGORE (Rathindranath). Father as I know him. In *Rabindranath Tagore: a centenary volume 1861-1961.* 1986. Sahitya Akademi; New Delhi; pp. 48-58.

THOMPSON (Edward). *Rabindranath Tagore: poet and dramatist.* 1979. Rddhi-India; Calcutta.

Visva-Bharati and its Institutions. 1956. Visva-Bharati; Santiniketan; 1956.

Visva-Bharati Annual Report 2002-07. Visva-Bharati; Santiniketan.

Viava-Bharati Bulletin no. 11. 1928. Visva-Bharati; Santiniketan.

Visva-Bharati Granthan Vibhaga panchasatvarsha parikrama: 1923-73. 1974. Visva Bharati Grantha Vibhaga; Calcutta.

Visva-Bharati: report of the high level committee. 2006. Raj Bhavana Press; Kolkata.

ZIPF (GK). *Human behaviour and the principle of least effort.* 1949. Addison-Wesley; Cambridge.

ZIPF (GK). *Selected studies of the principle of relative frequency in language.* 1932. Harvard University Press; Cambridge.

ZIPF (GK). *The psychobiology of language.* 1935. Houghton Mifflin; Boston.

Index